W9-CGS-732

2003 Men'sHealth® TOTAL FITNESS GUIDE

2003 Men'sHealth®
TOTAL FITNESS
GUIDE

RODALE®

Notice

The information in this book is meant to supplement, not replace, proper exercise training. All forms of exercise pose some inherent risks. The editors and publisher advise readers to take full responsibility for their safety and know their limits. Before practicing the exercises in this book, be sure that your equipment is well-maintained, and do not take risks beyond your level of experience, aptitude, training, and fitness. The exercise and dietary programs in this book are not intended as a substitute for any exercise routine or dietary regimen that may have been prescribed by your doctor. As with all exercise and dietary programs, you should get your doctor's approval before beginning.

Mention of specific companies, organizations, or authorities in this book does not necessarily imply endorsement by the publisher, nor does mention of specific companies, organizations, or authorities in the book imply that they endorse the book.

Internet addresses, telephone numbers, and product information given in this book were accurate at the time this book went to press.

Printed in the United States of America

Rodale Inc. makes every effort to use acid-free (∞), recycled paper ♻.

ISBN 1-57954-677-3 hardcover

2 4 6 8 10 9 7 5 3 1 hardcover

Visit us on the Web at www.menshealthbooks.com, or call us toll-free at (800) 848-4735.

WE **INSPIRE** AND **ENABLE** PEOPLE TO IMPROVE THEIR LIVES AND THE WORLD AROUND THEM

2003 Men'sHealth TOTAL FITNESS GUIDE

EDITOR-IN-CHIEF, *MEN'S HEALTH* MAGAZINE
David Zinczenko

EXECUTIVE EDITOR
Jeremy Katz

SENIOR EDITOR
Leah Flickinger

ASSOCIATE EDITOR
Kathryn C. LeSage

EDITORIAL ASSISTANT
Daniel Listwa

FITNESS DIRECTOR
Lou Schuler

EXERCISE ADVISOR
Michael Mejia, C.S.C.S.

CONTRIBUTING WRITERS
Mark Anders; Rick Ansorge; Christina Bilheimer; Ethan Boldt; Adam Campbell; Elizabeth Coleman; Jeff Csatari; Martin Dugard; Desi Gallegos; Brian Good; Jim Gorman; Steven Gourley; Scott Hays; Brooke Herman; Skyler Kensho; Joe Kita; Rebecca Kleinwaks; John Lacombe; Chris Lawson; Noah Liberman; James Mack; Matt Marion; Michael McNulty; Michael Mejia, C.S.C.S.; Myatt Murphy; Laura Ongaro; Ed Pavelka; Deanna Portz; Carol Potera; Allen St. John; Bruce Schoenfeld; Lou Schuler; Nicole Serr; Ted Spiker; Darren Steeves, C.S.C.S.; Bill Stieg; Bill Stump; Elizabeth M. Ward, M.S., R.D.; Mike Zimmerman

DESIGNER
Susan P. Eugster

PHOTO EDITORS
Darlene Malkames, Natalie McGill

RESEARCH EDITOR
Deborah Pedron

ASSOCIATE CUSTOMER MARKETING MANAGER
Matt Neumaier

CONTENT ASSEMBLY MANAGER
Robert V. Anderson Jr.

LAYOUT DESIGNER
Jennifer H. Giandomenico

PRODUCT SPECIALIST
Brenda Miller

OFFICE MANAGER
Alice Debus

ASSISTANT OFFICE MANAGER
Marianne Moor

ADMINISTRATIVE ASSISTANT
Pamela Brinar

Contents

Introduction

The Bottom Line

On my first day as a fitness journalist, my new boss warned me about confusing readers. His magazine had recently done a feature detailing the pros and cons of a specific exercise technique, expending thousands of painstaking words explaining every positive and negative.

He had been proud of the story—until he was inundated with calls and letters asking a question he hadn't anticipated: "So, which way do we actually do the exercise?" The lesson he learned? Give readers the bottom line. Never present two comparable strategies that have equal benefits and pitfalls.

The longer I write about fitness and exercise—I'm up to 11 years and counting—the more I see the weakness in that advice. I've gotten into just as much trouble presenting a technique as the one and only as he did with his pick-and-choose approach.

Why? Two reasons.

First, what the hell would I write about the next time I cover the same topic? If I identify one program as the best, does that mean the next one I highlight is, at best, second best?

Second, the bottom-line approach goes against what I know as a certified strength-and-conditioning specialist: *There is no single best program for any particular goal.* The world's top athletes continually tweak their workouts to stay competitive.

I have a good reason for telling you all this. This year's edition of the *Men's Health Total Fitness Guide* has a lot of workout programs in it. You'll find programs to improve endurance, strength, appearance, muscle size, and athletic performance. You'll find programs for beginner, intermediate, and advanced exercisers. In fact, you'll find so much great information here that you may feel overwhelmed by the choices. Not to worry. I assure you all the options are good.

My bottom-line advice: *Exercise should be fun and interesting.* Boredom means you need a new challenge. So pick any program that seems appropriate—and have at it. For a while. Then, when you think you've gotten all the results you can, try something else. The more advanced you are, the more often you'll need to mix things up.

The *Men's Health Total Fitness Guide* has enough new challenges to keep you mixing it up for a long time—or at least until we come out with next year's version.

Lou Schuler

—LOU SCHULER, FITNESS DIRECTOR, *MEN'S HEALTH*

GET SERIOUS

If you're like a lot of guys, you've told yourself you'll get serious about exercise in 2 or 3 weeks—as soon things settle down at work or at home.

Problem is, those 2 or 3 weeks always turn into another 2 or 3 weeks. Before you know it, months or even years have passed.

Let's face it: Life never really settles down, so you'll never run out of excuses. But eventually, you will run out of time.

So you may as well get fit right now. In this section, we'll show you what it takes to get and stay motivated.

What are you waiting for?

MH • QUIZ

Do You Lead a Fit Life?

Ultimate fitness takes more than a thrice-a-week weight toss at the gym. It's embedded in the decisions you make every day—like whether to walk six blocks to the nearest barbershop or drive to Silver Scissors across town. Take our quiz to find out if you need a lifestyle overhaul.

1 I live in a . . .
- ☐ City
- ☐ Suburban neighborhood
- ☐ Rural area

2 I share my pad with a . . .
- ☐ Dog ☐ Fish ☐ Bird

3 My job is . . .
- ☐ Very physically demanding
- ☐ Somewhat physical
- ☐ Sharpening my pencil is the most active I get at my job

4 For lunch I usually . . .
- ☐ Grab fast food or restaurant fare
- ☐ Get outside for a run or some hoops with the guys
- ☐ Have a salad or sandwich at my desk and work through lunch

5 In the evenings, I'm more likely to . . .
- ☐ Take a walk or toss a ball around with the kids
- ☐ Watch the game and then stay up late to catch the highlights on SportsCenter
- ☐ TV? There's no time for that with all the chores on my honey-do list

6 On the days when I can't motivate myself to work out, . . .
- ☐ I push it off until tomorrow, when I'll probably have more energy
- ☐ I focus on the results and that makes me do it
- ☐ I never miss a workout—my day isn't complete without it

7 My goal is to . . .
- ☐ Exercise at least three times a week
- ☐ Get rid of my gut
- ☐ Be healthier

8 The last time I played competitive sports . . .
- ☐ I was in high school
- ☐ Was just last week
- ☐ Does challenging my son on PlayStation count?

9 My ideal vacation would be . . .
- ☐ An adventure excursion such as hiking the Ozarks
- ☐ Lying on the beach
- ☐ A week off to relax and get some chores done around the house

WHAT YOUR ANSWERS SAY ABOUT YOU

1. Suburban sprawl has led to midsection sprawl. City dwellers are a step ahead of suburbanites because of one thing: the sidewalk. If you need a car to get to the grocery store, you're at a fitness disadvantage. But what you lack in roadside concrete you can make up for in property maintenance. Mowing, mulching, raking, and string trimming are physical activities that, when done on a regular basis, can lead to fitness gains.

2. Your choice of pet can impact your fitness level. Most mutts need to be walked at least once a day, giving dog owners built-in exercise partners.

3. Experts recommend at least 20 minutes of moderate physical activity 3 to 5 days a week. Obviously if you lug lumber for a living, you more than meet that each day. But if you have a desk job, you need to find slick ways to work fitness into your life. Some suggestions: Park several blocks from the office to work in a quick walk, sign up for the company softball team, or set up a Nerf basketball court in the empty cubicle down the hall.

4. Fit guys create opportunities to get off their duffs. So can you by turning your lunch hour into power hour. Have a lunch meeting? Invite your boss or client to join you for a run or at the gym. No time for a full workout? No problem. Exercise sessions as brief as 10 minutes count toward your total, so you'll still benefit if you squeeze in a walk along with your chow.

5. Here's a simple formula: Less TV equals greater fitness. The average guy spends a mere 2 hours exercising each week yet manages to watch 29 hours of TV. Not only does all that tube-time wreak havoc on fitness, it can impact your health as well. Your risk of developing diabetes, for example, jumps 73 percent if you watch 20 or more hours of TV a week.

6. If working out is something you do knowing you will feel good later, you're more than halfway there. Anything that keeps you coming back is good. But once exercise becomes its own reward—you do it because you look forward to it—chances are that you'll stick with it.

7. These are all worthy goals. But the best answer is (a), because it's specific. You're not promising yourself pie-in-the-sky success and then getting discouraged when you don't measure up. Here's a tip: If your goal is to work out three times a week, actually schedule in four sessions. That way if you have to ditch one when your boss slams you with a last-minute project, you'll still get in three.

8. Playing on a team ensures you'll have at least a moderate level of fitness. Sports teams have scheduled practices and games that last a full season. Plus, when you're up against competition and your teammates are counting on you, you're likely to put some effort into staying in shape.

9. Obviously, trekking through the Ozarks would require you to be physically fit (unless your cohikers plan to carry you off the mountain), but the other two options have potential as well. Exercise doesn't have to involve dumbbells or the gym. As we said in answer #1, chores count toward your daily sum of physical activity. So stop paying the neighbor to mow your lawn or shovel your sidewalk.

As for the island vacation, turn that into a fit guy's getaway: Walk on the beach, swim laps in the hotel pool, play volleyball, and leave plenty of time for vacation sex. (You'll burn anywhere from 80 to 120 calories per 1-hour session.) Plus, according to a recent *Men's Health* survey of over 1,000 guys, a trip to the beach was the top reason they'd try to lose their gut fast.

—DEANNA PORTZ

BY SCOTT HAYS AND ADAM CAMPBELL

Get Fit in No Time

Too swamped to work out? If a TV talk-show host, a billionaire CEO, and a former governor of New Mexico can find time to stay in shape, you can, too

You'd like to exercise. You'd love to shape up. But you're simply . . . too . . . busy. If you're singing that song, you're the brother of every out-of-shape, overweight, overworked man in America. So why don't you just ditch that overused excuse once and for all and join a better club? 'Cause it ain't gonna work no more. You won't let it. Not after reading about the men on these pages—an ESPN anchor, a billionaire CEO, a governor among them—guys who have just as much on their plates as you do, enjoy successful careers, and still maintain athletes' bodies.

These aren't typical men. But then, neither are you. Got an all-consuming career? Have young kids at home? Travel more than some pilots do these days? The gentlemen here have faced these challenges, but they've learned to apply the same hustle, intensity, and ingenuity to their fitness as they've brought to their jobs. You'll find yourself somewhere in the profiles below. Steal their tricks, try out their tips, then toss the old time-crunch excuse forever.

The Overscheduled Boss

Gary Johnson, 48

Former governor of New Mexico

Gary Johnson may have been the nation's most physically fit public servant. After his election in 1995, Johnson competed in several Ironman triathlons and 500-mile, cross-state bike endurathons. To train for these events, the then-governor ran, biked, or swam nearly every day.

All this seems hard to fathom when you look back at his political schedule: first appointment at 8:00 A.M., and his day was filled with them, until he arrived home after 9:00 P.M. Even with such a busy agenda, Johnson made fitness a priority. In fact, it was part of his political strategy. "When I work out, I don't get rattled," he says. "I sleep well at night, and I have a positive attitude."

Strategy: Use a Point System

Johnson created a point system in 1984 to track his weekly exercise goals, and it's served him well ever since. He assigns a point value to every fitness activity—for example, 1 point for running 1 mile, biking 3 miles, swimming a quarter of a mile, or lifting weights for 10 minutes. He strives to score 80 points a week, 3,200 a month. (Do the math; that's a lot of exercising. If you're not an ultra-endurance athlete like Johnson, add up your normal weekly points, following his system, and make that your weekly goal.) The log makes it easy for Johnson to recognize when he's falling short of his weekly or monthly point goals so he can adjust to make them up. "I don't have anxiety over not working out because I'm confident that I'll ultimately end up logging the exercise," he says.

Tips from the Real World

▶***Use a logbook.*** Studies show that people who record their workout results stick with regular exercise longer than people who don't. Even the simple act of marking a big black "X" on your calendar on the days you exercise can keep you motivated. Canadian researchers found that people who did just that made more progress in their exercise programs than those who didn't. "It's another way to make yourself accountable," says John Jakicic, Ph.D., an exercise psychologist at the Brown University school of medicine.

▶***Vary your workouts.*** To keep his exercise program fresh, Johnson cross-trains

To make sure he gets enough exercise, Johnson keeps a point system.

by hiking, kayaking, or inline skating. But he still assigns points to everything that makes him sweat. Follow his rule: Give yourself 1 point for every 10 minutes of any exercise you do.

▶***Set your internal alarm clock.*** Johnson lives by an ironclad rule: Always be on time. "If you schedule everything and you're never late, you'll always be able to fit everything in," he says. He even schedules his sleep. Johnson tries to be in bed by 10:30 every night and gets up religiously at 4:45 A.M. to exercise—even when a fund-raising dinner keeps him out late.

▶***Carry two jockstraps.*** If you exercise during work hours, keep two full sets of workout clothes and two towels (and duplicate toiletries) in two washable mesh bags. One bag is for your current workout; you'll take this stuff home to launder. The other remains at work. Rotate them.

The Frequent Flyer

Scot McLernon, 43

Executive vice president of sales/ marketing CBS MarketWatch.com

As head of a national sales department, Scot McLernon is captive to an unpredictable schedule, 12-hour workdays, and lots of travel. He typically spends 4 days a week away from his northern California home, which means he lives nearly half of his life in hotels—a huge obstacle to anyone's fitness program.

But for McLernon, exercise is how he purges job stress. "You need a pressure valve," he says. "I've never once regretted [making time] for a run or a bike ride."

Strategy: Plan Ahead

"When you're in sales and marketing, your schedule is generated for you by your clients," says McLernon. So he wrestles control back into his life by scheduling his workouts, without deviation or excuses. If he has a client dinner on Monday night, he reserves a time slot on Tuesday for exercising. No exceptions. And when he's on a multiday business trip, he always schedules a "previous

When McLernon books the client dinner, he books a workout as well.

engagement," that is, a running or swimming session, into his planner. "If it's on paper, it's an appointment that must be kept," he says.

Tips from the Real World

▶***Pop aspirin, get thin.*** To make sure you're ready to get moving when you land, take half an aspirin once a day, starting 2 days before your flight, to keep your blood thin. "When you sit for long periods of time—especially on a plane, where you have very little room to move—you may be susceptible to clotting," says Stanley Mohler, M.D., director of aerospace medicine at Wright State University. Exercise can trigger a clot to cause a stroke. If your feet are swollen—a sign of clotting—avoid exercising until they're back to normal. During long flights, get up once an hour and move around to help keep your blood from pooling and clotting.

▶***Run after the plane.*** When traveling to a new time zone, go for a run as soon as you can after the plane lands. "It helps to clear the postflight fog," says McLernon. First thing the next morning, go for a walk or run outdoors. Morning light stimulates receptors in your retinas that trigger your brain to reset your internal clock and fight jet lag.

▶***Pick a sweaty hotel.*** "I always try to stay close to the places where I enjoy exercising, like Central Park when I'm in New York," says McLernon. Find the best places to run in more than 90 cities—along with listings of nearby hotels—at www.runnersworld.com. For a listing of pools at your travel destination, surf to www.swimmersguide.com. If you weight-train, stay at a hotel that's located in the same building as a health club. When you call for a reservation, ask if complimentary passes to the club are included. If they aren't, request a price package that includes the health club or spa facility. "Often, by bundling the health club into the price of the hotel, you'll get a cheaper rate than if you paid just the regular room rate," says Tom Parsons, CEO of bestfares.com.

TOUGH TALK

"Everyone thinks of changing the world, but no one thinks of changing himself."

LEO TOLSTOY

▶***Take stuff with you.*** Essential gear: Pack the Amphipod Micropack Land Sport ($13; www.amphipod.com). This neoprene pouch has a tiny pocket that holds your hotel key, ID, and cash.

The Family Man

Karl Ravech, 36

Anchor
ESPN's *Baseball Tonight* and *College Hoops 2Night*

Three years ago, Karl Ravech was flabby and unhealthy. Fitness took a backseat to work and spending time with his young family. One day, he ate a tuna fish sandwich before playing basketball with some buddies from ESPN. What he thought was heartburn during the game turned out to be a heart attack. Fortunately, he had the brains to get checked out, and doctors were able to clear his clogged artery with an angioplasty procedure.

The experience changed his life. He started eating smarter and exercising in earnest by running between 5 and 12 miles a day, cramming the runs into a work schedule that starts at 4:30 in the afternoon and often ends around 2:00 A.M. His cardiologist says he's now as healthy as most professional athletes. And his family life didn't suffer as a result of his renewed commitment to fitness. In fact, it got better.

TOUGH TALK

"Working out? Even when I'm in a hurry, I never rush anything."

DAVID BOWIE

Strategy: Put Family First

Ravech's kids, Sam and Max, are 7 and 2, respectively. "I want to spend as much time with them as possible while they're still young," he says. So he forces himself out of bed between 6:00 and 7:00 every morning—even if he didn't hit the feathers until 2:00. "The lack of sleep can be brutal, but my family and health are worth it," says Ravech. He spends the morning playing with the kids and getting them ready for school and day care. Once they're out the door, he runs out the door.

Tips from the Real World

▶***Pick the right time to run away.*** Ravech gets in his daily run when his kids are busy with school, so he's not eating into family time. You can do the same thing even if you work a normal schedule. Just wait until your children go to sleep, then exercise. Contrary to popular thought, late-night workouts may not make you toss and turn in bed. Researchers at the University of California found that men who finished an exercise session 30 minutes before going to bed experienced no greater difficulty falling asleep.

▶***Crunch your kids.*** Instead of spending "quality time" in front of the TV, get the kids outside for wrestling, a game of tag, whatever. You'll get exercise by default, says Kevin Waters, M.D., director of the Duke Executive Health Program, a special program formed at the medical school 10 years ago to address the health needs of stressed-out, time-starved execs. Bonus: "Children emulate their parents. If more adults practiced a healthy lifestyle, more children would, too," says Waters. Think of it as recess for your family.

▶***Do everything faster.*** Instead of sacrificing other tasks in order to squeeze in exercise, Ravech structures his day around workouts, which forces him to get everything else done quicker. "I know I have to exercise, so that gives me less time to do the laundry and mow the yard—I've actually become more efficient," he says. And the simple act of moving more quickly boosts your heart rate and fries more calories.

The Workaholic

Henry Nicholas, 42

President and CEO
Broadcom Corporation

When Henry Nicholas launched his microelectronics company, Broadcom, in 1991 with just a few thousand dollars, he was told he'd fail. Today, he's worth nearly $3 billion. He's built a reputation as a cutthroat negotiator and workaholic. He regularly racks up 20-hour days—jetting back and forth on short notice between Silicon Valley and his company headquarters in southern California. And he brings this same fervor to exercise, squeezing in three 2-hour predawn weight workouts per week and two cardiovascular sessions, either a 6-mile run or a bike ride of up to 70 miles. It's all worth it to Nicholas. "I believe the reward in terms of happiness is directly proportional to the sacrifice," he says.

Nicholas marries his work and fitness goals—and schedules time for both. "The reward in terms of happiness is directly proportional to the sacrifice."

Strategy: Make Your Workout Part of Your Work

"Being in good physical condition is a key to my success in business," says Nicholas. It helps him push harder, stay mentally focused longer, and cope with business pressures. New research at Texas A&M University supports his approach: "Fit men experience less physical and psychological stress than unfit men," says the study author, Camille Bunting, Ph.D.

Nicholas pairs his career goals with his fitness ones. He'll choose lofty, long-term goals that may take up to 5 years to reach. Example: Right now his target is to gross $10 billion in revenue, bench-press 350 pounds, and run 6 miles in 36 minutes—all in the same year. Marrying a physical goal with a career goal is a smart strategy, says Kevin Waters, M.D., director of the Duke Executive Health Program. "You're more likely to achieve both, because as you progress with one, you're reminded to stay focused on the other."

Tips from the Real World

▶***Carry a notepad or PDA when you work out.*** "I get my best ideas when I exercise," Nicholas says. And new research supports this notion. The subjects in this study who exercised at a high intensity for 30 minutes processed information faster and more accurately 50 minutes after the exercise session than they did when they took the test prior to working out. "It's possible that you can multitask much more efficiently because there's more blood feeding your brain," says Charles Hillman, Ph.D., an exercise psychologist at the University of Illinois at Urbana-Champaign. Bring a Palm Pilot or Handspring or low-tech notepad to record your brainstorms before you get sidetracked by the spandex.

▶***Invest in some motivation.*** Nicholas keeps a personal trainer on call 24 hours a day. And he's not about to waste money by not using him. You might not have the dough for a 24-7 exercise physiologist, but you can offer a local trainer payment in advance for a discounted rate. "Paying ahead of time definitely improves adherence—it's extra motivation to follow through," says Michael Mejia, C.S.C.S., *Men's Health* exercise advisor.

▶***Find a partner.*** Whenever it's possible, Nicholas schedules exercise sessions with workmates in place of normal meetings and business lunches. "You'll probably be just as productive as you would be in a conventional meeting, if not more so," says Waters. It's a smart way to multitask.

The After-Hours Schmoozer

Craig Kilborn, 39

Host

CBS's *The Late Late Show with Craig Kilborn*

Hosting your own late-night talk show comes with its share of perks—money, fame, the Dixie Chicks. But while Kilborn's official workday starts at 10:00 A.M. and culminates with the filming of his show from 6:00 P.M. to 7:00 P.M., his nights are often spent networking with agents, producers, and celebrities. To put a workout in the picture, he stops at a nearby gym for 25 minutes on a treadmill, followed by a short weight routine. "I like to exercise before going to work; carrying the young male demo for CBS is hard on my lower back," he says.

Strategy: Make Exercise Convenient

Kilborn asked the network to build him a basketball court on top of the CBS Building in L.A. "It's a convenient escape whenever I need to relax before a show," he says.

All right, so you might not have that kind of clout at your job, but you can still use the logic—do the activity that's most convenient to work or home, or leave a pair of dumbbells under your office desk so you can do a couple of quick sets of shoulder presses and squats when you need to recharge. Don't own weights? One of the best ways to get an intense, convenient, full-body workout is by pushing your car (your buddy steers while you push). Think we're nuts? Try it. "You'll burn a ton of calories while you build functional strength and muscle," says Mark Philippi, C.S.C.S., strength coach at the University of Nevada at Las Vegas. Start by pushing your car as fast as you can for 30 yards. Do five sets, resting 60 seconds after each. (Hey, don't be stupid; if you're out of shape or have heart trouble, don't mess around with this.)

Tips from the Real World

▶ ***Work out early.*** "Making time to exercise in the morning, as Kilborn does, may be the only way to guarantee you'll get it in," says John Raglin, Ph.D., an exercise researcher at the University of Indiana. Not a morning person? Here's how to turn yourself into one, according to Raglin: For the next 4 weeks, force yourself to get up 15 minutes earlier than normal to crank out pushups, do calisthenics, or run up and down stairs, for instance. Make the exercise so convenient that you don't even have to change into workout clothes. As you near the end of the 4 weeks, you will have created a habit and will then be able to work on getting out of your jammies and into a gym.

Kilborn grabs a workout where he can—like on top of the CBS Building in Los Angeles. "Carrying the young male demo for CBS is hard on my lower back."

The No-Excuses Workout

Anybody who owns a TV or drinks coffee can find a measly 900 free seconds in his day to exercise. That's just 15 minutes—less time than the typical man spends on coffee breaks or watching TV commercials, or daydreaming—but it's enough to do the body and mind right. We asked Stephen Maxwell, owner of Maxercise Sports/Fitness Training Center in Philadelphia, to devise a 15-minute total-body workout you can do almost anywhere, with no special equipment—just something heavy that you can get a good grip on.

The Workout

This routine builds strength and endurance while burning fat. Do the workout as a single circuit—performing one exercise followed by the next without resting or putting the "heavy thing" down between moves. If you have time, repeat the circuit once or twice.

The Equipment

All you need is something that weighs about 45 pounds. A weight plate works well; grab it as you would a steering wheel, at 3 and 9 o'clock (except where noted). Use a lighter weight if you find that 45 pounds is too heavy. A dumbbell, cinderblock, or laptop will work in a pinch.

The Exercises

Overhead plate swing. Keep your arms straight and swing the plate over your head as you stand upright by pushing your heels into the ground. Do 10 to 15 repetitions.

Bear-hug front lunge. Hold the plate across your chest with both arms. As you lunge, your front lower leg should be perpendicular to the floor, and your torso should remain upright. Do 10 to 15 repetitions with each leg.

Hammer curl. Grab the weight plate (with both hands on the top third of the plate) and curl it toward your face until the top of the plate nearly touches your forehead. Do 10 repetitions.

Nonlockout squat. Hold the plate above your head with your elbows locked, and lower your body until your thighs are parallel to the ground. Don't straighten your legs or pause at the top of the movement. Do 15 to 20 repetitions.

Single-arm bent-over row. Grab the weight plate by putting your right middle three fingers in the center hole. Bend over and rest your right hand on your thigh. Pull the plate to your shoulder. As you do, squeeze your shoulder blade toward the middle of your back. Do 10 repetitions with each arm.

Rotating deadlift. Lower your upper body by bending your back and your left leg—while keeping your right leg straight—until the bottom of the plate nears your left ankle. Repeat with your left leg bent to complete one repetition. Do 10 repetitions.

Pushup (plate optional). You know how this is done (do 20 repetitions), but to make pushups more challenging, try this: Have a friend delicately place the weight plate on your back when you're in position. The key is to make sure you keep your back straight; your hips may dip under the weight. Bad. Do only 10 weighted repetitions.

▶ ***Slow down a little.*** Because he leads a hectic day and night life, Kilborn needs time to recharge. "At least one night a week, I try to get to bed by 9:30 P.M.," he says. That helps him avoid the inevitable crash that accompanies a lifestyle of late-night partying and early-morning wake-up calls.

▶ ***Mix your drinks.*** If the cocktail scene is a necessary part of your work, keep it from hurting your workout. Learn to dilute: "Each time you finish an alcoholic beverage, have a glass of water," says Chris Rosenbloom, Ph.D., R.D., a professor at Georgia State University. It'll not only keep you hydrated—which will help you avoid a hangover—it'll also slow down your drinking pace.

▶ ***Walk when you can't run.*** "If I know I'm not going to be able to exercise, I make a conscious effort to pace more in my office," says Kilborn. Science shows that breaking exercise into little bits still leads to profound improvements in your health. "In terms of fitness benefits, there isn't much difference between splitting up your workout and doing it in a single bout," says Raglin. In fact, he says you're more likely to stick with an exercise plan if you do three 10-minute sessions a day than if you do a single session of 30 minutes or more.

Secrets of America's Best Gyms

Iron seems lighter when you lift it on the Gold's standard.

BY LOU SCHULER

Here's what you can learn from the places where the biggest, strongest, and fastest go to get even bigger, stronger, and faster

I've rarely met a gym I didn't like. As long as there's a bench, weight set, squat rack, pullup bar, and some form of population control, I can get a decent workout almost anywhere. My results are proportional to the effort I put in and have nothing to do with the quality of the juice bar or the high-speed Internet access on the treadmills, or whatever else the gyms are offering this month to lure in the suckers who don't want to exercise anyway.

And yet, some clubs are different in ways that have nothing to do with cosmetics or marketing. The best places have a center-of-the-universe feel to them. Take Gold's Gym in Venice, California. On any given day, you might see Kobe Bryant or Mike Piazza pumping iron next to a 300-pound bodybuilder, who's ogling Gabby Reece, who's leg pressing more weight than you and I could lift with all four of our legs. Then there's the Alabama Sports Medicine and Orthopedic Center in Birmingham. You and your strained ACL could be parked in the waiting room next to a future Hall of Famer and his torn rotator cuff.

The coaches and trainers and doctors who run these places must know something the rest of us don't. Which explains why the careers of the world's top athletes are put into their hands—and why we set out to learn their secrets.

Feel free to take these tips with you wherever you normally exercise. You're sure to raise the standards in your little corner of the fitness world, even if you can't single-handedly make it one of the best gyms in America.

BEST PLACE TO ADD AN INCH TO YOUR ARMS

Gold's Gym

360 Hampton Drive
Venice, CA 90291
(310) 392-6004
Day passes are $20
www.goldsgym.com/venice

Wander aimlessly in Gold's for 5 minutes, and chances are good you'll come across at least one man the size of a lunar orbiter. How does anyone become so huge? "Bodybuilding is both an art and a science," says Karl List, a personal trainer and former bodybuilder who has worked at Gold's for 11 years. The science involves every muscle-building technique known to man (helped along by extreme pharmacology in many cases). The art is figuring out which of these techniques works best with your frame and your genetic potential for building muscle.

One universal rule from List: Your muscles work best when they work together. "The nervous system is basically a loop. If you isolate the muscle groups, you end up with an uncoordinated body," he says.

PULLOVER/SKULL CRUSHER

▶Grab a pair of dumbbells and lie on your back on a bench. Hold the weights overhead, with your elbows bent slightly and palms facing forward.

▶Lower the weights behind your head as far as you can. Be careful not to arch your back excessively.

▶Pull the weights back to the starting position.

▶Now turn your palms toward each other and bend at the elbows to lower the dumbbells to your forehead. Straighten your arms. That's one repetition.

To Get Big Arms

The multipart exercises shown below and on the previous page take into account the fact that your biceps and triceps do more than bend and straighten your elbows. Do three sets of 6 to 10 repetitions of each. Go from one exercise to the other without rest until you finish all your sets. (Our lawyers want us to tell you not to do this sequence if you have a history of shoulder injuries; if you get shoulder pain during either of the exercises, stop.)

BICEPS CURL/SHOULDER PRESS

- ▶**Hold a pair of dumbbells straight down at your sides, your palms turned toward each other.**
- ▶**Curl the weights up, rotating your wrists inward.**
- ▶**When you've curled the weights as high as you can, pause, then press them overhead, rotating your palms forward as you do so.**
- ▶**Reverse the motion to return to the starting position. That's one repetition.**

BEST PLACE TO STAY FIT ON THE ROAD

Guest Lodge at Cooper Aerobics Center, Dallas

12230 Preston Road
Dallas, TX 75230
(972) 386-0306
www.cooperaerobics.com

The average hotel fitness facility would have to improve to match the equipment in your neighbor's basement. But the Cooper Guest Lodge is different. Not only does it have all the usual stuff you find in a hotel—restaurants, meeting rooms, clean sheets—but it also offers access to everything on the 30-acre campus of the world-famous Cooper Aerobics Center: a 40,000-square-foot gym plus running loops, lap pools, and tennis courts. And the price is down to earth: $165 to $295 per night for room and gym fees.

Isn't it time you paid a visit to the Dallas branch office?

Traveling without Unraveling

Before leaving on your trip, memorize this phrase: If I can't gain, at least maintain. "Breaking even is better than losing ground," says Conrad Earnest, Ph.D., an exercise researcher at the Cooper Institute.

Earnest recommends a circuit session, featuring a combination of chest, back, and leg exercises with no rest in between. "This redistributes bloodflow, which is what cardiovascular exercise does," he says. Combine the circuit with some exercise on an aerobic machine, and you can maintain your cardiovascular fitness and muscle mass until you return to your regular home workouts.

Here's how.

HOTEL MINICIRCUIT

- ▶5 minutes on aerobic machine
- ▶Circuit 1 (perform three times without rest): chest exercise, back exercise, leg exercise
- ▶5 minutes on aerobic machine
- ▶Circuit 2 (perform three times without rest): chest exercise, back exercise, leg exercise
- ▶5 minutes on aerobic machine

You should be able to perform this entire workout in about 45 minutes, Earnest says.

How many repetitions you do per set depends on your goals (6 to 12 for strength and muscle mass, 12 to 15 for muscle endurance).

The equipment on hand determines which exercises you can do. For example, if the gym has a mix of free weights and machines, you might do bench presses, rows, and squats in Circuit 1, then incline bench presses (or shoulder presses, if you prefer), lat pulldowns, and step-back lunges in Circuit 2.

BEST PLACE TO WIN A NATIONAL CHAMPIONSHIP

Stanford University

For more information, visit www.stanford.edu

Stanford's commitment to athletics goes beyond its noted ability to recruit 6-foot-10-inch basketball players who score 1200 on their SATs. This is a school that attracts and nurtures the best and brightest in all sports. In fact, Stanford won the Sears Directors' Cup, naming it the best overall athletic program in all of Division I, in each of the past 8 years.

Surprisingly, Stanford's athletes all train from the same page, whether they play football or golf. "Athletes' muscles contract in the same manner for all sports," says Andy Campbell, a Stanford strength coach who works with the soccer, golf, tennis, and volleyball teams, among others.

The First Step Is the Quickest

Campbell uses this drill to help his athletes improve first-step quickness, a key asset in instant-reaction sports like tennis and soccer.

THE DRILL

- ▶Stand in an athletic position (feet shoulder-width apart, butt back, knees slightly bent, torso leaning forward slightly, hands in front of your body) with your toes on a line. Step over the line and back with one foot as fast as you can for 15 seconds, tapping your toe on the other side of the line and then returning to the starting position. Rest 15 seconds, then repeat with the other foot.
- ▶Repeat, stepping to the side instead of forward. Then repeat going backward.
- ▶Finally, repeat the whole sequence, but with both feet hopping over the line at once—forward, then sideways, then back. "The hopping also helps increase ankle stability, which is important in all the sports I work with," Campbell says. Even if you'll never get a chance to play them in college.

BEST PLACE TO GET BETTER

Alabama Sports Medicine and Orthopedic Center

1201 11th Avenue South
Suite 200
Birmingham, AL 35205
(205) 939-3000
www.asmoc.com
Note: ASMOC is part of the HealthSouth hospital network: www.healthsouth.com.

Elite athletes spend a lot of time in airplanes, often traveling in weather that would frighten Chuck Yeager into therapy. But by far the scariest trip an athlete can make is to Birmingham, Alabama, to see if the orthopedic surgeons at ASMOC can put him back together again. Michael Jordan, Troy Aikman, Greg Norman, and Kerry Wood have all made the trek.

On a typical Monday morning, however, the clinic is filled with men who look a lot like you and me. "I've treated some of the world's elite athletes, but my day normally consists of taking care of weekend athletes who play a little too hard," says Lawrence Lemak, M.D., a sports-medicine orthopedist at ASMOC and medical director for NFL Europe, Major League Soccer, and LPGA.

Stay in the Game

Almost every athlete who throws or lifts strains his rotator-cuff muscles at some point. Here's a three-exercise routine you can do to strengthen these small but crucial muscles.

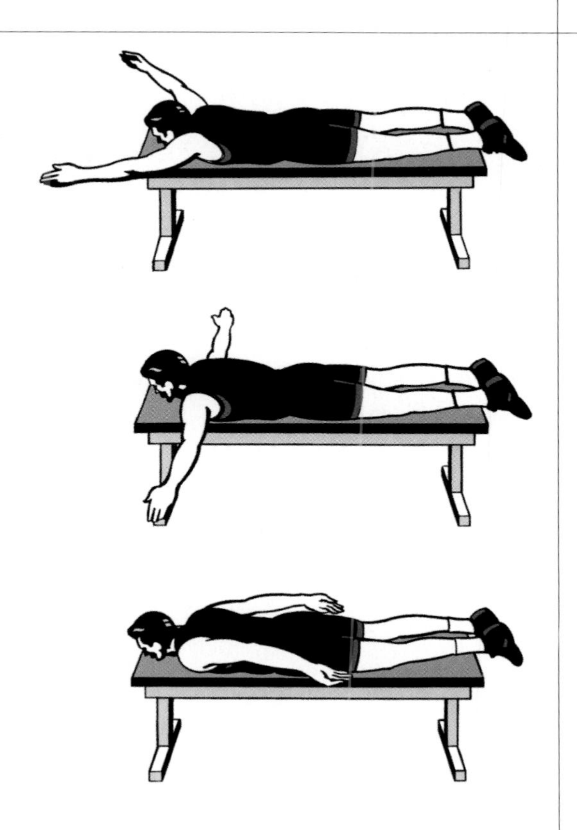

_Y, T,_ AND _I_

▶Lie on your stomach on a bench and extend your arms in front of you, forming the letter _Y_, with your thumbs toward the ceiling. Try to lift your arms by squeezing your shoulder blades together in back. They won't move much, but you should really feel that squeeze. Slowly lower your arms and repeat.

▶Now form the letter _T_, with your palms turned toward the floor. Again, lift your arms by squeezing your shoulder blades together. Slowly lower and repeat.

▶Finally, do the letter _I_, with your palms toward your sides.

▶Do three sets of 10 repetitions of each, starting with no weights, then very light weights, then slightly heavier weights.

BEST PLACE TO PICK UP A STEP

The UCLA Track

HSI
www.hsi.net

Everyone knows the world's top sprinters compete for the United States in the Olympics. But only the most devoted track-and-field fans know that the best of these sprinters—Maurice Greene and Jon Drummond among them—compete for HSI when they aren't representing the red, white, and blue.

HSI is a legal firm/track club based in southern California. On almost any weekday morning, you'll find Greene, the 100-meter world-record holder, and his fellow HSI afterburners at the UCLA track, where they're coached by John Smith, who also works with UCLA's sprinters.

"In order to run fast, you have to practice running fast," says Smith. But not all-out fast. Smith recommends repeated sprints of 40 or 50 yards at 90 percent intensity, with 3 to 4 minutes' rest in between. "The most important thing is not how fast you do a sprint, but to finish it every time. The quality of that 90 percent will go up with each passing week."

Build Fast-Track Muscle

Another key component of a sprinter's training is weight lifting. Smith uses the snatch, an Olympic lift that develops flexibility and coordination, along with squats, pullups, and power cleans, and lots of work for the abdominals and lower back. "The snatch is the most athletic movement in the weight room. I find that when people master that one, they have tremendous leaps in their physical development," Smith says.

THE SNATCH

▶Start with a broomstick or, if you're strong already, a barbell. Set your feet hip-width apart; grab the bar with a wide, overhand grip; and squat with the bar hanging a few inches over the balls of your feet. You want your lower back slightly arched, shoulders back, head up, feet flat [1].

▶The first part is a combination jump, shoulder shrug, and calf raise. Stand, shrug, and pull the bar upward. Rise up on your toes to generate momentum [2]. Keep the bar as close to your body as possible while bending your elbows and lifting the bar as high as you can [3].

▶Flip the bar upward, then quickly drop back down into a squat while holding the bar overhead with straight arms [4]. Stand. That's one repetition.

▶Lower the bar to your shoulders, then thighs, then the floor. Try three to five sets of five repetitions to learn the exercise.

BEST PLACE TO LEARN TO RUN LIKE A KENYAN

Fila Discovery USA Marathon Program

www.fila.com

It doesn't seem fair. How come the Kenyans suddenly get to win all the important long-distance races? Is there something about Kenya's skinny little guys that's different from our skinny little guys? Or is it the Kenyans' Italian coach—Gabriele Rosa, M.D.—who gives them the edge? The Fila athletic foundation decided to find out when it started the Discovery USA training camps last year. After carefully selecting a handful of athletes with good running form, average builds, high aerobic capacity, and strong motivation, Fila took them to a camp in the mountains east of San Diego.

The first results of the program were encouraging. After 10 weeks in the program last summer, Josh Cox sliced 6 minutes off his previous best marathon time.

So what are the Kenyans' secrets? Primarily that there are no secrets. "As Americans, we tend to look for the simple answer, and it's not simple. The Kenyans clearly understand that being your best has to do with paying attention to what you're doing all hours of the day," says Fred Treseler, who manages the Discovery USA marathon project. In other words, what you do on training runs is important, but how you eat, rest, and sleep matters, too.

To Run Farther Faster

Recreational distance athletes can incorporate the following techniques Rosa developed for the Kenyans.

Work those abs. "If your abdominal muscles are weak, you lose your posture, and your hamstrings and lower back start to bother you because your pelvis has shifted," says Treseler. Try the standing crunch shown in the strength section on the next page. Treseler also recommends upper-body strength training—pushups, pullups or lat pulldowns, and shoulder presses. In addition, the Kenyan athletes do incredible amounts of hill running, which strengthens their abs.

Climb those hills. "People get into trouble when they do a flat run at a slow pace every day. You don't have to have good form to do that," Treseler says. Hills improve both form and leg strength, and Treseler recommends traversing them in most, if not all, of your runs.

Hit that accelerator. Rosa asks his athletes to run slowly for the first third of a run, then at a normal pace in the middle third, then at a faster-than-normal pace at the end. Gradually increase the starting pace and you'll increase your normal and fastest paces, too.

HARD TRUTH

Priority game

Number of men who would rather work out than have sex:

1 in 7

Percentage of men (and women) who think that gyms are pickup joints:

14

Percentage of men who don't belong to a gym:

88

BEST PLACE TO DOUBLE YOUR STRENGTH

Westside Barbell

A private club in Columbus, Ohio
www.westside-barbell.com

Louie Simmons is 53 years old. He weighs 235 pounds and has broken his back twice. Given these three facts, you'd expect to find the man collecting disability checks from his ratty sofa. But in June 2000, Simmons squatted 920 pounds in a power-lifting meet, one of the best lifts of the year in his weight class.

Simmons founded Westside Barbell in 1970 as an experimental club, and that's what it remains today: a 20-by-40-foot strength lab in which the rats are Simmons and, on average, 18 of the strongest mofos on the face of the earth. Half of his current members can bench-press more than 600 pounds.

You'd think that these goliaths spend all of their time hoisting loads close to those they use in competition, but in fact they spend half their workouts using about 50 to 60 percent of their maximum weights. On these days, they try to bang out three repetitions with the lighter weights in the time it would take them to lift a maximum load once. "Having large muscles doesn't mean anything if you can't contract 'em quickly," Simmons says.

To Get Strong as Heck

Here are two exercises Simmons uses in his training programs. They'll help you develop your abdominal and lower-back muscles, which are crucial to a heavy lifter. Try one to three sets of 6 to 10 repetitions of each.

STANDING CRUNCH

▶Attach a rope handle to a high cable pulley. Stand with your back to the weight stack, and hold the ends of the rope behind your head.

▶Now crunch. Simmons likes standing abdominal exercises because that's how you use the muscles in real life—standing up.

CHEST-DOWN GOOD MORNING

▶Stand holding a barbell across your shoulders, as if you were going to do a squat. Make sure you have a tight grip on the bar.

▶Now tuck your chin down as you bend forward at the waist and hips. Start with a very light weight to get comfortable with the motion. And definitely avoid this exercise if you have lower-back problems.

BY DARREN STEEVES, C.S.C.S., AND SUE STENDER

3 ESSENTIAL READING

Stay on the Wagon, Get with the Program

Six ways to stop yo-yo exercising and get the results you want

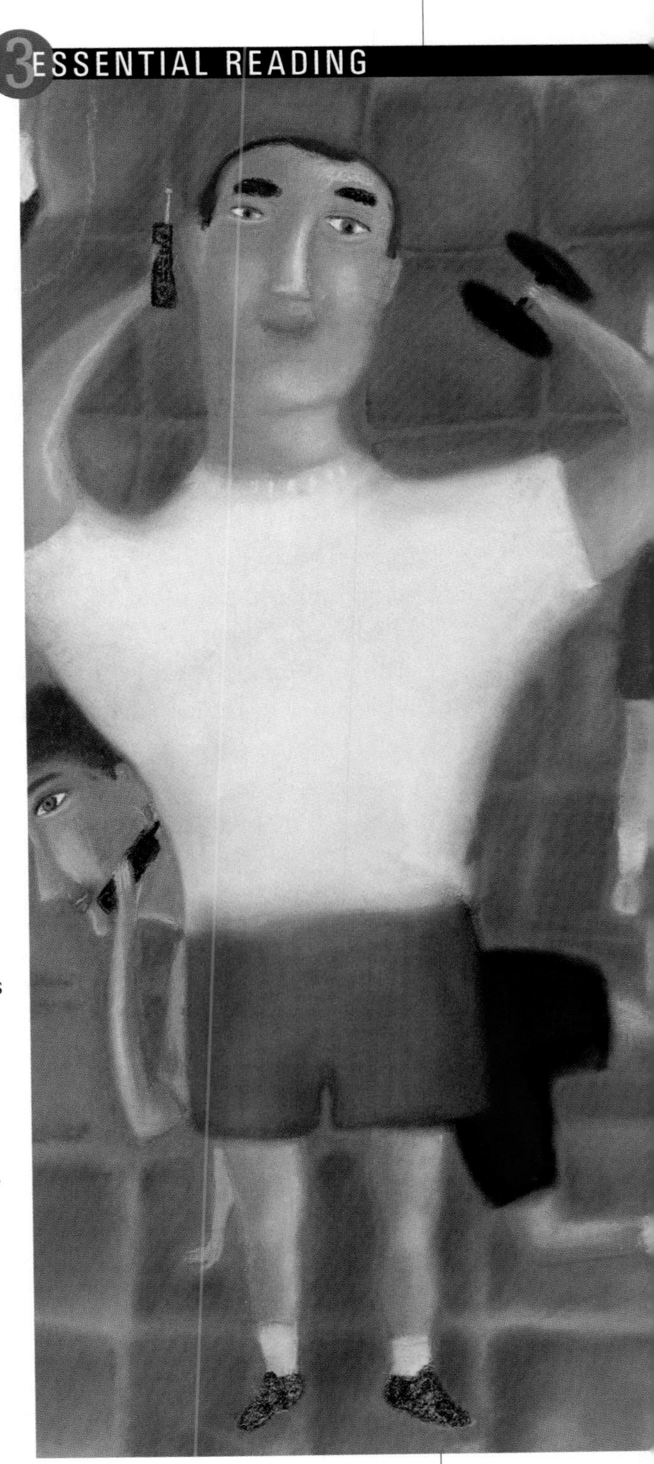

Some famous smart guy once declared that consistency is the hobgoblin of small minds. He probably was right when it comes to politics (5 minutes of listening to AM radio would confirm this). But for exercisers, consistency is the harbinger of small waistlines.

See, the benefits of exercise—the great stuff like bigger muscles, smaller fat stores, lower blood pressure, higher levels of "good" cholesterol, and an improved outlook on life—are all transient.

Scientists call this the reversibility principle. What you have today could be gone next month if you don't work to maintain it. Doesn't matter if you're a world-class marathoner or a guy who just signed on for the local gym's "How Many People Can We Squeeze In?" special offer. If you don't exercise, you eventually lose most of what you gained, if not all of it. (The marathoner will probably keep some of his hard-earned aerobic endurance, but the guy who's been jogging 3 weeks is screwed.)

We don't tell you this to make you feel bad about yourself. At some point, we all succumb to yo-yo exercising. We're consistent for weeks or months or even years, and then something comes up—a family crisis, a work crunch, crummy weather, or simple boredom with an unchanging routine. And we fall off the wagon.

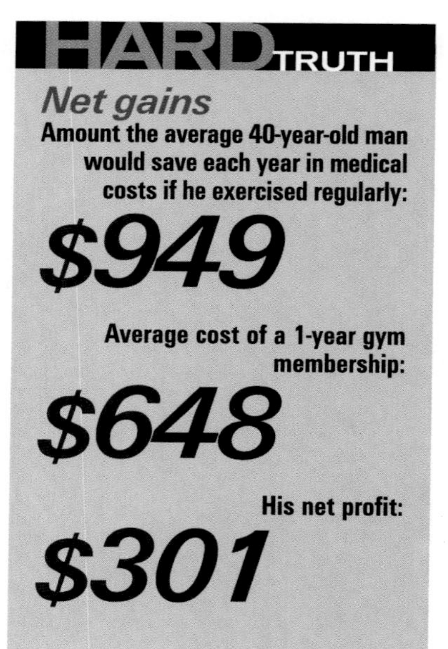

Obviously, we can't control the weather (although there'd be a nice little profit if we could). And we can't tell your boss never to hit you with a sudden deadline that requires you to work around the clock. What we can do is show you how to be more consistent in ordinary circumstances. That way, when a real crisis arises, you can afford to take some time off and still be ahead of the game.

STRATEGY #1
Find the Time

A week has 168 hours. All you need for exercise is a few of them. Some ideas:

Book it. At the start of each week or month, block out chunks of exercise time on your calendar. Then do your damnedest to keep anything from interfering with those workouts. If something does come up, move your workout to another slot on your calendar. Just don't give yourself the option of erasing the workout altogether.

Choose convenience first. Studies show that you'll stick with an exercise program longer if your workout facility is within a 4-mile radius of your home or office. It's even better if the gym is on a straight line between the two places. Rule of thumb: The number of reasons to miss a workout is directly proportional to the inconvenience imposed by that workout.

Get buy-in from everyone who matters. The average guy is surrounded by people who lay claim to chunks of his time—the wife, the kids, the boss, the direct reports, the parole officer. You have to convince each of them that your workout is important and that you can't be pulled away from it on a whim. You may have to go so far as to post this sign on your fridge: "Dad's exercising from 6:00 to 7:00. Your allowance will be paid at 7:05."

STRATEGY #2
Anticipate Problems

No matter how well you implement Strategy #1, the world remains imperfect. So your next goal is to figure out ways to exercise even when fate strikes down Plan A.

Use your home-field advantage. If you belong to a gym, have an at-home fallback routine for when you can't get out, or for when the health department finds a rare fungus in the health club and shuts it down. Stash some dumbbells and a bench in a corner of the laundry room, keep some exercise bands in your dresser drawer, or have a walking or jogging route figured out in advance.

Be a workout connoisseur. Whether you exercise in a home or a gym, it's a good idea to keep a file of alternative workouts you can try when you can't or don't feel like doing your regular program. When you see a good routine in a magazine or on the Web, clip or copy it and keep it in your gym bag. That way you always have something new to try.

Investigate alternative lifestyles. Or, at least, alternative exercises. If all the bench-press stations are stacked three-deep, you need to know some other chest exercises you can substitute.

Figure your family into the mix. The wife is sick and you're in charge of the brood. There goes the workout, right? Not necessarily. Many gyms now offer babysitting. More and more offer programmed activities for your tots. If you pick a gym that offers these, you've lost a bunch of excuses to skip a workout.

Kids and dogs can also join you at the local park. If your kids are old enough, they can ride a bike next to you while you jog. If they're small enough, you can stow one of them in a backpack and go for a hike. And don't underestimate how good a sweat you'll work up while pushing a stroller up and down hills.

Plan your travel around your workouts. Business travel has probably shut down more fitness programs than anything else. So book yourself into a hotel with a gym or pool—or both. If not, make sure you know where to find the nearest gym, and how much you'll have to pay for a daily or weekly pass. The price will be outrageous if you're staying in a downtown hotel in a big city, but your company may allow you to put it on your expense account (if the strip club is allowable, why not a gym?).

TOUGH TALK

"There are all kind of theories about heart rate . . . but you know what? Just get your ass moving. That's going to get you in shape."

ACTOR STEPHEN BALDWIN

STRATEGY #3
Stay Motivated

Everyone has days when he doesn't feel like lifting a bunch of inert iron plates or dragging his ass around a jogging trail like all the other fitness lemmings. You have to anticipate and remain prepared for those moments.

Find a workout buddy. You can always find someone who's in about the same shape as you and would be willing to start a fitness program. Even if you work in an office filled with women, find the one who shares your passion for Frisbee golf. Trust us: There will be days when the only reason you can find to get off the couch and into the gym is the knowledge that your workout partner will be pissed off if you don't.

. . . Especially when you travel. It's the end of a long day of meetings at the Omaha office. Before heading back to your hotel, you ask, "Anyone else feel like working out tomorrow morning?" All of a sudden, you've improved your life in two ways. Someone is bound to say yes—if for no other reason than to look more gung ho than the other schlubs at the meeting—and as soon as someone does, you know you won't be able to wiggle out of it without looking bad. Second, you know you're not going to drink too much or stay out late when you have a morning workout scheduled with a highly motivated coworker.

Picture this. Ever stop and wonder why you're doing all this sweaty, exhausting, uncomfortable exercise? If you haven't, you will. For those moments, it helps to have some visual aids left around in strategic locations. Let's say you've lost a bunch of weight, but you've hit a wall and your enthusiasm is flagging. It helps to have a picture of your most bloated, out-of-shape self taped to the fridge. That'll startle you back into the right frame of mind.

If you're just starting, find a picture of yourself back when you were in the best shape of your life. Hang that where you can't miss seeing it. Tape it to the dashboard of your car, and just try to drive past the gym on the way to Wendy's.

STRATEGY #4
Find a Great Program, and Stick with It . . . for a While

Exercisers seem to come in two varieties: Those who stick with one program forever, despite not seeing improvements in strength and body shape after the first 3 months, and those who change their workout as often as they change their socks. Both are about 5 percent right and 95 percent wrong. Here's a better way.

Start with an even dozen. Studies link exercise programs lasting 12 weeks or more to higher adherence. This may be because you incorporate them into your lifestyle over a period of time. That doesn't mean you should do the exact same thing for all 12 weeks. Whether you focus on strength training or aerobic exercise, increase the volume and intensity of the exercise gradually, with a built-in series of peaks and valleys.

And after that, try something else. Once you've completed the program, try a new one. For example, if you were working toward general goals—losing weight, increasing endurance, and/or building some muscle—try something specific: building *lots* of muscle, running a 10K, stripping 2 inches off your waist.

STRATEGY #5

Remember, This Is Supposed to Be Fun

Exercise isn't punishment. It's something you do *for* yourself, not to yourself. With that in mind . . .

Build your program around stuff you like. Sounds incredibly, ridiculously simple. But how many people join gyms despite the fact they hate formal exercise? How many people buy treadmills when walking in place is about as interesting to them as watching milk curdle? If you hate the very thought of doing something, don't imagine that you're going to stick to a program that's based on the thing you hate.

So, for example, if you love golf but hate formal exercise, make golf your workout. Give up the cart and walk as many rounds as you can, weather permitting. Practice when you can. Then add in some exercises to improve your golf game—flexibility and strength exercises to lengthen your drives, along with aerobic exercise to improve your stamina.

And find new things to like. After 6 months of jogging, let's say you decide to try inline skating. Now you're working your leg muscles differently, you're developing new coordination (and if you're not, you're creating new revenue for your

PEAK performance

Talk the Talk

Nothing firms up a commitment like going public. Listen to this *Men's Health* reader: "I tell everyone in the office that I'm going to go to the gym every lunch hour. If I don't go, I'll lose face. Plus, everyone asks me how the workouts are going. It's positive reinforcement. Now I've noticed that more people in the office are going to the gym. So I've sort of become a leader, and leaders can't quit."

dentist and orthopedist), and you're getting a little adrenaline rush from moving really fast with no guarantee you can stop.

But the best part of starting new fitness pursuits is you get to buy new gear—skates, clubs, rackets, bats, and, best of all, sport-specific shoes. Make this your motto: Anything worth pursuing is worth buying specialized footwear.

Mix and match. A quick way to take the fun out of exercise is to pursue something that doesn't provide any yin to the yang of your day-to-day life. Got a solitary job? The last thing you need is a solitary workout—join a team or a club or at the very least find a workout buddy. By contrast, if your job is one unrelieved series of meetings and interruptions, a solitary hour on the road or surrounded by dumbbells (the noninterrupting kind) might be the best stress relief you'll find.

PEAK performance

Tell Yourself Off

So you missed a workout and now you want to exorcise your guilt.

Step 1: Remember that muscle needs to rest in order to rebuild and grow.

Step 2: Know that "it would take a 10- to 15-day hiatus from working out for you to see any significant effects on your body," says John Silva, Ph.D., a professor of sports psychology at the University of North Carolina.

Step 3: Tell yourself that even God took a day off from bench-pressing mountain ranges.

STRATEGY #6

When You Stumble, Get Back Up

Everyone falls off the horse, but only the real cowboys climb right back on. Unless you're hurt, you need to get back into an exercise routine as soon as you can. Just keep these tips in mind.

Don't get sore. Muscle soreness doesn't mean you got a good workout. It means you did more than your body was prepared for, producing millions of microscopic tears in your muscles. Serious gym rats can live with it—they know it's a sign they overreached, and the next step is to train their bodies to handle this type of workload.

But for an on-again, off-again exerciser, postworkout soreness compromises the next workout because it generally peaks 2 days later. If you exercise on a Monday-Wednesday-Friday schedule, overdoing it on Monday will make Wednesday's workout a pure pain fest. And there may not be a Friday workout.

Remember the 10 percent rule. Increase the intensity or duration of your workout by 10 percent each week. And for each week of exercise you miss, decrease the intensity or duration of your next workout by 10 percent. So if you missed 2 weeks of workouts, start back at 80 percent of what you did before. Give yourself 2 full weeks to catch up.

On the bright side, by the third week, you'll be 10 percent better than when you quit.

Keep it real. No matter how many hours you spend in the gym, you're not going to build arms like that guy on the cover of

Modern Muscularity. No matter how many miles you run, you're not going to win the Boston Marathon. If you had the genetic potential to do any of those things, you'd know it by now, and you'd be writing articles on exercise, not reading them.

We don't say this to make you feel bad. We've just seen too many guys bury themselves with unrealistic expectations. When a tape of Karl Malone is running through your head, it's hard to accept that you perform like Karl Malden.

For just 1 month, limit your ambitions to these goals.

▶Three workouts a week.

▶A 10 percent improvement in some parameter each week. For aerobic exercise, increase distance or speed by 10 percent. For weight training, increase the weight or volume (sets and repetitions) by 10 percent.

When you reach those goals, set the bar higher and go for another 4 weeks, then another 4.

After 12 weeks of steady, progressive exercise, stop and assess. Look at how your body changed. Look at how you performed and take stock of how it feels—where you feel supercharged, where you feel drained and sore.

Now you can set realistic goals for yourself—muscle to gain, weight to lift, pounds to lose, miles to run.

With goals perfectly matched to your body and schedule, you may find you'll never miss another workout again.

HARD TRUTH

It doesn't take much

Percentage of men who would never skip another workout if . . .

. . . They could build twice the muscle with half the effort:

40

. . . Women began wearing see-through spandex:

16

Trainer's Forum

with MICHAEL MEJIA

CLOCK WORK

Q: I have about a half-hour to work out in the morning and again at night, 2 or 3 days a week. How can I make the most of these narrow time constraints?

L. K., FAYETTEVILLE, ARKANSAS

A: Plan to do strength training at one session and cardio at the other. You've probably heard that doing cardiovascular exercise on an empty stomach may help burn fat. But it won't have the type of pronounced effect on your metabolic rate that a tough session with the weights will. So to maximize your workout time, start your day with intense, muscle-building exercises like squats, bench presses, and pullups and save the cardio work for later that evening. This way you get both a long-term metabolic boost and a quick fix to help guard against any little dietary indiscretions you might have made during the day.

HARD TRUTH

Smart guys

Exercise equipment the average guy is most likely to own:

Dumbbell

MOTIVATION

Take a Shot

For this trick, you'll need a camera and a mirror—or a friend. Put on your swim trunks. Shirt off. Let out the gut. Now take your picture in the mirror, or have your friend take it. This is how you'll look in summer beach snapshots unless you get your act together. It's still early. Make a copy and tape it to the rice pudding.

CONSISTENT PATTERN

Q: My motivation varies from one workout to the next. How can I get pumped up every time?

A. J., STATEN ISLAND, NEW YORK

A: Even a workout nut like me feels the enthusiasm wane every now and then. No matter how fit you are, that first 5 minutes of your run or your first couple of sets are going to be uncomfortable. But after that, the rest of the workout usually isn't too bad. Think about the payoff. Or, look at those first 5 minutes as the difference between being just a guy with an average body versus being one of the few, the proud . . . the strong.

Believe it or not, getting mentally pumped also can be related to the nutrients you pump into your body. To find out if food is affecting your mood, keep track of what you eat for a week. Say you notice that after consuming a protein-rich meal, you tend to feel energetic for the next several hours, yet a meal high in carbohydrates makes you sluggish and tired. The solution is obvious: Restrict your carbohydrate intake for a few hours prior to your workout.

HOME OR AWAY?

Q: I can't decide if I should join a gym or just work out at home. What are the pros and cons of each?

R. D., HEMPSTEAD, NEW YORK

A: It's hard to say, since we all perceive things differently. What one person sees as a major drawback, might be a no-brainer to someone else. The following charts should help you decide.

TOUGH TALK

"Fear is a great motivator. It's also a sign of intelligence. A year ago, my cholesterol was 300 and my triglycerides were 750. If that's not motivation for change, see a shrink."

THE SHIELD STAR MICHAEL CHIKLIS

TRAINING AT HOME

WHY IT'S GOOD	WHY IT'S BAD
Cost. A weight set and a bench, or an exercise ball, can serve as an effective, inexpensive alternative to a gym membership.	Cost. Unless you're in P. Diddy's income bracket, don't count on having too elaborate a setup.
Not having to wait in line to use the equipment.	No access to a spotter if you train alone—a huge concern given the amount of people who are hurt, or even killed, lifting weights alone each year. According to the National Injury Information Clearinghouse, hospital emergency rooms treated an estimated 68,054 people for weight-lifting injuries in 2000.
Your own music. This is big! Especially if you don't find listening to Britney Spears inspirational.	No motivation. Sure, not having a gym commute is nice, but it also can work to your disadvantage. Once you get home after a tough day at work, your mind and body automatically go into "relaxation mode," not to mention the distractions offered by your wife, your kids, the Victoria's Secret catalog.
No commute.	

TRAINING IN A GYM

WHY IT'S GOOD	WHY IT'S BAD
Atmosphere. Some people get pumped just from the high energy levels in most commercial gyms.	Crowds. Nothing interrupts your groove more than waiting in line for the bench press or the treadmill.
Equipment selection. Unless you live in the sticks, most gyms are equipped with numerous high-tech machines complete with all the bells and whistles.	Cost. Despite the fact that many gyms now offer monthly, or "pay as you go" installment plans, at anywhere from $20 to $75, monthly membership can still be too expensive for some guys.
Easy to find a spotter. A mere grunt in your fellow Neanderthal's direction will usually do the trick.	Other people's sweat. Not everyone is kind enough to wipe down the equipment when he's done.

FEED THE BEAST

Smart eating doesn't mean you have to subsist on a diet of carrot sticks and mineral water. Guy-specific research shows you can lose weight, build muscle, and rev up your sex life without giving up the foods you love.

Peanut butter, chocolate, Chinese take-out—all of these and more can be part of a hearty, healthy eating plan. We'll even tell you what you should wash 'em down with. So turn the page and grab a plate: Here's some food you can use.

MH • QUIZ

What Kind of Loser Are You?

Can't lose your gut? Maybe the problem's all in your head. For each question below, pick the answer that best describes you. Then check off the appropriate box at the end of the quiz. Mark the score box carefully—the letters aren't in alphabetical order. When you're finished, add up the number of checked boxes in each column. The column with the most checks is your personality type. (In case of a tie, read both descriptions and pick the one that's most like you.) Then find the weight-loss strategy that matches your personality type.

1. When picking a movie, I . . .
   a. Ask friends for suggestions
   b. Read the reviews first
   c. Go for number one at the box office
   d. Decide what to see while standing in line

2. When going to a party, I . . .
   a. Put on clothes I chose earlier
   b. Grab my newest, coolest shirt
   c. Choose whatever is clean and comfortable
   d. Wear something like what I think everybody else will wear

3. When I shop for food, I . . .
   a. Always buy the same 10 items
   b. Grab whatever's on sale
   c. Buy what I'm hungry for
   d. Make a list and stick to it

4. When ordering in a restaurant, I . . .
   a. Ask what others will order before deciding
   b. Choose something I've had before, instead of something new
   c. Wait until the last second to decide
   d. Know what I want in advance and try to find it on the menu

5. When surfing the 'Net for fun, I . . .
   a. Browse from link to link based on whatever seems interesting
   b. Read e-mail first, then check my favorite sites
   c. Look for sites I've heard about from friends or ads
   d. Spend most of my time chatting with people or reading message boards

6. When driving somewhere new, I . . .
   a. Ask a friend for directions
   b. Grab a map, fill my tank, and step on it
   c. Consider getting lost an adventure
   d. Follow the most interesting route, even if it takes longer

7. When trying to pick up a woman at a bar, I . . .
   a. Say the first thing that comes to mind
   b. Often see someone even better looking and go after her instead
   c. Spend several minutes planning what to say before approaching
   d. Take a buddy along so I feel more comfortable

8. My coworkers would describe me as a guy who . . .
   a. Is a multitasking master
   b. Would rather work as part of a team than be the leader
   c. Loves the big ideas but doesn't want to bother with the details
   d. Sets a goal for the department and makes sure everybody sticks to it

	FREE SPIRIT	PLANNER	SHORT-ATTENTION-SPAN MAN	CROWD PLEASER
1.	d ☐	b ☐	c ☐	a ☐
2.	c ☐	a ☐	b ☐	d ☐
3.	c ☐	d ☐	a ☐	b ☐
4.	d ☐	b ☐	c ☐	a ☐
5.	a ☐	b ☐	c ☐	d ☐
6.	d ☐	b ☐	c ☐	a ☐
7.	a ☐	c ☐	b ☐	d ☐
8.	c ☐	d ☐	a ☐	b ☐
TOTAL				

THE FREE SPIRIT

A guy like you: Jack Nicholson

You are: Independent and rebellious. You're also easily bored and love spontaneity or variety. If there's too much planning or repetition in an activity, you tend to lose int—hey, are those doughnuts over there?

Your weight-loss strategy: Don't go on any more diets. "You won't follow them anyway," says Hillary Wright, R.D., a Boston nutritionist. Instead, keep a magical, rebellious number in your head: 500. That's the number of calories you need to cut from your diet each day to lose a pound of fat a week. "Having a single goal provides the structure you need to lose weight," says Wright.

How to do it:

▶***Prioritize your snacks.*** "It's okay for you to snack. If you don't, you'll end up craving certain foods and ultimately eating even more of them once your willpower finally caves in," says Wright. The key (and the catch) is making a list of the six snacks you eat every day, and then ranking them in order of importance. Got it? Now cut that list in half. Eat your usual amount of the top three, but say goodbye to four through six.

▶***Substitute X for Y.*** Go ahead and order that Sausage McMuffin—but ask for an extra slice of cheese instead of the recycled pig parts. Or eat a cinnamon-raisin bagel in place of a cinnamon roll. You still get what you want, but you cut calories while you do it. "It's important for an impulsive person to feel that he's making his own choices," says Kathleen Vohs, Ph.D., a psychologist at Case Western Reserve University. "You just have to make those choices healthier."

▶***Don't trust yourself.*** That's right, you are not to be trusted with "Family Size, 75% More Free!" packages of anything on your list of favorite munchies. Pick up single-serving sizes of the stuff instead. "If you're incredibly impulsive, you're also very likely to cheat," says Wright.

▶***Take a menu to the gym.*** Give yourself plenty of options. Make a list of three or four different weight-lifting programs and cardiovascular workouts, and each day pick the one that gets you most psyched. "The only rule is that you have to do something each day," says Craig Ballantyne, C.S.C.S., a strength coach in Toronto.

MH•QUIZ

THE PLANNER

A guy like you: Bill Parcells

You are: Conservative and focused—lost without a schedule in hand. Spontaneity? That never quite makes your to-do list.

Your weight-loss strategy: Put your organizational skills to good use. You already enjoy making lists and schedules and keeping track of numbers, so, according to Vohs, "You just have to help that love of order cross over into another part of your life." The part called your stomach.

How to do it:

▶***Keep a journal.*** "Journals help you to see how much you're eating during the day," says Ross Andersen, Ph.D., an associate professor of medicine at Johns Hopkins. "Once you see that, it's much easier to find ways to cut back."

▶***Pencil in your workouts.*** You write everything else on your calendar, so why not jot down when you're going to the gym? At the beginning of each month, block out 30- to 45-minute chunks of time on the days when you plan to exercise. Then keep the appointment—no matter what.

▶***Plan meals.*** "Not knowing what they're going to eat until mealtime is a prime reason planners end up cheating," says Andersen. "Instead of leaving things to chance, sit down once a week to write out your entire week's menu." Or, log on to www.menshealth.com and sign up for our Belly-Off Custom Weight-Loss Planner. You'll get a weekly shopping list and a daily meal planner. Cost is $6 a month.

▶***Score points with yourself.*** For instance, give yourself four points for each time you lift weights, two points for each mile you jog or bike, one point for every game of tennis you play, and half a point for every 20 minutes you spend walking or having sex. Try to accumulate at least 25 points each week. If you miss a workout, make up the points the following day.

THE SHORT-ATTENTION-SPAN MAN

A guy like you: Emeril Lagasse

You are: Eager and excited, but lacking commitment. Blame it on your hunter-gatherer past. Evolution has bred you to be the ultimate searcher, constantly looking for something better, whether it's a woman, a job, or a way to burn fat. Your downfall? The second you can't find a quick fix or easy answer—bam!—there goes your interest.

Your weight-loss strategy: Incorporate order into your life. "You need to work on your follow-through in order for a diet to work long term," says Andersen.

How to do it:

▶***Start slowly.*** "The more passionate you are about a program in the beginning, the harder it is to maintain that passion and stick with the program," says Andersen. Instead of a big, revolutionary goal, like eating more healthfully, give yourself a specific goal—like eating one additional piece of fruit each day, or avoiding beer on weeknights.

▶ ***Chew on this. Slowly.*** You do everything fast. But experts say that when you inhale food from your plate, your brain doesn't have time to tell you to stop eating. To figure out how long it should really take you to eat a meal, try this exercise: After each bite, put down your fork and take a sip of water. Keep doing it until your plate is clean and your cup runneth dry. "That's how long it should really take you to finish a meal," says Wright. Repeat the process—without the water—next time you eat. You'll eat less and feel full sooner.

▶ ***Be more consistent.*** "The biggest reason men don't get the results they want is that they constantly jump from plan to plan," says Alwyn Cosgrove, C.S.C.S., a personal trainer and the owner of Cosgrove Fitness and Sports Training Systems in Santa Clarita, California. Instead of following the latest fad, Cosgrove suggests picking short-term programs—under 4 weeks is ideal—that involve very specific goals. "It's easier for guys with a short attention span to stick with a 3-week arm-building program or a month-long weight-loss program than a longer-lasting program," he says.

THE CROWD PLEASER

A guy like you: Bill Clinton

You are: The life of any party. The attention you get from people boosts your ego, motivating you to be a better person. Unfortunately, too much partying also turns you into a bigger person.

Your weight-loss strategy: Build your own social support system. "A true crowd pleaser enjoys being around people and the support that being part of a group provides," says Andersen. For you, the best chance of sticking with a diet is to find a group of friends, coworkers, or even total strangers from whom you can gain inspiration.

How to do it:

▶ ***The easy way.*** Visit the Men's Health Belly-Off Club at www.menshealth.com. It offers the cyber camaraderie of tens of thousands of men like you—men who want to lose weight and improve their health, but who need motivation to make it happen.

▶ ***Team up.*** Join a league, or start a regular game of basketball with the guys at work. "If you're part of a team and have built-in peer pressure, that makes it harder to quit," says Vohs.

▶ ***Be accountable.*** Tell a friend or significant other that you're trying to lose weight. Then ask your cohort to play bad cop with you at least once a week. "Knowing that you have to account to another person can have a positive influence on your behavior," says Andersen.

▶ ***Clone yourself.*** Find a picture of yourself at your heaviest, and another of yourself at your fittest. Run 'em both through the copier a dozen times and stick them in places where you'll frequently see them—like in your car and on the refrigerator.

—ELIZABETH M. WARD, R.D.

BY BRIAN GOOD

Drink Away 10 Pounds

A bottoms-up plan for siphoning off the weight

Two hundred gallons. That's the amount of liquid the average man guzzles each year. Approximately 34 gallons of beer, 53 gallons of soda, 24 gallons of milk, and a whole lot of gallons of other stuff. Feeling bloated? You should. But the great thing about drinking so much is that all you have to do to lose weight is make a few adjustments to the types of drinks you're already pouring down every day. Juice with pulp instead of pulp-free. Green tea instead of regular. Do it all and you're gulping 35,456 fewer calories in 4 weeks. That's a savings of 10 pounds. So fill 'er up. This one's on us. And off you.

Your A.M. Juice

Unless you're an astronaut or a skinny 10-year-old boy, trade in your Tang, Sunny D, and pulp-free OJ for the thick stuff—juice with extra pulp. It may help you resist the lure of the office bagel basket. Researchers at Purdue University found that people stayed full longer when they drank thick drinks than when they drank thin ones—even when calories, temperatures, and amounts were equal. "Thicker drinks help to fight off hunger longer," says Richard Mattes, Ph.D., the study author.

Calories saved in 4 weeks: 5,460

Your Midmorning Break

Even if your taste in tea runs more toward Long Island than iced, there's a reason to consider adding a bit more of the stuff to your diet: It's a natural fat burner. But not just any tea will work. You need to buy the stuff marked "green." A Swiss study found that substances in green tea called catechin polyphenols can significantly increase your body's metabolism of fat so you burn the stuff at a faster rate.

You can drink prebrewed greens from Snapple, SoBe, or Arizona, but they're filled with sugar and average more than 200 calories a bottle. Look for Honest Tea brand instead—it has just 34 calories per bottle. Or buy tea bags and brew the stuff yourself.

Calories saved in 4 weeks: at least 4,872

Lunch in a Can

Meal replacements really work. In a study presented at the annual meeting of the North American Association for the Study of Obesity, researchers found that regularly drinking meal replacements increased a man's chances of losing weight and keeping it off for longer than a year. But which one should you drink? "Men trying to lose weight need about 600 calories per meal, with 25 percent of those calories from protein, 25 percent from fat, and 50 percent from carbohydrates," says Liz Ward, R.D., a Massachusetts nutrition consultant. That's about what you get from this drink, the strawberry power blast. Blend together 1 cup low-fat vanilla yogurt, 1 cup 1% milk, 2 teaspoons peanut butter, a banana, 1½ cups frozen unsweetened strawberries, 2 teaspoons sugar, and 2 ice cubes or ½ cup crushed ice. Mix the concoction on high speed until it's smooth (4 to 5 minutes). Drink it immediately. Each serving provides 608 calories, 25 grams of protein, 106 grams of carbohydrate, and 11 grams of fat.

Calories saved in 4 weeks: 9,856

Your Afternoon Indulgence

Need something thick and creamy from a drive-thru? Head to White Castle. The damage from its regular chocolate shake is just 220 calories, compared with a small McDonald's chocolate shake, which has 360 calories. Burger King is nearly as bad, with 305 calories per small shake, but Dairy Queen wins the crown for the most fattening shake going: A small DQ chocolate shake is packed with 560 calories.

Calories saved in 4 weeks: 9,520

Your Postworkout Smoothie

Bananas don't just fend off muscle cramps. They also fight hunger, according to Alan Hirsch, M.D., neurological director of the Smell & Taste Treatment and Research Foundation in Chicago. "The scent of bananas tricks your brain into thinking you've eaten a lot more than you really have, making you fuller faster," says Dr. Hirsch.

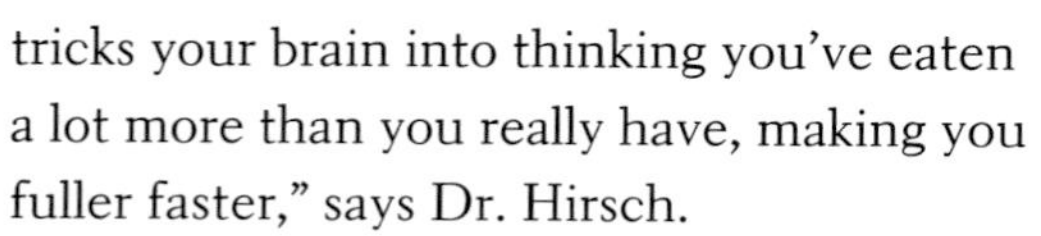

To make your own appetite-busting smoothie, blend together a banana, 1/2 cup nonfat vanilla yogurt, 1/8 cup frozen orange-juice concentrate, 1/2 cup 1% milk, and 1/2 cup crushed ice. Mix until it begins to get frothy; the extra air will also fend off your hunger pangs. A Penn State study found that men who drank yogurt shakes that had been blended until they doubled in volume ate 96 fewer calories a day than men who drank shakes of normal thickness. "The extra volume helps to fill you up and curb your appetite," says Barbara Rolls, Ph.D., the study author. And it'll be that much easier to belch Beethoven's "Ode to Joy."

Calories saved in 4 weeks: 2,688

Soda for the Drive Home

The best place to get used to the taste of diet soda is a minimart, according to Ward. The soda at those places is always ice cold. "The colder a diet soda is when you're drinking it, the less you'll notice the difference in taste," she says. Or try hitting the self-serve drink station at a fast-food place. "If you can't stand diet but want to start drinking it, try filling your cup three-fourths of the way with regular soda and topping it off with diet," says Ward. "Then gradually adjust the ratio until you can wean yourself off regular altogether."

Calories saved in 4 weeks: 2,024

Your Evening Beer

There's nothing wrong with "lite" beer, unless you count not tasting anything like the real thing. Unfortunately, a bottle of Sam Adams or Heineken can set you back around 170 calories. Here are some better regular beer choices:

BEER	CALORIES PER 12-OZ BOTTLE
Cerveza Tecate	110
Keystone	122
Busch	133

Calories saved in 4 weeks: at least 1,036

BY MICHAEL McNULTY

Fuel Your Fire

Eight challenging days in the life, and eight rocket meals to propel you through them

You wouldn't go into a meeting without your lies and evasions in order, right? Toe the line at a marathon with just your left shoe on? Hell no, you say. But tell us: Why do you step out the door on the most important days of your life with any old swill in your stomach?

Guilty as charged, right? The thing is, a nutritional edge is such an easy advantage to claim. Your premeeting, pregame, prebacchanalia foods can bring mind and body in tune and supply you with fuel that will sustain you through the last Power Point, the final fit with the caddie, the last snog in the corner. To help you find that edge, we consulted a team of Machiavellian nutritionists and tactical snackers to determine the absolute best foods to send you into the fray and welcome you home. On your mark, get set, eat.

When You're Playing Catch-Up at Work

You've spent the last 3 days cruising fantasygirls.com and napping in an empty third-floor office, but now you've got to produce.

Eat: Small meals with snacks in between. Start the morning with a low-fat blueberry muffin and a cup of whole grain cereal with low-fat milk. An hour or two later, grab a block of cheese and a banana. At noon, go Chinese—chicken or vegetable stir-fry and steamed rice is ideal. Finish the day with more snacks: an orange at 2:00, and a pack of peanut-butter cookies or a bag of nuts at 4:00.

When: Try to eat once every 2 hours.

Why: Frequent snacking prevents the dips in blood sugar that lead to Brian Wilson–like lulls in productivity. "Large meals trigger a surge of energy-sapping insulin, but small meals help to keep insulin and energy levels at their peak," says Jackie Berning, Ph.D., R.D., a University of Colorado nutritionist.

Avoid: Too much protein without carbs to counterbalance it. Since your brain runs on carbohydrates, you need a steady supply in order to perform at your peak.

After Your Workout

When you're not savoring the pump or preening by the water fountain . . .

Eat: An energy bar with a four-to-one ratio of carbohydrates to protein. A chocolate-chip Clif bar has a perfect ratio of 40 grams of carbs to 10 grams of protein.

When: As soon as you finish your last rep.

Why: The minutes following a workout are the easiest time to replenish your carbohydrate reserves. And the four-to-one ratio of carbs and protein is ideal for triggering a spike in your body's production of insulin. "Having extra insulin in your system after working out stimulates protein synthesis, making your body's muscle-building system more effective," says Thomas Incledon, M.S., R.D., director of sports nutrition for Human Performance Specialists.

Avoid: Calorie-dense protein shakes.

Drink 1,500 calories after burning 1,000 calories and you still gain weight.

When You Have a Tee Time

John Daly can drive the ball 350 yards after eating Taco Bell food, but you'd better hope you're not downwind in the gallery. Instead of going Mexican, you should . . .

Eat: A cup of low-fat yogurt and 2 tablespoons of peanut butter on a slice of whole wheat bread.

When: 1 to 2 hours before tee time.

Why: "The yogurt and peanut butter provide 20 grams of protein, which will slow digestion and keep your energy levels high for an entire round of golf," says Roxanne Moore, M.S., R.D., a nutritionist at Towson University in Maryland.

Avoid: A pregreens pizza feast. "Spices and tomatoes can trigger an upset stomach," says Robert McMurray, Ph.D., a professor of sports nutrition at the University of North Carolina.

Before a Job Interview

Your future is on the line, and your brain is thrashing like a speed metal band.

Eat: Dark chocolate.

When: Immediately before you step into the waiting room.

Why: Chocolate has the perfect mix of sugar and caffeine to help you do well under pressure. "Caffeine makes you feel sharper and more aware of your surroundings," says Richard Anderson, Ph.D., a USDA scientist. As for the sugar, researchers at Yale found that mental activity actually saps sugar from your bloodstream. By spiking blood-sugar levels with a bit of chocolate, you can think longer before feeling drained.

Avoid: An energy drink like Red Bull, which has less caffeine than an average cup of coffee. As for the "revitalizing herbs," there's not enough of them per can to have any effect on your body.

TOUGH TALK

"My strategy was simple: I didn't eat anything that was fattening, fried, fast food, or just plain not good for me."

JOEY CALLOWAY, *MEN'S HEALTH* BELLY-OFF CLUB MEMBER, ON LOSING 185 POUNDS

Before a Marathon

Try to sneak a bite of whatever the Kenyans are eating. But if they won't share . . .

Eat: A handful of macadamia nuts.

When: Half an hour before race time.

Why: Pasta and beer are a prerace tradition, so go for it. But unless there's some fat in your system when you cross the starting line, your body won't efficiently burn your energy reserves. "Macadamia nuts are a good source of unsaturated fat, which can slow your metabolism and leave you with a longer-lasting supply of energy," says Anderson.

Avoid: Skipping breakfast. Eat at least an egg and a small bowl of oatmeal, and drink a cup of low-fat milk. "Avoid high-fiber foods; they'll leave you stopping at a Porta Potti during the race," says Moore.

During a Long Bike Ride

You can pack your bag with hard-to-swallow sports gels, or you can go for something a bit closer to real food.

Eat: Dehydrated fruit, low-fat granola bars, and Fig Newtons.

When: At the bottom of that next grueling hill.

Why: "You need to keep your energy up and stay hydrated," says McMurray. "Fruit and granola are ideal. They're packed with protein and carbs, without a lot of fat."

Avoid: Bulky foods high in fiber. "Salad, watermelon, and fruits with seeds, like strawberries, are all bad," says McMurray—who recently completed a 330-mile ride. "To digest high-fiber foods, your stomach diverts the flow of blood away from muscles, making each stroke of the bike's pedals harder," he says.

At Your Best Friend's Wedding

The bar is open, and so are the bridesmaids.

Eat: A good mixture of protein and fat. Look for appetizers with cheese, meat, or cream-cheese toppings. A pig-in-a-blanket is a good choice. Or, if there's a buffet, eat thin slices of turkey, chicken, or ham, along with a medium-size roll with a dab of mayo or butter.

When: Before you order your fourth G&T.

Why: To avoid doing your "funny drunk" impersonation, eat foods with a nearly equal ratio of protein to carbohydrates to fat. Each nutrient plays a specific role in keeping you sober. "Carbohydrates and fiber soak up alcohol, blocking its release into the bloodstream," says Anderson. "Protein slows down your body's rate of processing the alcohol, while fat helps to trap the booze in your stomach, delaying the start of the digestive process," he adds.

Avoid: Mini-quiches. Just one has 226 calories and 18 grams of fat, most of it saturated.

Before the Clock Starts

Wade Boggs ate chicken. Michael Jordan preferred steak and potatoes. You should . . .

Eat: 1½ cups of spaghetti with three 2-ounce meatballs, a small salad with light dressing, and a piece of garlic bread.

When: 3 hours before suiting up.

Why: You want a meal that gives your body a continuous supply of oomph during play. This blend of 55 percent carbohydrates, 25 percent fat, and 20 percent protein provides the perfect combination of instant and long-term energy to help you make it through double OT.

Avoid: High-fat foods, which take longer to digest and end up sucking oxygen away from your muscles instead of helping to create more energy.

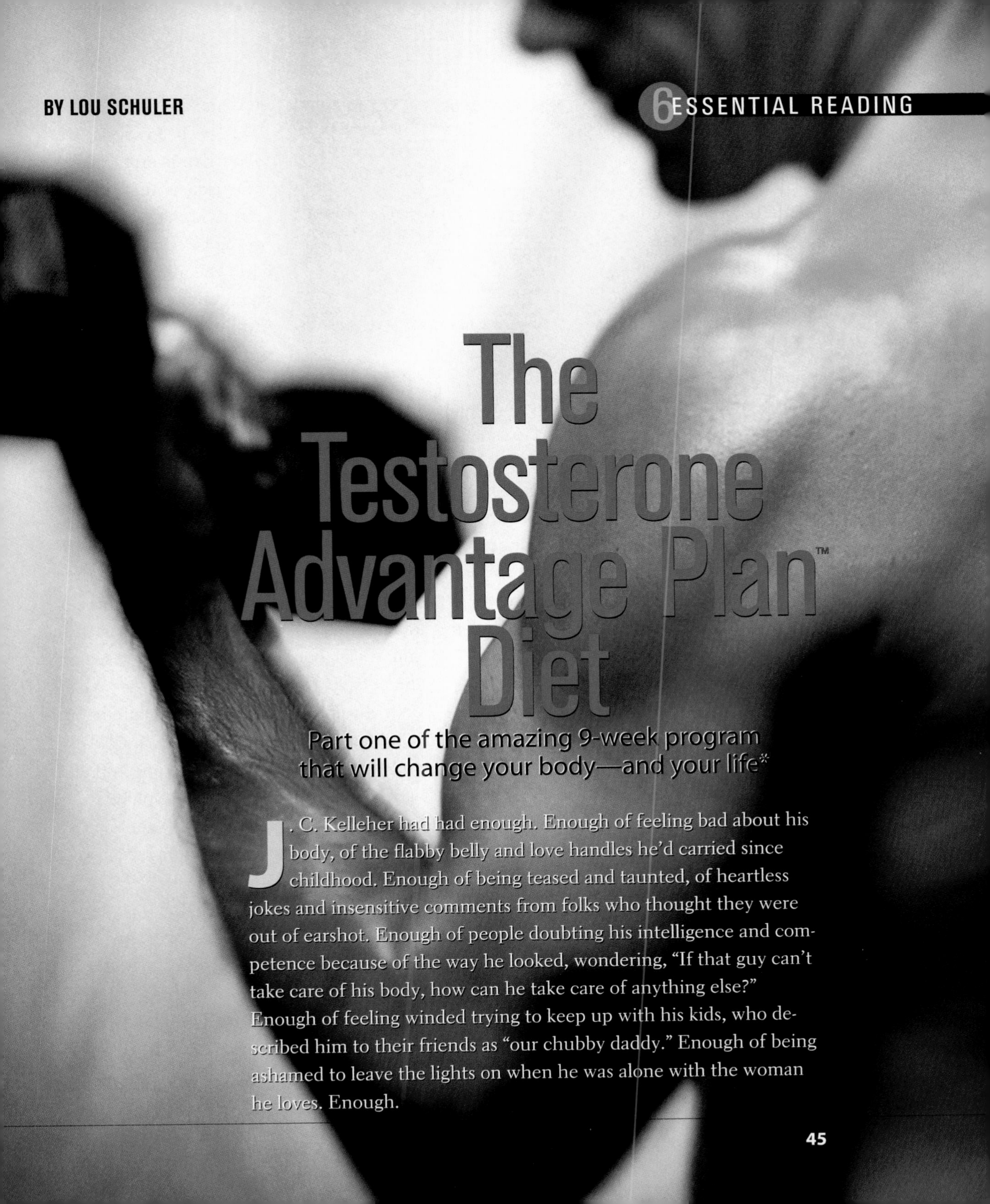

BY LOU SCHULER

The Testosterone Advantage Plan™ Diet

Part one of the amazing 9-week program that will change your body—and your life*

J. C. Kelleher had had enough. Enough of feeling bad about his body, of the flabby belly and love handles he'd carried since childhood. Enough of being teased and taunted, of heartless jokes and insensitive comments from folks who thought they were out of earshot. Enough of people doubting his intelligence and competence because of the way he looked, wondering, "If that guy can't take care of his body, how can he take care of anything else?" Enough of feeling winded trying to keep up with his kids, who described him to their friends as "our chubby daddy." Enough of being ashamed to leave the lights on when he was alone with the woman he loves. Enough.

So Kelleher took control. And in just 9 weeks, his entire life changed.

"I knew I needed to do something. I just didn't know what," he says.

Like most men who try to lose weight, Kelleher found that traditional diet-and-exercise programs simply didn't work. The diets were hard to stick to, and they cut out all his favorite foods, from sirloins to sandwiches. Worse, the traditional aerobic workouts often prescribed for weight loss—run, run, run—tend to leave men with aching joints and miles and miles of frustration.

> **HARD TRUTH**
>
> ***Makes a plain ol' cheese bomb seem dietetic***
>
> **Number of calories just four slices of pepperoni add to your piece of pizza:**
>
> ***108***
>
> **Source: U.S. Department of Agriculture**

In the past several years, however, research has shown two things: 1) Low-fat diets may not work because they suppress the manufacture of testosterone, the hormone that may be our most potent weapon in the fight to build muscle and burn away fat; 2) aerobic exercise can reduce muscle mass. In fact, one study showed that men with higher levels of testosterone were 75 percent less likely to be obese than men with lower testosterone levels. They were also 72 percent less likely to have a heart attack and 31 percent less likely to have high diastolic blood pressure.

Fortunately for Kelleher, he and 15 other men were among the first to try a new testosterone-boosting diet and exercise program. And the changes they saw were simply extraordinary.

"This program was an opportunity to change the way I'd been living for the past 20 years," says Kelleher. "This has been so easy to follow that everything fell into place naturally. It was a lifestyle change, much for the better. The kids don't call me their chubby daddy anymore. Now I'm just their dad, like I always wanted to be."

Today, Kelleher is 5 foot 10 inches, 172 pounds, with a 32-inch waist. He can toss a football around with his 11-year-old son and not have to quit because he's winded. His wife likes to look at him naked.

And strangers treat him . . . like a person. "People respond to me differently. They're more receptive to my thoughts and ideas," Kelleher says. "I hate to say that people are superficial, but if they like what they see on the outside, they're more receptive to what's on the inside. I find I'm more accepted now."

A transformation like this—82 pounds and 12 inches of waist girth stripped off at age 35—takes time. It takes discipline. It takes a plan. Fortunately, we've got one. We call it the Testosterone Advantage Plan. You might just call it a miracle.

How the Diet Works

Throughout the diet wars, one notion has remained fairly constant: Fat makes you fat, while carbohydrates make you slim. Another assumption has also gone largely unchallenged: Fat has no effect on muscle mass, while carbohydrate preserves muscle.

Add these two bits of nutritional folklore together and you get the idea that a low-fat, high-carbohydrate diet is ideal for weight loss and muscle preservation.

Meat eaters have much higher testosterone levels than vegetarians

But evidence is building that the opposite could be true. A 1989 study in the *American Journal of Clinical Nutrition* placed six men on either a high-carb diet, in which the ratio of carbohydrate calories to fat calories was two to one, or a high-fat diet, in which the ratio was one to one. The men had higher nitrogen levels—meaning their bodies preserved protein better—on the high-fat diet.

A more recent study looked at what happens when you cut calories of fat in the diet without reducing total calories. The answer: Triglycerides go up, increasing your risk of heart disease, but no fat is lost.

"I Wasn't Hungry at All"

Ed Stash is the embodiment of what's wrong with homemade workout programs and so-called healthy diets: They don't work.

On life before the T plan: "I was lifting weights every day, close to an hour and a half a day. I was also trying to keep in shape by eating low-fat foods. I thought I was watching what I ate, but it turns out I was probably taking in 1,000 calories a day that were a total waste. I was on that diet for 3 years, and I worked out religiously. In those 3 years, I went up two pants sizes."

On the T diet: "I wasn't hungry at all. There was more than enough food."

On his results: "I am the strongest I've ever been in my life. I got the greatest increases in strength in my biceps and triceps and in my back. I had to buy a whole new wardrobe."

On others' reactions: "People who hadn't seen me in a couple of months were shocked. When I was home visiting my parents, I saw a neighbor who was 20 or 21 years old. She hadn't seen me in about 8 years. She just came right out and said, 'You have a very nice ass.'"

Bottom line: "I feel more confident everywhere I go. Just seeing what I was able to accomplish, I feel better about myself."

Ed Stash, 28, 5'10"

	BEFORE T PLAN	AFTER T PLAN
Weight	187 lb	172 lb
Waist	35"	32"
Chinups	7	11

Moreover, many studies have found that meat eaters have much higher testosterone levels than vegetarians. Men increase testosterone on a fat-rich diet and lose it on a low-fat diet.

Another study of 1,522 men ages 40 to 70 found that the men following low-protein diets had decreased testosterone activity, which then led to—egads!—decreased sexual performance.

Unfortunately, the U.S. government, along with most dietitians, is still stuck on the idea that low-fat eating is better for everybody—men, women, and everything in between. This philosophy is symbolized by the Food Guide Pyramid, which recommends huge quantities of breads and other grains, smallish amounts of protein-rich foods, and almost no fat at all. In fact, fats and sweets are lumped together in a tiny prison cell at the top of the pyramid, meaning our preeminent nutritional guide-

"She Wants Me to Model"

Though not our most impressive subject in terms of pure strength, J. C. Kelleher underwent one of our most dramatic personal transformations.

On his reasons for trying the T plan: "I was having problems with headaches and chest pains. I wasn't feeling too good about myself."

On his past attempts at losing weight: "I'd go faithfully to a gym and work out three or four times a week and see absolutely no results." He did manage to lose 30 pounds in the 6 months before the T plan, but had to use an ephedra-based supplement, Metabolite, to do it.

On the T plan itself: "I never felt empty. I made my meals the prior night, and I was dedicated to it."

On his results: "This is basically the least I've ever weighed as an adult. I'm doing a lot more with my kids. We'll play soccer or shoot hoops; I can maneuver around now like I couldn't before. I have more energy. I even stopped snoring."

On his wife's reaction: "Last night, she looked at me and said with a smile, 'I lost half my husband.' She wants me to model clothing for her. She checks me out in the dressing room as I'm changing. She wants me to turn around so she can see my backside. I have more 'quality time' with her."

Bottom line: "It changed my life."

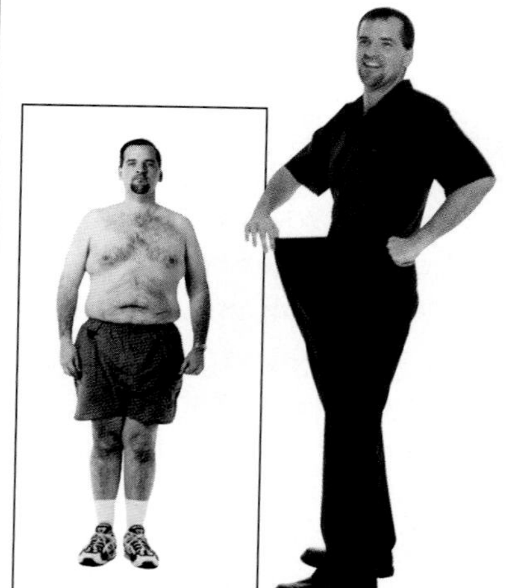

J. C. Kelleher, 35, 5'10"

	BEFORE T PLAN	AFTER T PLAN	TODAY
Weight	224 lb	199 lb	172 lb
Waist	43"	38"	32"

line makes no distinction between olive oil and Ding Dongs.

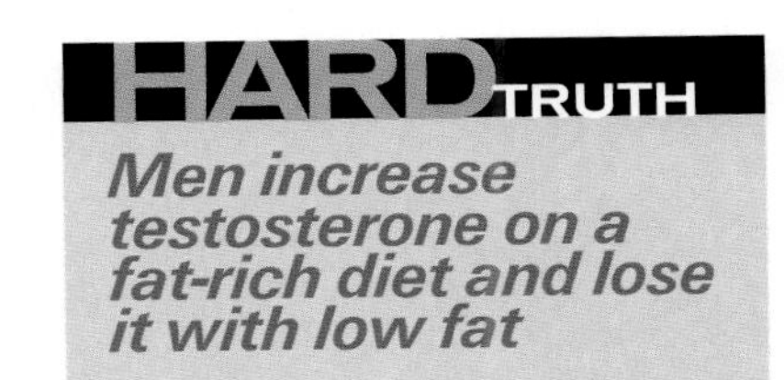

We say it's time to junk the pyramid. In its place, we'd like to suggest the *Men's Health* T, created by Jeff Volek, Ph.D., R.D., a nutrition researcher at the University of Connecticut. Our T, as you may have guessed, stands for testosterone. That's because our diet increases your testosterone by increasing your intake of healthy fat.

The base of the T is protein, 2 grams for every kilogram (2.2 pounds) of body weight. Of the three macronutrients—fat, carbohydrate, protein—it's the one that makes you feel fullest fastest. In addition, your body uses more energy to process protein than it does to process the other two.

Your protein intake will remain constant as long as you stay on the T diet. But protein as a percentage of the total calories in your diet will increase or decrease depending on your goals, and the proportions of your *Men's Health* T will change to reflect this.

For an idea of what a typical day's meal plan will look like, check out pages 50 and 51. You'll see that this "diet" requires you to eat an awful lot of food—not just three squares, but five meals and snacks spread throughout the day. (Note: You will get best results from following the diet in conjunction with the workout on pages 86 to 89.)

All the meals are important, of course, but two matter more than the others.

Breakfast: A hearty breakfast helps prevent food cravings later in the day. It gives your body protein to work with, preventing it from cannibalizing your biceps to get the amino acids it needs to keep your systems running. And a good breakfast stabilizes your blood sugar, giving you a source of steady energy to start your day.

Postworkout snack: The hormone insulin speeds nutrients to your muscles after a workout and also stops muscle breakdown. All it takes is carbohydrate and protein, eaten as soon as possible following exercise.

The rankings among your other three feedings are mostly equal, although your pre-exercise meal deserves a bit more consideration. That's because you won't get as good a workout if you're ravenously hungry or sluggishly full. A good rule of thumb is to exercise 1 hour after a snack or 2 hours after a meal.

So if you like to exercise in the morning, we recommend a snack as soon as you wake up, followed an hour later by a workout, followed immediately by a full meal—in this case breakfast. Or if you like to work out before lunch, just make sure you have your mid-morning snack 1 hour before you hit the weight room. And if you're an after-work exerciser, time it so you train 1 hour after your mid-afternoon snack.

What's Your Goal?

Whether you want to slim down, bulk up, or just change your body composition, there's a *Men's Health* T plan for you.

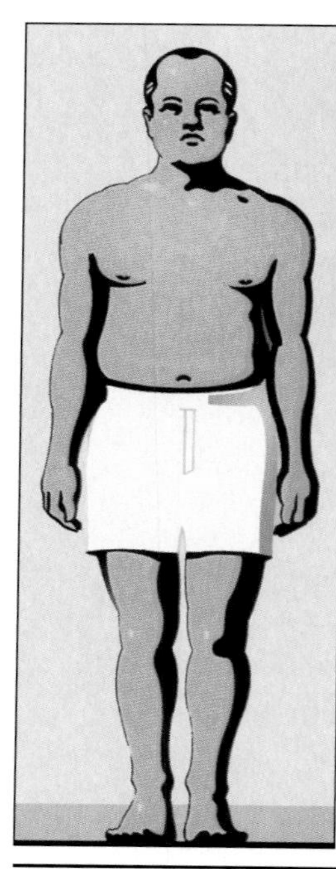

GUY #1

AGE: 45 WEIGHT: 230

GOAL: 2-pounds-per-week fat loss

FAT: 30 percent

CARBS: 30 percent

PROTEIN: 40 percent

Breakfast

▶1 cup Shredded Wheat and Bran with 3/4 cup 1% milk

▶5 links turkey breakfast sausage

Snack 1

▶1 ounce dry-roasted peanuts

▶1 cup 1% milk

▶1 cup 1% cottage cheese

Lunch

▶Sandwich made with 2 slices multigrain bread, 1 tablespoon Miracle Whip, 6 ounces fat-free turkey lunchmeat, 1/2 cup spinach, and 2 tomato slices

Snack 2

▶Sandwich made with 2 slices multigrain bread, 1 tablespoon Miracle Whip, relish, and 1 can tuna (drained)

Dinner

▶1 serving stir-fry with 3 ounces chicken, frozen stir-fry vegetables, fresh ginger, minced garlic, and soy sauce

DAILY CALORIES: 2,000

GUY #2

AGE: 35 WEIGHT: 180

GOAL: More muscle, less fat

FAT: 38 percent

CARBS: 38 percent

PROTEIN: 24 percent

Breakfast

▶1 3/4 cup Shredded Wheat and Bran with 1 cup 1% milk

▶3 links turkey breakfast sausage

▶1/2 cup pineapple chunks

Snack 1

▶2 ounces dry-roasted peanuts

▶1 cup 1% milk

Lunch

▶2 sandwiches, each made with 2 slices multigrain bread, 1 tablespoon mayonnaise, 3 ounces turkey lunchmeat, 1/2 cup spinach, and 2 tomato slices

▶1 orange

Snack 2

▶1 ounce dry-roasted peanuts

▶1 cup 2% chocolate milk

Dinner

▶1 serving chicken-and-vegetable stir-fry with 6 ounces chicken, plus 1/4 cup brown rice

DAILY CALORIES: 2,700

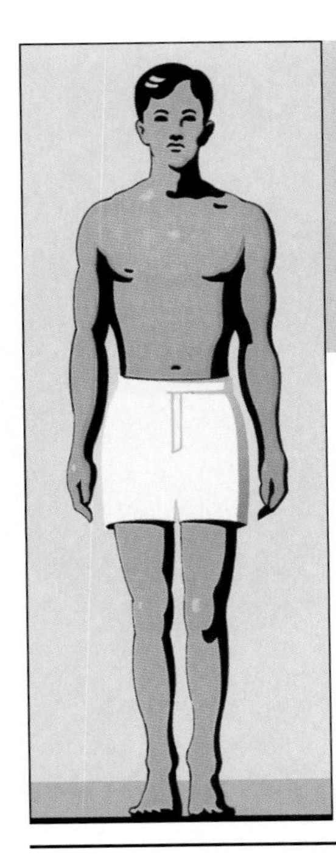

GUY #3

AGE: 25 WEIGHT: 150

GOAL: 1-pound-per-week muscle gain

FAT: 41 percent

CARBS: 41 percent

PROTEIN: 18 percent

Breakfast

▶ $1\frac{3}{4}$ cup Shredded Wheat and Bran with 1 cup 1% milk

▶ 3 links turkey breakfast sausage

▶ $\frac{1}{2}$ cup pineapple chunks

Snack 1

▶ 1 plain bagel with 2 tablespoons peanut butter

Lunch

▶ 2 sandwiches, each made with 2 slices multigrain bread, 1 tablespoon mayonnaise, 2 ounces turkey lunchmeat, $\frac{1}{2}$ cup spinach, and 2 tomato slices

▶ 1 orange

Snack 2

▶ 3 ounces dry-roasted peanuts

Dinner

▶ 1 serving chicken-and-vegetable stir-fry with 4 ounces chicken, some walnuts, and $\frac{1}{2}$ cup brown rice

DAILY CALORIES: 3,000

* Turn to page 86 for The Testosterone Advantage Plan Workout, part two of the amazing 9-week program that will change your body—and your life.

Adapted from the book *The Testosterone Advantage Plan*, by Lou Schuler, with Jeff Volek, R.D., Ph.D., Michael Mejia, and Adam Campbell. © 2002 by Rodale Inc. Available wherever books are sold.

Trainer's Forum

with MICHAEL MEJIA

PROTEIN PLUSES

Q: My friends swear by their protein powders to help maintain energy and gain muscle. Are there advantages to adding any of these "mixes" to my diet as opposed to just eating more lean meat or other protein? What kind, if any, do you recommend?

T. R., ROANOKE, VIRGINIA

A: Whenever you can, you should eat "real food." That said, in today's fast-paced world sometimes you just can't. But when you don't eat for prolonged periods, you face a twofold problem: 1) Your blood sugar levels drop, leaving you with far less energy. 2) Your body doesn't get the protein it needs every 3 to 4 hours to build muscle. More than anything else, meal replacement drinks such as Met-Rx, Myoplex, and the like offer a quick, nutritious alternative to your typical fast-food fare.

The only time you're better off with a supplement than a sit-down meal is after you've finished your workout. After an intense training session, your muscles crave protein—immediately. Your best bet here is a straight whey protein powder mixed with fruit juice, which your body can absorb more rapidly than either a solid meal or other protein drinks.

TOUGH TALK

"I hate the word *diet*, so I prefer to call it *food-consumption modification*."

JEFFREY CHADWICK, *MEN'S HEALTH* BELLY-OFF CLUB MEMBER, ON LOSING 80 POUNDS

STRATEGIES

At Breakfast

EAT THIS	NOT THAT
2 Egg McMuffins	**Sesame bagel with 2 Tbsp cream cheese**
580 calories	643 calories
24 g fat	28 g fat
34 g protein	20 g protein

At the Ballpark

EAT THIS	NOT THAT
Hot dog with mustard and sauerkraut **16-oz light beer** **Soft pretzel**	**Chili dog** **16-oz regular beer** **Cheese nachos**
680 calories	904 calories
19 g fat	37 g fat
20 g protein	28 g protein

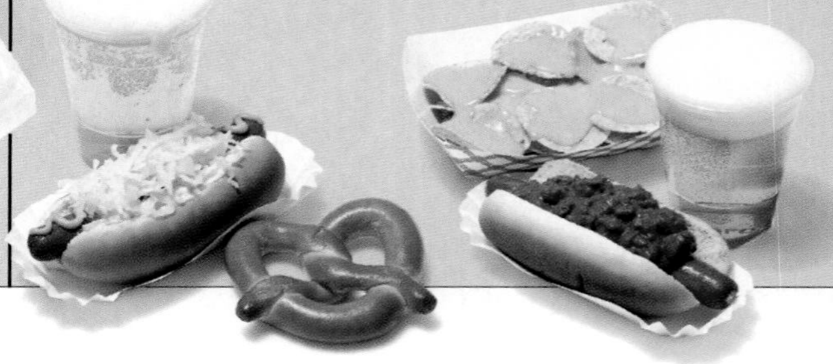

METABOLIFT

Q: What should I do to get the greatest and longest boost of my resting metabolic rate? Will this burn fat even while I'm resting?

D. W., HELENA, MONTANA

A: Two words: Strength training.

You won't just get the long-term metabolic boost you get from adding muscle to your frame—although that's a nice perk. Depending on how you do it, strength training can cause an immediate, and often prolonged, spike in your metabolic rate compared to typical steady-state aerobic exercise. In fact, programs that use moderate to heavy loads (60 to 80 percent of your one-rep max) and brief rest intervals (45 to 60 seconds) can cause your metabolism to remain significantly elevated for hours on end.

The reason for the metabolic afterburn associated with this kind of strength training is its tremendous intensity. If you're looking to get a similar effect from your aerobic workouts, ditch the slow, steady stuff and try interval training. Several intervals of all-out running for 30 to 60 seconds followed by a jog or brisk walk of twice that duration will produce much better results than zoning out for that half-hour on the treadmill.

TOUGH TALK

"You can find your way across the country using burger joints the way a navigator uses stars."

CHARLES KURALT

HARD TRUTH

The eyes don't have it

Number of pounds you could lose in a year by using a measuring cup for your cereal instead of eyeballing the portion:

10

SOURCE: ***Journal of the American College of Nutrition***

At the Steakhouse

EAT THIS	NOT THAT
6-oz grilled top-round steak	6-oz grilled rib-eye steak
Baked sweet potato	2 cups french fries
Ear of corn with pat of butter	½ cup broccoli with cheese sauce
603 calories	968 calories
21 g fat	60 g fat
56 g protein	52 g protein

At the Sushi Bar

EAT THIS	NOT THAT
1 California roll (9-piece serving)	1 orange roll (9-piece serving)
6 salmon nigiri	1 spicy shrimp hand roll (1 cone-shaped roll)
1 cup miso soup	1½ cups salad with ginger-sesame dressing
804 calories	1,262 calories
9.6 g fat	32 g fat
28 g protein	59 g protein

BUILD MUSCLE

You want the truth? Can you handle the truth? Here it is: Building muscle takes motivation, dedication, and a lot of hard work. But it's worth it, because in the end, might feels right. Not to mention the fact that it looks damn fine.

So we enlisted a few good muscle men, from certified strength-and-conditioning specialists to U.S. marines, to show you the best drills you can use to become a man of arms . . . and abs . . . and pecs. Here's your battle plan—get ready to see some action.

MH•QUIZ

Are You Fit for Battle?

Today nearly 1.5 million members of the United States military are on active duty, an elite 12 percent of them belonging to the Marine Corps. Do you have what it takes to join that echelon of strength, stamina, and bravery? The Marine Corps uses the following test to gauge the physical fitness of its troops. Take it and find out if you pass muster.

1 CHINUPS

Grasp the bar using whatever hand position feels comfortable. With feet off the floor, pull up until your chin is above the bar, then lower yourself until your arms are fully extended again. Repeat to exhaustion.

2 MODIFIED SITUPS

Lie on your back with knees flexed, feet flat on the floor, and arms folded across your chest. (Arms must remain against the chest throughout the exercise; a buddy can hold your feet or legs below the knees for added leverage.) Raise your upper body until your elbows or forearms touch your thighs, then return to the starting position. Do as many as you can in 2 minutes.

3 THREE-MILE RUN

Done as fast as possible over reasonably level terrain.

YOUR SCORE

1. Chinups: ______ (number done × 5)
2. Situps: ______ (number done)
3. Run: ______ (points, based on the following scale: time of 18:00 = 100 points, 18:10 = 99 points, 8:20 = 98 points, 18:30 = 97 points, and so on; round time to the next highest tenth)

TOTAL SCORE: ______ (add the three numbers)

	YOUR AGE			
YOUR RANK	**17–26**	**27–39**	**40–45**	**46+**
1st Class	225+	200+	175+	150+
2nd Class	175	150	125	100
3rd Class	135	110	88	65
Fail	<105	<94	<88	<65

NOT MARINE TOUGH? We'll fix that.

The following program, designed exclusively for *Men's Health* by marine martial-arts instructors at Quantico, Virginia, includes 14 exercises that can be done in 30 to 40 minutes with nothing more than a folding chair and an inner tube. It's a total-body workout designed to build not only strength and endurance, but also explosiveness and power—the battle cry of the new marine. Do it daily if you want, moving quickly from one exercise to the next for extra aerobic benefit. (Be forewarned: This is not a get-back-in-shape, beginner's program. It assumes a respectable level of fitness and a desire to go beyond it.)

1. Grippers: Extend both arms straight overhead, then quickly open and close your hands for 30 seconds. Repeat with arms extended in front, and then to either side.

2. Shadowboxing: 10 lead-hand jabs, 10 rear-hand jabs, 10 left hooks, 10 right hooks, 10 left uppercuts, 10 right uppercuts. Repeat this series two or three times while moving on your feet like a boxer; as fitness builds, increase the repetitions or hold light dumbbells.

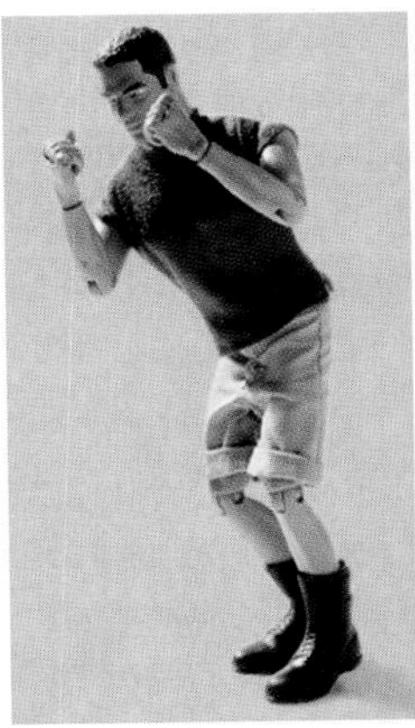

3. Resisted punching: Tie a bicycle inner tube to a doorknob. Close the door, then practice punching while you grip the tube: 10 to 20 with the lead hand, 10 to 20 with the rear hand. For extra power, twist your hips before delivering the punch.

4. Wall chair: With your back against a smooth wall, slowly squat and walk your feet out until your thighs are parallel to the floor. It should look as if you're sitting on an invisible chair. Hold for 60 seconds.

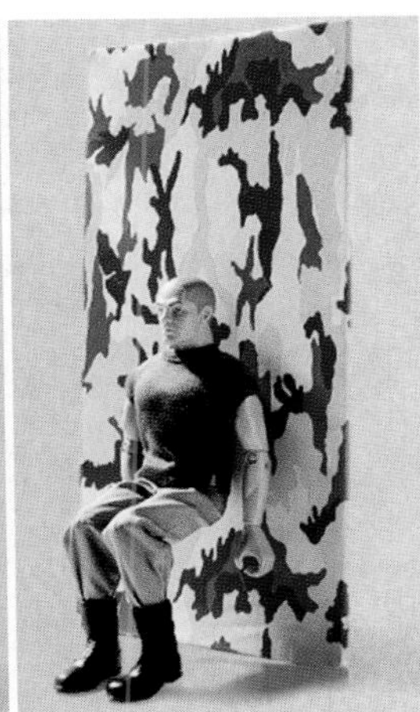

5. Side kicks: Ten left-leg kicks, 10 right-leg kicks. Repeat this series two or three times, holding the back of a folding chair for support if necessary; as fitness and flexibility increase, kick above the chair seat and then, eventually, above the chair back.

6. Chinese pushups: Bend over and put your hands on the floor. Walk them forward until your torso and legs form an inverted V, as shown. Make a triangle with your hands by bringing the tips of your index fingers and thumbs together. Then use your arms to lower your-

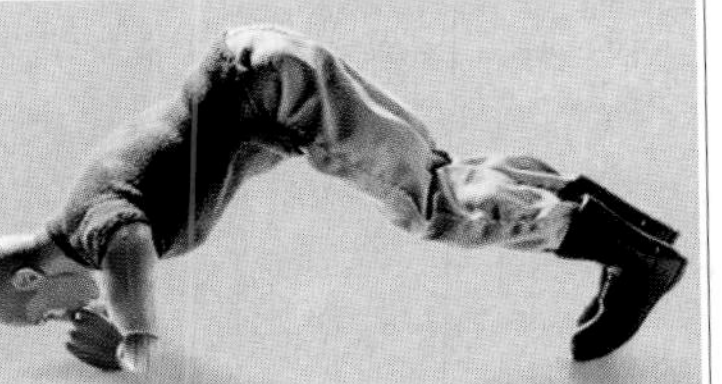

self until your nose touches the triangle. Repeat 5 to 10 times.

7. **Boot slappers:** Stand with legs slightly more than shoulder width apart, squat down, slap the sides of your ankles, then stand back up. Repeat 10 to 20 times.

8. **Dive-bombers:** Put your hands and feet on the floor so your body forms an inverted V. In one fluid motion, bend your arms, sweep your upper body down and forward, and drop your butt. Then push your torso up until your head is up, your back is arched, and your arms are straight, with your elbows locked. Hold this for a few seconds, then push back to the start. (Only your hands and toes ever touch the floor.) Repeat 5 to 10 times.

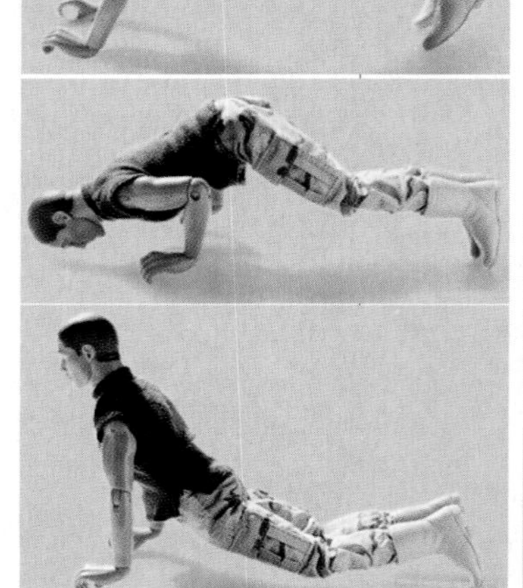

9. **Korean jumping jacks:** Stand with your hands behind your head, then drop down onto one knee. Stand back up, then do the same with the other leg. Alternate for a 20 count.

10. **Bicycle:** Lie on your back with your hands behind your head, legs extended, and feet a few inches off the floor. Touch your right elbow to your left knee as shown, then your left elbow to your right knee. Continue alternating for a total count of 20. (Keep your feet off the floor and your lower back against the floor at all times.)

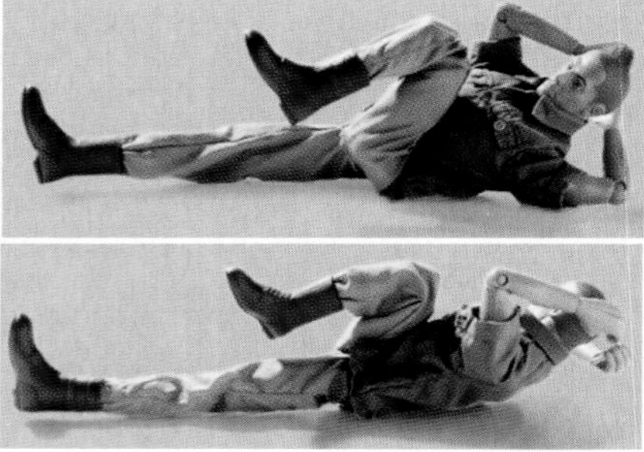

11. Star jumpers: Just like boot slappers, only after squatting, explode upward while extending your arms and legs. Do 10.

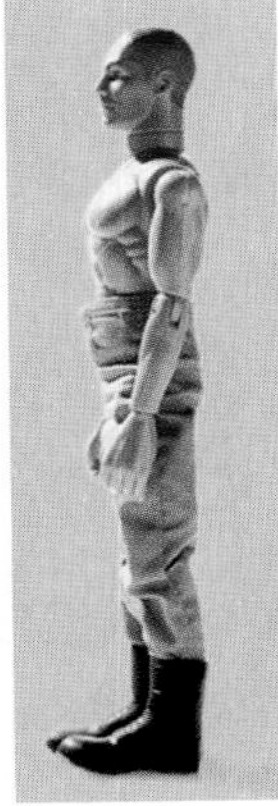

12. V-ups: Lie on your back with legs and arms extended. Keeping your knees and elbows locked, simultaneously raise your legs and upper body while trying to touch your fingers to your toes. Repeat 5 to 10 times.

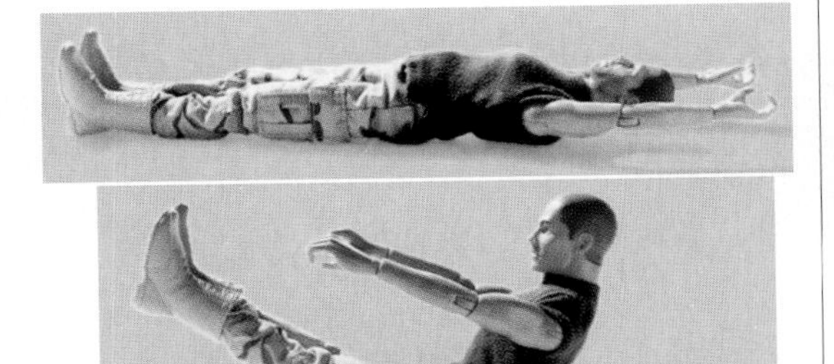

13. Push-aways: Lie on your back with your hands on your chest, legs extended, feet a few inches off the ground, and head curled forward. Alternately bring each knee toward your head, then forcefully kick forward. (Don't let your feet touch the floor.) Do 10 with each leg.

14. Hip raises: Lie on your back with your palms on the ground and your legs extended overhead. Raise your hips a few inches off the floor, using as little arm leverage as possible. Repeat 10 to 15 times.

–JOE KITA

BY JOE KITA

Martial Laws

Follow these Marine Corps rules of engagement and you, too, will become a hard body

It was 0600 at the Marine Instructor-Trainer School in Quantico, Virginia, and someone had parked in Lieutenant Colonel George Bristol's spot. A small squad of marines, dressed in fatigues, had surrounded the offending vehicle and was plotting a predawn strike. Finally, one of them popped the lock and pulled the trigger on the parking brake, and together they heaved it out of the way . . .

Bristol is a big gun of a man with a personality like cold steel, but he tells this story as sweetly as if he were reminiscing about a childhood Christmas. As he lounges in his foxhole of an office at Quantico, his bayonet-blue eyes suddenly lose some of their usual glint and he swipes a callused knuckle across a nose that's been broken multiple times. "I have a very strong bond with all my marines," the 44-year-old 26-year veteran tells me. "I don't say this to them a lot, but they're like my sons. Sometimes you have to kick 'em, and sometimes you have to lick 'em. For a marine, the team is everything."

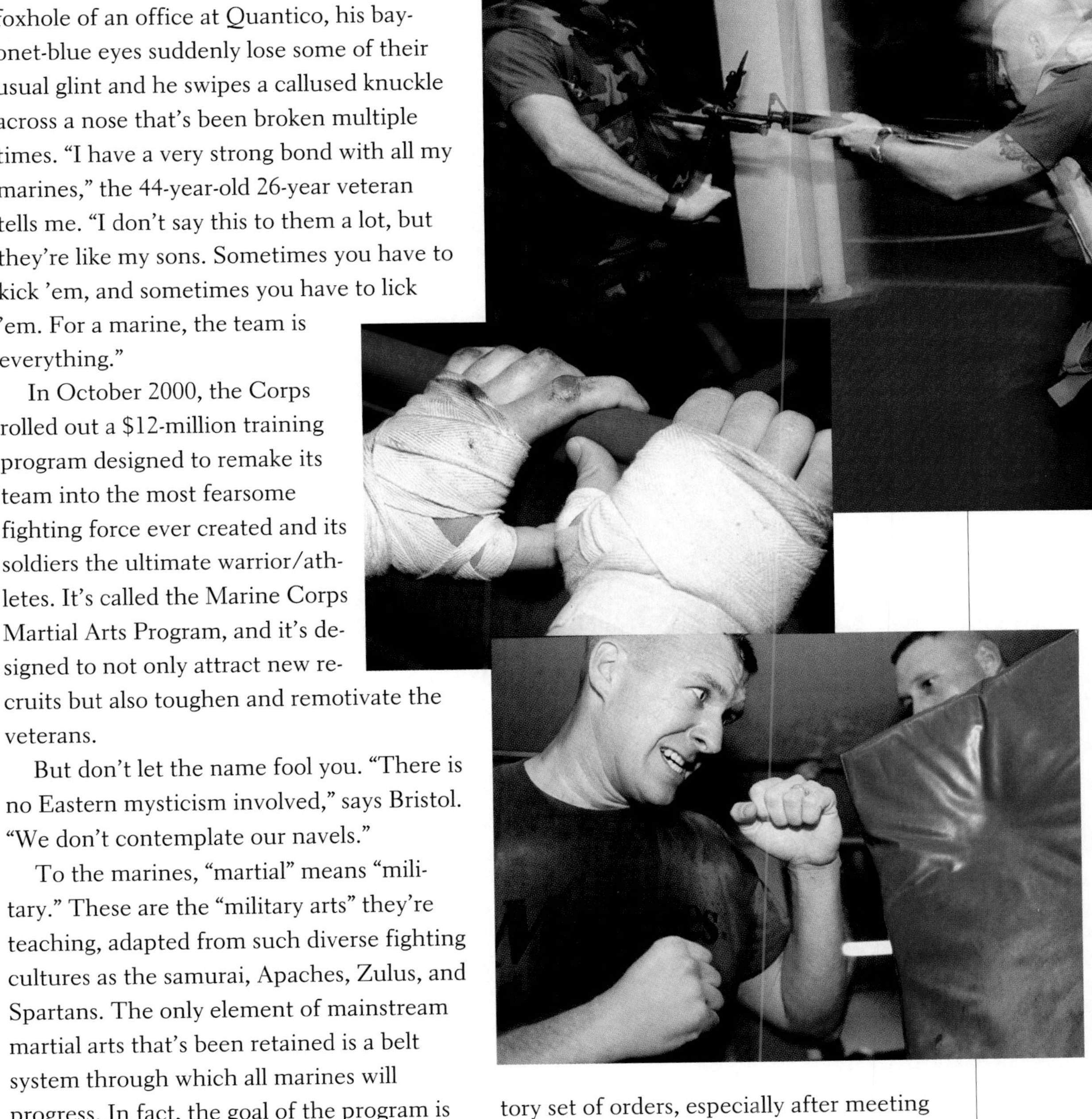

In October 2000, the Corps rolled out a $12-million training program designed to remake its team into the most fearsome fighting force ever created and its soldiers the ultimate warrior/athletes. It's called the Marine Corps Martial Arts Program, and it's designed to not only attract new recruits but also toughen and remotivate the veterans.

But don't let the name fool you. "There is no Eastern mysticism involved," says Bristol. "We don't contemplate our navels."

To the marines, "martial" means "military." These are the "military arts" they're teaching, adapted from such diverse fighting cultures as the samurai, Apaches, Zulus, and Spartans. The only element of mainstream martial arts that's been retained is a belt system through which all marines will progress. In fact, the goal of the program is to make every enlisted man not only an accredited black belt but also a gentleman.

At first, this may sound like a contradictory set of orders, especially after meeting some of the program's leatherneck creators. Bristol, whose specialty is bayonet fighting, often snarls when he speaks. Master Gunnery Sergeant Cardo Urso, 42, whose knuckles are so thickly callused they resemble little noses, is an expert in chokeholds, face rips, nerve strikes, and a death point called "stomach 9." Lieutenant Jesse Lee Sjoberg, 28, whose everyday expression is as intense as a butane flame, keeps a set of large knives, a copy of *The Dark Side of Man*, and a jug of Fierce Lime Gatorade on his desk. And their half-dozen drill instructors all wear black sweatshirts with blood-red lettering that reads, "One Mind, Any Weapon."

No doubt about it, these are intense men in the business of training others to be proficient killers. Depending on your opinion of the military, they may or may not be role-model material. But what you can't help wanting to emulate is their level of physical conditioning. While few have Adonis physiques, they all possess a lean, do-anything hardness more impressive than that of most athletes. And even more remarkable is that this fitness has been built in the simplest of ways, using body weight, partner resistance, and gritted teeth.

At the heart of the new training program is a concept called "conversion conditioning." The goal of Bristol and his officers is to convert the basic strength, endurance, and callusing that marines acquire at boot camp into power, toughness, and integrity. With their help, we're going to show you how to do the same. The benefits that accrue will be more than physical. You'll start to get a sense of the core marine values of honor, courage, and commitment. You'll handle life with greater confidence. As Bristol puts it, "We're out to create a person who is so highly skilled that he can function in the cauldron of combat, yet has ethics, compassion, and discipline. This is the warrior gentleman."

All of us do battle every day in some small way. Our cauldron of combat may be the commuter lane, the workplace, or the dinner table across which we face our teenagers. Here's how the marines get ready for it. Here's how they build combat fitness. Here, sir, are the seven rules of engagement.

RULE #1
You'll Push Yourself Harder If You Train with a Partner

I am so wet, cold, and exhausted that I feel like one of Private Ryan's dead brothers. My fatigues are soaked, my helmet is askew, and with 30 pounds of gear on my back, I can hardly move.

My platoon is in the midst of an outdoor "thrash session"—12 exercises done in an open field as quickly as possible and interspersed with fighting drills. A big lieutenant and I alternate throwing one another to the ground. After hitting the deck a half-dozen times, I honestly cannot tell if it's the sod squishing or my intestines.

TOUGH TALK

"No gains without pains."

BENJAMIN FRANKLIN

Each time I get up, I remind myself that I don't have to do this, that I'm not enlisted. But the sergeants have split our class into two competing groups of a dozen marines apiece. If I go AWOL, my team suffers. And therein lies the first lesson.

A common reason exercise programs fail and fat wars are lost is that it's only you against the enemy. A training partner supplies motivation, exerts subtle peer pressure, and threatens your fragile ego. Whether you're grunting out final repetitions of a bench press or running one last interval, you'll respond better and push yourself further if there's someone to encourage and challenge you.

"C'mon! You can make it!" yells that big lieutenant.

And although it hurts, I do.

RULE #2
Never Let Yourself Get into a Rhythm

Not far from the aforementioned field of screams is a 3-mile stamina course that winds across broken terrain. There's one particularly steep hill, crowned by scrub brush, where Lieutenant Colonel Bristol likes to hide out. With a banshee yell and a bayonet thrust, he springs out at every marine who approaches. "I push 'em back down that hill six or seven times before I let 'em move on," he says. And this isn't the only interruption. As the marines run the course with rifles and packs, they're stopped every quarter mile or so by their drill instructors and made to fight back. Punches, kicks, falls . . . It's impossible to find a rhythm.

But that's the point. When you get into a rhythm, you get into a comfort zone. After you become proficient in an activity, conversion conditioning requires you to modify that activity in order to keep it challenging. For example, instead of running 3 miles every day on the road at a steady pace, try running on trails, where you're constantly refining balance and speed. Or instead of cycling steadily at 15 mph, do a series of surges in which you raise your speed to 18 mph for 30 seconds. The idea is to disturb the body's equilibrium and, by doing so, raise fitness.

This theory holds true for training programs as well. Too many guys exercise the same way every workout. Other than weaponry, the marines don't specialize in anything. They're cross-trainers. Try changing your primary fitness activity every 3 months and see how much fitter you become.

RULE #3
Hit and Be Hit

In the early morning, a line of already-sweaty marines kneels on mats in the base gymnasium. Their hands are raised in front

PEAK performance

Semper Fit

You don't need a gym, pogue!

Post this picture on your wall and you'll never again mutter a lame excuse for missing a workout. U.S. Marine Corporal Joshua Mount of Sugar Grove, Ohio, was fighting a war, yet still found time to stay in shape, using nothing but a sack of Afghan sand. He did what marines are trained to do: adapt, improvise, overcome.

This move is called the hammer curl, which mainly works your biceps. It also calls on your shoulders, since you're lifting the weight to your forehead. Gripping a thick bag like this hits your forearms harder than usual, too.

Stand upright like this guy—back straight, shoulders pulled back. Keep your arms tucked in to your sides and curl the weighted bag up to your forehead. We'd prefer that you keep your neck straight and your eyes front. But don't tell that to the marines. They're doing just fine.

of their chests, and on each whistle blast they fall forward onto their forearms. It makes for strange music: Tweet! BLAM! Tweet! BLAM! Tweet! BLAM! This is a body-hardening drill designed to toughen skin and deaden nerves. They do it every morning, to the front, the sides, and the rear, until the sting of the vinyl subsides and they wear a natural armor veneer.

Body hardening is a big part of conversion conditioning. It's akin to making jerky from fresh meat. Besides these impact drills, the marines also toughen themselves by boxing—2 minutes in a quartered-off ring, wearing huge gloves that feel as if you're swinging sledgehammers by round's end. "The Corps had gotten away from boxing for fear somebody would get hurt," says Bristol. "Well, guess what? This isn't the Girl Scouts. Close interpersonal violence brings you to a new level of physical and mental awareness."

We're not advocating going out to the nearest bar and slugging someone. But it's beneficial to rough yourself up a little. Practice tumbling on mats, wrestle with someone other than your girlfriend, take boxing lessons, or order some 18-ounce gloves and headgear from www.ringside.com and start your own Fight Club. All that padding will prevent anyone from getting hurt, but it'll accustom you to getting hit and expose another dimension of fitness. It'll make you resilient.

RULE #4
If You Don't Have a Goal, You Don't Have a Soul

A year-2000 survey of the U.S. armed forces found that 7 percent of marines had not exercised in the last week. That was better than the air force (23 percent), navy (16 percent), and army (9 percent), but far from the steely ideal. The new marine training program is designed to stomp out sloth by keeping troops marching toward a higher goal. This is done by way of a martial-arts belt system. A tan belt is awarded upon graduation from boot camp, and advancement through gray, green, brown, and six degrees of black belts follows. (Instead of wearing them decoratively like karate sashes, marines use them functionally, to hold up trousers.)

Such a system is important because, in Bristol's world, there are two states of existence: being and becoming. The former is where most men get stuck, defining themselves either by what they are now or by what they used to be. It's an end state. The latter, however, is where most men should be, defining themselves either by where they're heading or by what they'll one day achieve. It's a beginning.

This is the secret to reaching increasingly higher levels of fitness. An exercise program without a goal is doomed to failure. The mistake most men make is thinking that "losing weight" and "getting back in shape" are adequate goals. They're not. Just like the qualifications for earning green, brown, and black belts, they must be specific. Better that your goal be "to lose 10 pounds by December 1" or "to get in good enough shape to take this month's *Men's Health Challenge*." Specific goals are like crosshairs in a rifle sight. You need them to hit your target.

RULE #5
It's Not the Gear That Makes You Fit, but the Will to Use It

You won't see any Capilene or Synchilla labels on clothes the marines are issued. Rather, it's mostly cotton and wool, with only a grudging nod to Gore-Tex. Nor is the base gym filled with rows of high-tech fitness machines. It's striking how the Corps can train the ultimate warrior/athlete with so little help from exercise science.

But there's a reason the brass prefers canteens to CamelBaks. As part of their training, marines study martial cultures such as those of the Spartans, Zulus, and Apaches. These were some of the fiercest fighters in history, yet they succeeded with little more than a spear backed by spirit.

"Lots of guys today are gear freaks," says Bristol. "They think they need all this fancy stuff to get fit. But that's bullshit. If you want aerobic fitness, hike with a pack. If you want to strengthen every muscle in your body, do bench presses, squats, and power cleans."

If you're skeptical that it can be this simple, do the workout Bristol's officers designed, starting on page 56. It calls for only a folding chair and an inner tube.

RULE #6
To Build Power and Speed, Exercise Explosively

Marines are like coiled springs. On the surface they may appear relaxed and well polished, but deeper down, at a muscular level, they are tightly wound. Should the situation warrant, they're capable of striking with deadly force in a moment. Warriors are intimidating because you can sense this ability, this tethered power. It's a daunting something you'd love to have. And you can. Because it's not natural; it's cultivated.

The marines develop it in two ways. First, they exercise explosively. Once they've acquired basic strength and endurance, they do their drills faster and more forcefully. For example, instead of traditional leg squats, they substitute "star jumpers" (see page 59). Instructors make even traditional weight exercises more explosive by requiring troops to lift fewer pounds more quickly or take less time between sets. Standing in waist-deep water and kicking as hard as possible is another drill that builds explosive power. "We're not as interested in forklift strength as we are in strength times speed," explains Bristol.

The second way it's developed is through weighted aerobic training. Marines are legendary for marching great distances with 50-pound packs. And this has not changed. But when they take those packs off, they suddenly feel like a warmup bat minus the weighted doughnut.

You can achieve the same training effect by walking or running with a backpack. But if you're confined to urban wilderness, a less-conspicuous alternative may be a weighted vest. Called "extra-load conditioning," the process is akin to exercising in hypergravity. Studies have found significant improvements in explosive power (jumping) and cardiovascular stamina (running to exhaustion) after 3 to 6 weeks of wearing approximately 10 percent of body weight. The $150 to $195 SmartVest by Training Zone Concepts (available at www.smartvest.net, or 888-797-8378) is a well made, surprisingly comfortable model that carries up to 32 pounds.

RULE #7
Heroism Is Endurance for One Moment More

By the end of day one in the Martial Arts Program, there is blood, snot, skinned knuckles, and hound-dog exhaustion among us. I'm about to lay down arms in a hot tub, but somehow my comrades must endure 6 full weeks of this. Still, what's most important is that we've survived, and in a battle of any kind, that's sweet victory. The state we're in now is where we're most malleable. It's at this moment that the warrior/athlete begins to take shape.

"Most men don't exercise," says Bristol with a scowl, "but hard physical exercise is the basis for character development. If you're able to do these things, break through these barriers, you'll develop mental toughness. This is how integrity is built."

It's important for marines to possess these qualities because combat is, above all else, confusing. The first time Bristol was shot at (Somalia, 1993), he says he forgot about "all that John Wayne crap and wanted another flak jacket and two more helmets." But what got him through was knowing that his mind could overrule his body when it demanded surrender and, conversely, that his body would instinctively do the right thing when his mind hesitated.

Bristol learned this through training, by continually pushing past his "uncle point" and resisting the temptation to quit. The marines use physical demands, sleep deprivation, and even verbal abuse to teach this. Eventually, they hone not only mental toughness but also basic motor skills. These are the mechanics that keep a man marching or fighting long after his energy deserts. They form the bedrock that makes a fearful situation more stable.

Instilling this in yourself is as simple as gutting out a few extra repetitions on every lift, or sprinting for 10, 20, or 30 seconds at the end of each run. You'll soon find that there's always a little more left, that you have a reservoir of strength. Try a marathon, a century, or a long-distance hike next. You will reach a point during it when your body insists on stopping, but you won't let it. Then, farther along, will come another point when your mind no longer cares but your body automatically continues. When this happens, you'll have met your warrior/athlete. And Bristol, by God, will salute you.

BY MICHAEL MEJIA, C.S.C.S., AND LOU SCHULER

Muscle: A to Z

26 quick ways to build a letter-perfect body

Muscle magazines and supplement companies are determined to make the simple principles of strength training as complex as third-world epidemiology. They publish unworkable workouts and inedible pills—all in an effort to make you think you've got to pay more and do more in order to look good.

Hooey, we say. Muscle building is as easy as the ABCs, and we're here to prove it with our version of the alphabet. For each letter we give you a little lesson in muscularity—something you can use to form new brawn, if not new words. The advice offered for each letter should help you slap on more muscle, shake you out of a slump, or make you appear smarter than the other dumbbells down at the gym. So buy yourself a vowel or two and crank out a few consonants, and you'll find whole new ways to spell M-U-S-C-L-E.

Arnold

If Schwarzenegger weren't around, not only would we miss out on a few great movies, but we might all be skinny runners. Arnold had lots of ideas about building muscle; one of his best is the exercise that bears his name, the Arnold press. It builds your shoulder muscles better, and more safely, than any other.

Hold two dumbbells in front of your shoulders, your palms facing you. As you lift them overhead, rotate the dumbbells so your palms are facing outward at the end of the movement.

Barbell

It's easy to figure out how much weight you've put on a barbell. You just add up the numbers on the sides of the weight plates.

But how much does the barbell itself weigh? The folks at York Barbell gave us the following answers.

BAR	WEIGHT
Olympic bar (7') (the kind you find in gyms)	45 lb
Olympic EZ-curl bar	25 lb
Standard bar (80") (1" wide, for home use)	20 lb*
Standard EZ-curl bar	11 lb*

* With collars; also, remember that the collars you put on an Olympic bar at the gym can weigh between 1 and $5^1/_2$ pounds each.

Inside tip: The bar on the Smith machine—that barbell-on-rails device—looks like a 45-pound Olympic bar, but it's counterbalanced, so it's much lighter: just 15 pounds.

Chicks

Women may like money more than they like muscles, but at the gym they can't see your wallet. So you have to build muscle. But not where you think. "We want to see guys with great legs and a good butt," says Liz Neporent, C.S.C.S. The stepup builds the entire lower body, particularly the gluteals.

Grab a pair of dumbbells and pick a step about 8 to 12 inches high. Place one foot on the step, and lift yourself by pushing down on the bottom of that foot. Don't push off with the trailing leg. Step back down with the trailing leg, and do 8 to 15 repetitions the same way. Then switch legs and repeat.

Dumbbells

You probably don't use dumbbells for really heavy exercises because it's too hard to get them up over your head or chest to start the set. Two tricks:

Use Power Hooks. Clamp them onto your

dumbbells, and then hook your dumbbells over a bar that's set up for bench presses. Besides having a better starting point for your dumbbells so that you're at less risk of shoulder injuries, you'll have a place to rack them at the end of the set, an evolutionary step beyond the old drop-'em-on-the-floor trick. $49.95 plus shipping; call (888) 669-6316.

Use your leg muscles. Squat down and lift the dumbbells off the floor. Rest them against the front of your thighs. Sit on the end of the bench [A]. As you lie back, raise your legs to boost the dumbbells over your chest [B].

A B

Equipment

The free weights-versus-machines debate has raged as long as exercise machines have existed. We say, use both. But the smartest way is to start with the exercises that require the most balance and move on to those requiring the least.

Here's why: Small muscles stabilize your body, and they get tired faster than the big muscles. Once they're worn out, you won't be able to handle weight safely. That's when you should switch from free weights to machine exercises. So in your next workout, do the following exercises in the order given.

MUSCLE GROUP	DO . . .	BEFORE YOU DO . . .
Back	Pullups, barbell or dumbbell rows	Pulldowns, machine and cable rows, machine-assisted pullups
Chest	Dips, barbell and dumbbell presses, dumbbell flies	Machine presses, machine flies, machine-assisted dips
Arms	Barbell and dumbbell curls and extensions	Cable and machine curls and extensions
Legs	Lunges, squats, deadlifts	Leg presses, leg extensions, leg curls
Abs	Hanging leg raises, crunches, slant-board situps, cable crunches	Machine crunches, ab-roller exercises

Failure

Failure in life builds character, along with surprisingly varied pharmacological dependencies. But in the weight room, doing a single set to failure—the point at which you absolutely can't do another repetition—will produce only limited results. Most guys will get better results with multiple sets that don't necessarily end in failure. Here's how to decide which is best for you:

Do a single set if . . .

▶You're a beginner.

▶You're pressed for time but don't want to lose muscle.

▶You've been doing the same program for a long time and haven't seen any improvement in a while.

Do multiple sets if . . .

▶You've been working out longer than 6 months and have made progress.

▶You're trying to increase your strength in a specific exercise, like the bench press.

▶You're trying to increase your overall muscularity.

Glutamine

Glutamine is the most abundant amino acid in your body, and taking it as a supplement is thought to improve the immune system—leading to fewer colds and flus—and keep muscle tissue from breaking down. But only in athletes who are training really, really hard.

"Although promising for the more advanced athlete, glutamine may not be quite as beneficial for the everyday athlete," says Doug Kalman, R.D., a nutrition researcher at Peak Wellness in Greenwich, Connecticut.

Our advice? Save your money.

PEAK performance

Cause for Pause

Unless a Tara Reid look-alike asks for a spot, we hate interruptions in the gym. But pausing at different points while you're lowering a weight (it's called negative interruption) can make you stronger, says Michael Mejia, C.S.C.S., *Men's Health* exercise advisor. The pauses keep your muscles under continuous tension longer and increase the load at various points in the range of motion, which means greater gains in size and strength. You can incorporate this technique into nearly any exercise. If you're doing a biceps curl, lower the weight about a third of the way and pause for 3 seconds. Then lower it to about the halfway point and pause again. Finally, lower it all the way and pause for 3 seconds before pulling the weight back up to the starting position.

Heavy

Want bigger muscles? Lift heavier weights. Here are two secrets to doing that.

Don't try to lift heavy all the time. Pick several 2- to 4-week periods each year, and increase the weight every week during those periods. Increase the number of sets (from three to five, say), and decrease the number of repetitions (from 10 to 12 per set to 5 or 6).

Microload. There's no rule that says you have to increase the weight 10 or 20 pounds at a time. Instead, increase the weights by the tiniest possible increments each week. If your gym has 1¼-pound plates, use them. Your muscles will adapt better to a little challenge each week than to a bigger challenge every third or fourth week.

Idiots

Maybe the reason so many people exercise at home is because people at the gym do stupid things. But the only thing worse than being annoyed by idiots is realizing you're one of them. Here are two things you do to piss off the rest of us:

You talk too much. Too much socializing

means you spend more time on a piece of equipment than you should. Excessive chatter also throws off the concentration of the more serious lifters.

You block equipment when you exercise. Every gym has a guy who does lateral raises or dumbbell flies right next to the dumbbell rack, keeping other people from getting to the weights they need. Don't be that guy. Make sure you find a wide-open spot to do your raises, flies, lunges, and any other exercise that takes up an unusual amount of space.

Jack LaLanne

We think Jack is a great guy and everything, but he was famously disparaging of warmup exercises. We find that odd, just like those funny jumpsuits and ballet slippers he wears.

Guys do need to warm up before lifting. But few of us understand how, says Patrick Hagerman, C.S.C.S., an exercise-physiology instructor at Oklahoma State University. Breaking a sweat with 10 minutes on a stationary bike is fine for starters, but it won't prepare your muscles for sudden exertion—the kind you do when lifting weights. The idea is to stretch your muscles at the most extreme point of their range of motion, where they have to do their hardest work and where they're most vulnerable to injury. So if you're going to start your workout with bench presses, lie on a bench, holding just the bar at arm's length. Lower the bar to your sternum and do three or four quick, controlled repetitions, but lift the bar only a few inches above your sternum each time.

You can also do this with squats, shoulder presses, pullups, or any other heavy-weight exercise you do at the beginning of your workout.

HARD TRUTH

Going nowhere

Percent increase in treadmill sales in 2000:

11

SOURCE: Sporting Goods Manufacturers Association

Kansas City Strip

Lifting weights will help anyone increase strength, but if you want more muscle too, you have to eat your meat, according to a 1999 study in the *American Journal of Clinical Nutrition*.

A good 4-ounce piece of beef, like the Kansas City strip (also known as New York strip or just plain strip loin), provides 21 grams of high-quality, muscle-building protein. "You don't need a steak every day. But small portions a few times a week is fine," says Heidi Skolnik, a nutritionist who works with the New York Mets and Giants.

Low Glycemic Index

Those are the secret code words nutritionists use to describe carbohydrates that your body burns at a slower, steadier pace. Your incentive: Load up on carbohydrates that have a low glycemic index, and your body will burn more fat for fuel.

In the box below are six simple ways to switch from foods with a high glycemic index to those with a moderate or low glycemic index.

MEAL	INSTEAD OF...	SUBSTITUTE...
Breakfast	Cornflakes or Rice Chex cereal	All-Bran or muesli with a peach
Morning snack	Bagel	Low-fat yogurt
Lunch	Sandwich	Soup with meat and vegetables
Afternoon snack	Cantaloupe or watermelon	Apple or orange
Dinner	Steak with baked potato and French bread	Steak with pasta and mixed green salad
Dessert	Cake	Ice cream

Max

Some people will tell you there's no real point in going for a "one-rep max"—the most weight you can lift on any given exercise. But there is a good reason, and not just to include the numbers in your annual Christmas letter: If you don't know your maximum, you don't really know that you're using the right weight for your goals.

Here's how to match your one-repetition maximum to your workouts:

To get huge: Use 65 to 80 percent of max. If your maximum bench press is 200 pounds, that means you should work out with between 130 and 160 pounds to build your chest muscles.

To get strong: Use 80 to 95 percent of your maximum, or 160 to 190 pounds if your maximum is 200.

For a quick and foolproof way to increase your max in any lift, see "Undulating Loads," on page 76.

Negatives

Each lift has two components: the "positive," or lifting phase, and the "negative," or lowering phase. If you want to get the most benefit from weight lifting, you should lift the weight as fast as you can and then control the descent, says Jose Antonio, Ph.D., an exercise researcher at the University of Nebraska at Kearney. Lots of guys lift fast, but most lower the weight just as quickly, robbing themselves of half the muscle-building equation. Next time you lift, try this: Take 1 second to lift the weight but 6 seconds to lower it. It's hard, and you'll probably have to use less weight. But the strain of putting the brakes on the barbell or dumbbells will produce more muscle.

Two exceptions: Don't lower the weight this slowly on deadlifts or bent-over barbell rows, since that would be too tough on your lower back.

Obliques

The muscles on the sides of your waist help to bend your torso from side to side. But that's beside the point. They just look cool—if you can see them, of course. The most effective way to work those muscles: Bend to the side while struggling to hold your torso in place. Next ab workout, try the crunch/side-bend combo pictured on page 74: Lie on your back, knees bent, hands behind your head. Curl up so your shoulder blades are off the floor [A]. Now bend at the waist to the right, aiming your right armpit toward your right hip [B]. Straighten, then bend to your left. Do eight to each side.

Pump

A few sets into your workout, you notice that your muscles feel heavier and that they look different, too: bigger, fuller, more veiny. This is the blessed pump, a sensation that Arnold Schwarzenegger once compared to orgasm. (We assume he was kidding. If not . . . well, let's just say we feel even more sympathy for Maria.)

Here's how to get the pump: For each muscle group, do three or four sets of 10 to 15 repetitions using light weight, resting 40 to 60 seconds after each set. This works great for the beach muscles—chest, shoulders, arms—but it's really exhausting for the bigger leg and back muscles.

The pump serves five main purposes.

1. Looks cool.

2. Kicks muscle-building enzymes into high gear.

3. Improves the muscles' ability to store nutrients, which creates more muscular endurance and gives them a fuller, harder look.

4. Generates a lot of lactic acid. This stimulates growth hormone, which leads to bigger muscles and smaller fat cells.

5. Looks cool.

Quaker Oats

For a guy interested in building lean muscle, oatmeal comes close to being the perfect food. "It's a food with a low glycemic index, so it gives you more energy to burn longer," Skolnik says. That means you can eat it a couple of hours before a workout and feel fully energized by the time you hit the weights. Even on the days when you don't work out, having oatmeal for breakfast means you eat less at lunch, which can help you stay leaner.

Ripped

On the off-chance that you're one of the guys looking for the ripped, shredded, sliced, diced, grated, chipped, stripped look, here's how to achieve extremely low body fat: Do sets of 12 to 15 repetitions with slightly less weight.

Try high-intensity techniques like supersets (one set of an exercise followed by another with no rest in between), and rest 30 to 60 seconds between sets or supersets. Do more aerobics on the days you don't lift, and immediately after you lift.

Give yourself 2 months, and take a picture when you're done.

Sucker

That's anyone who buys alleged testosterone boosters like androstenedione, DHEA, or any of the so-called prohormones. All these substances fall under the designation "Can't help, might hurt."

> **TOUGH TALK**
>
> **"I started going to my local gym, where I met the woman who changed my life: my personal trainer."**
>
> MICHAEL SCHIDLOW, *MEN'S HEALTH* BELLY-OFF CLUB MEMBER, ON LOSING 38 POUNDS

Time

You should never work out with weights for longer than an hour. After that, your body starts producing more of the stress hormone cortisol, which can have a testosterone-blocking, muscle-wasting effect. "If you're working out longer than that, then you're either trying to crowd in too many exercises or too many sets, or you're spending too much time between sets talking," says Dave Pearson, Ph.D., an exercise physiologist at Ball State. Do no more than 24 sets per workout—three sets of eight exercises, for example. If that doesn't exhaust your muscles, then you need to make those sets tougher.

Undulating Loads

This advanced lifting technique sounds a lot sexier than it is. The idea is this: Most guys do the same number of repetitions per set. Your body gets used to that in a hurry and stagnates. Undulating loads vary the number of repetitions to confuse your body about what you're going to do next. That way you can lift heavier weights and build more muscle. Hey, it's worth a try.

Let's say you normally do sets of 10 with 155 pounds when you bench-press, and your maximum is about 210 pounds. Next time you bench, try the workout below.

Take a full 3 to 5 minutes between sets. And make this the only exercise you do for any muscle group. In other words, if you normally do three sets each of flat and incline presses for your chest, perform only the flat presses if you're doing undulating loads.

You can use this technique for any exercise, from squats and deadlifts to arm curls and calf raises (although we don't recommend it for moves like lateral raises, in which your shoulder joints would be vulnerable to injury). Use perfect form always, and recruit a spotter when appropriate (for squats and bench presses).

SET	REPS	WEIGHT
1	8	170
2	3	195
3	5	180
4	2	210
5	4	200
6	1	215–220

V Shape

The two best things you can do to create the ideal shoulder/waist V shape: wide-grip pullups or pulldowns, and lateral raises. The first exercises build the latissimus dorsi muscles, in the middle of the back; the second thicken the deltoids. And keeping the waist trim will make anyone look more wide shouldered.

Waste of Time

Here's how to waste time in the gym.

Do any one thing for a prolonged period. "You have to incorporate training variations," says Antonio. Adjust your workout every 3 to 4 weeks, changing the exercises and the system of sets and repetitions.

Perform an abdominal twist while holding a stick. "I see so many people trying to get rid of their love handles by doing these twists. But you can't spot reduce," says Pearson. The move can be dangerous, too. You might hit people with the stick.

Live there. "Going to the gym six or seven times a week has not been shown to be any more effective than going three or four times," says Pearson. When you're a beginner, working your entire body three times a week is the most you should attempt.

Do hundreds of crunches, and do them every day. See "Xylophone Abs," below.

Xylophone Abs

If you want a midsection that she can play music on, you'll need to:

▶Train those muscles two or three times a week.

▶Do two or three different exercises.

▶Limit your sets to 12 to 15 repetitions, and use progressive resistance where possible. That is, strengthen your abdominal muscles by using more weights from set to set and workout to workout.

Some of the best exercises:

Hanging knee and leg raises. Raise your knees toward your chest, curling your pelvis upward at the end. When you can do that more than 12 times for three sets, make it tougher by extending your legs or holding a medicine ball between your knees.

Weighted crunches. Hold a weight plate or dumbbell across your chest and use progressively heavier weights. (Don't do this if you have any history of back problems.)

TOUGH TALK

"I look forward to going to the gym every night. Before, I would find myself in a bar after work for 2 hours."

FRANK SERAFINI, *MEN'S HEALTH* BELLY-OFF CLUB MEMBER, ON LOSING 80 POUNDS

Cable crunch. Hold a rope cable handle against your forehead; crunch your abs, keeping the rest of your lower body stationary.

Yeow!

The most common weight-room injury isn't torn biceps or blown-out spinal disks. It's smashed fingertips, which account for about 14 percent of all serious injuries related to strength training.

One of the easiest ways to smash your fingers is by piling 45-pound weight plates onto a seated-calf-raise apparatus. Here's a little trick to avoid that: Use smaller plates in between the bigger ones. That gives you a little margin for error when layering on the bigger plates and gives your fingers room to latch onto the plates when you're taking them off.

Zzz

Sleep is the best workout partner you'll ever have. Depriving yourself of those Zzzs not only limits your ability to grow muscle—your body releases most of its growth hormone during sleep—but also severely impairs your coordination and mental focus, according to a 1994 study. This translates to less strength and a greater chance of getting hurt.

So if you work out, you should sleep for the optimum amount of time each night—7 or 8 hours a night for most guys. And if for any reason you have to go a couple of nights with limited sleep—you're a medical intern, a new dad, or a fitness editor trying to come up with 26 fresh tips about building muscle—don't plan on being in good shape for your best performance.

Now, if you'll excuse us, we'll retire for the evening.

BY LOU SCHULER

The Genius of Dumbbells

Live longer, get stronger, and bulk up or trim down with the greatest exercise tool ever invented

The first time I heard The Truth about dumbbells, I wasn't ready for it. I was talking to a gym owner, a remarkably short man with a remarkably short message.

"If I have to help someone lose 10 pounds, I'd rather use a pair of dumbbells than a treadmill," he told me. On a profundity scale, it ranks somewhere between "Guns don't kill people" and the serenity prayer. But it did mark the first time in my career that someone hinted at The Truth as I now understand it.

Since then, I've learned that dumbbells

are not only the best muscle-building tool ever created, but also the greatest weapon a man can use in the fight against overweight, aging, illness, irritability, and even stupidity.

A doctor today could prescribe dumbbells for almost any ailment and stand a pretty good chance of getting it right (although herpes patients may prefer to seek a more immediate solution). These humble cast-iron configurations can help any man live longer and better, with increased vigor, a smaller waistline, and a more optimistic attitude.

PEAK performance

Strong Deal

Gravity ruins everything: It spills beer and makes your Vince Carter impression look pathetic. But you can put gravity to work for you to build more muscle in less time. Take, for example, the Saxon side bend. Michael Mejia, C.S.C.S., *Men's Health* exercise advisor, says this over-the-head dumbbell side bend forces your obliques—the muscles on the sides of your waist—to work extra hard. And because you're holding the weights over your head instead of at your sides, the lift works your shoulders and back as well.

Grab a pair of lightweight dumbbells with an overhand grip and hold them overhead, in line with your shoulders, with your elbows slightly bent [A]. Keep your back straight and slowly bend directly to your left side as far as possible without twisting your upper body [B]. Pause, return to an upright position, then bend to your right side as far as possible. Do two or three sets of 6 to 10 repetitions on each side.

A

B

But like any drug, dumbbells work only if you use them. That's why we've provided a workout with enough variations to keep you busy for months, if not years.

First, though, let's take a closer look at The Truth about the world's strongest medicine—if you think you can handle The Truth.

How Dumbbells Beat . . . Decrepitude

If you never picked up a dumbbell, your body's muscles would peak at about age 25. By age 30, they'd start shrinking and taking on more fat between the fibers. By the time the average man hits 70, he needs three grunts to get up from a chair and risks fracturing a hip just by watching other people exercise.

The solution to this problem is easy: Lift weights. Unless you were a world-class athlete in your youth, you can probably become leaner and stronger at 40 than you were at 20. Studies have shown that hoisting heavy metal can increase muscle strength and size and decrease body fat at any age.

And if you're going to lift weights, dumbbells offer more versatility than barbells or machines. "You're limited only by your imagination," says Juan Carlos Santana, C.S.C.S., whose two-part dumbbell-training videos include hundreds of exercises and exercise variations.

How Dumbbells Beat . . . Dumpiness

The biggest fallacy about dumbbells is that they only make you big. In fact, dumbbells can just as easily make you small.

Let's say you do three intense hour-long workouts with dumbbells each week. Not only will you burn calories—probably between 400 and 500—during the workouts, you'll also burn calories at a higher rate after the workout (commonly called "afterburn"). On top of that, the muscle you build will cause your body to burn more calories on a moment-to-moment basis. On top of that, hard exercise increases your body's production of the enzyme creatine kinase, which over time seems to make daily activities easier to perform. The easier it is to do things, the more likely you are to do them.

Add it all up, and 3 hours a week of in-

(continued on page 85)

Home-Schooled Muscle

A home gym designed around dumbbells can be as cheap or expensive as you want it to be. Here are some of the options.

Fixed-Weight Dumbbells

Advantage: Convenience. They turn your home gym into a real gym.

Disadvantages: Price and storage. Simple hexagonal dumbbells from www.fitnessfactory.com are $229 for 10 pairs ranging from 5 to 50 pounds. And you'll probably want to buy the $180 rack so they don't end up scattered across your floor.

If price is no object: We like these Hampton Eclipse dumbbells [A] from www.hamptonfit.com; 5 to 50 pounds, $2,000. The Dura-Bells [B] are coated with rubber; 3 to 50 pounds, $1,300.

Adjustable Dumbbells

Advantages: Price and storage. You can use weight plates you already own, and the handles and collars take up very little space.

Disadvantage: Convenience. It's a bitch to unscrew the collars and move plates around every time you change exercises.

Best bets: You can get these Olympic handles [C] (the diameter of the bar is 2 inches) from Sports Authority for $70 (www.sportsauthority.com).

If price is no object: Iron-Master Quick/Change dumbbells [D] cost $250 (5 to 80 pounds) from www.ironmaster.com. The weight plates are easy to slip on and off the handles.

For more information about Santana's videos—*The Essence of Dumbbell Training, Vol. I and II*—check out www.opsfit.com.

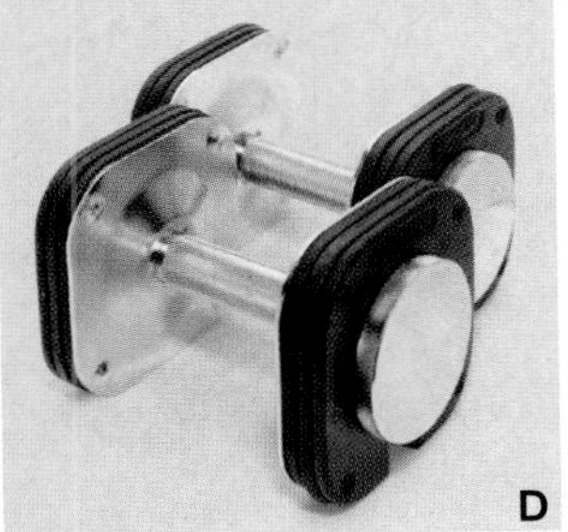

The Last Dumbbell Workout You'll Ever Need

We asked Juan Carlos Santana, C.S.C.S., to give us a dumbbell program that can work for any man, whether he's a beginner or a recently converted weight-machine operator. So Santana, who always delivers in triplicate, created three different programs based on the same exercises.

The basic program will work for anyone—even advanced guys can do these exercises and see gains. The intermediate variations (for men who've been working out steadily for 3 months or more) show how to take the basic exercises and make them tougher. The advanced variations (don't try them unless you've been lifting for at least a year) make them as tough as possible. An advanced lifter can also do all three variations in the same workout. For any muscle group, he can do the basic exercise to warm up, then the intermediate and advanced variations to challenge his muscles in every possible way.

No matter which level you choose, here's how to match it to your goals.

Basic strength and muscle building. Do one set of 8 to 12 reps of each exercise. Rest 1 minute between exercises.

Fat loss. Do the workouts in a circuit fashion—one set of 8 to 12 reps of each exercise; repeat once or twice, with minimal rest between exercises.

Aggressive muscle building. Do three sets of 6 to 10 repetitions of each exercise. You can substitute traditional chest presses (on a bench or ball) for the pushup or T-pushup. Rest 1 to 2 minutes between sets.

Aggressive strength and muscle building. Do three to five sets of three to six repetitions of the first four exercises in the workouts, and one set of 10 to 12 repetitions of the others. Again, you can substitute traditional chest presses for the pushup. Rest 2 to 3 minutes between sets.

Chest/Triceps

Dumbbell pushup (shown). Get into a pushup position with your hands holding hexagonal dumbbells, instead of being flat on the floor. Slowly lower your body, pause, then push back up to the starting position.

Intermediate: One-dumbbell T-pushup. Get into pushup position with your left hand on the floor and your right hand holding a dumbbell. Lower yourself to the floor, then push up, twisting your body so that you raise your right arm and the dumbbell straight up over your shoulder. Your body should form a *T.* Lower yourself and finish the set, then repeat the set with the dumbbell in your left hand.

Advanced: Two-dumbbell T-pushup (shown). Get into pushup position with both hands holding dumbbells. Do a pushup, and as you come up, twist to raise the dumbbell straight up over your shoulder. Lower yourself and repeat to the other side.

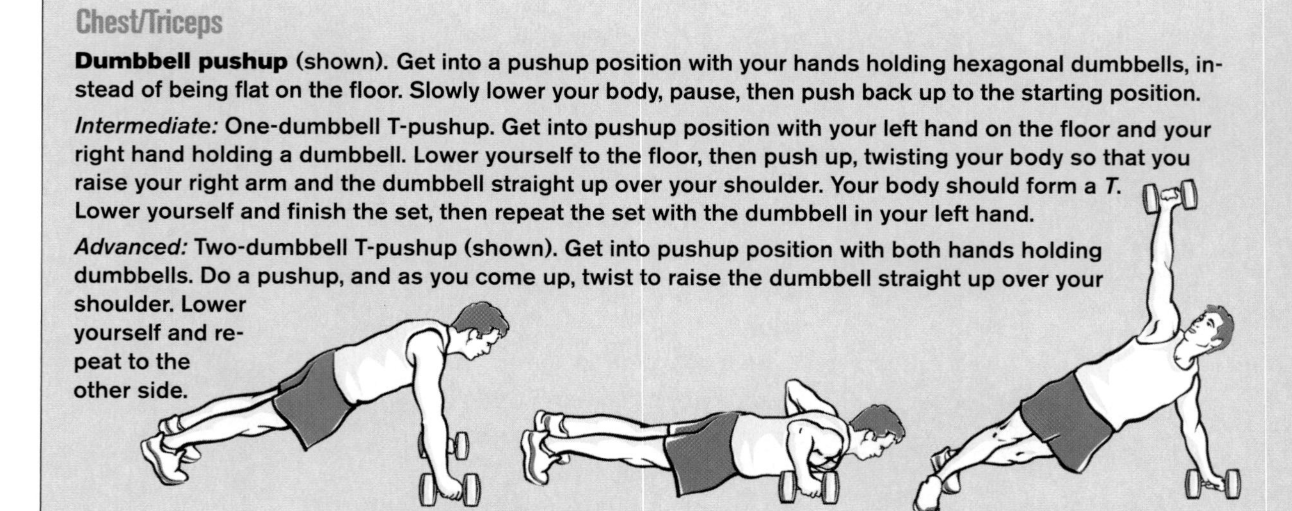

Dumbbell pushup

Two-dumbbell T-pushup

Upper Back

Bent-over row (shown). Stand with your feet parallel to each other and about shoulder-width apart. Bend at the hips until your chest faces the floor, and hold the dumbbells at arm's length beneath your shoulders. Pull them up to the sides of your chest, pause, then slowly lower them.

Intermediate: One-arm bent-over row. Stand with your right foot in front of your left, a dumbbell in your left hand. Bend and let the dumbbell hang. Pull it up, pause, and lower it. Finish the set, switch sides, and repeat.

Advanced: Alternating bent-over row. Stand with your right foot in front of your left. Bend at the hips so the dumbbells are hanging straight down from your shoulders, palms facing in. Raise the left dumbbell to the left side of your waist, and as you lower it, raise the right dumbbell. Alternate for half the repetitions in the set, then switch legs so your left foot is in front and finish the set.

Shoulders

Alternating shoulder press. Stand holding dumbbells at the sides of your shoulders. Lift the left one over your head while you bend to the right. As you lower that one, raise the other, bending to your left.

Intermediate: Rotation press (shown). Same as the shoulder press, but twist instead of bending on each repetition.

Advanced: Curl and press. Stand holding the dumbbells down at your sides, palms forward. Curl them to your shoulders, then rotate your hands outward as you press them overhead.

Biceps

Alternating biceps curl. Stand holding the dumbbells at your sides, palms forward. Curl one to your shoulder, then slowly lower it as you raise the other.

Intermediate: Cross uppercut (shown). Hold the dumbbells with bent arms. Lift one as you twist, as if you were throwing an uppercut. Repeat with the other arm.

Advanced: Do the curl and press described above for shoulders.

(continued)

The Last Dumbbell Workout You'll Ever Need (continued)

Abdominals

Cross crunch. Lie with knees bent and feet flat on the floor. Hold a dumbbell over your left shoulder with both hands. Curl your torso up and rotate to the right, bringing the dumbbell to your right hip. Lower yourself, finish the set, then repeat, going the opposite direction.

Intermediate: Speed rotation. Stand holding a dumbbell with both hands in front of your midsection. Twist 90 degrees to the right, then 180 degrees to the left. Keep your abs tight and move fast.

Advanced: Wood chop. Stand holding a dumbbell next to your right ear. Flex your abs and rotate your torso to the left as you lower the dumbbell to the outside of your left knee. Lift it back, finish the set, and repeat on the other side.

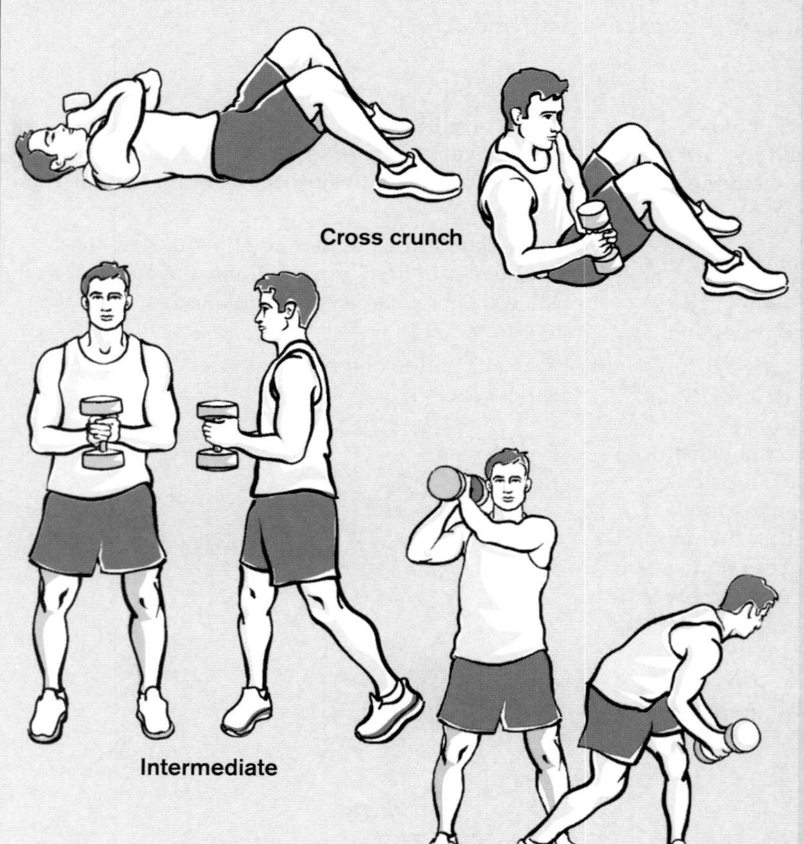

Lower Body

Squat. Stand holding the dumbbells outside your thighs. Slowly lower yourself until your thighs are parallel to the floor. Pause, then stand up to the starting position.

Intermediate: Jump squat (shown). Lower yourself, then jump as high as you can. Land with your knees slightly bent, immediately squat back down, and repeat.

Advanced: Split jump squat. Stand with your left foot farther forward than your right, dumbbells at your sides. Jump and switch leg positions in midair, so you land with your right foot in front. Land with your knees bent, quickly lower yourself until your front knee is bent 90 degrees, and repeat.

tense lifting can help your body burn an extra 650 calories a day, says Gary Hunter, Ph.D., who studies exercise and metabolism at the University of Alabama at Birmingham. Since a pound of fat has 3,500 calories, you can burn 2 to 4 pounds off your midsection each month if you hit the iron and hit it hard. To achieve the same results from a low-intensity exercise like walking, you'd have to exercise 100 minutes a day, seven times a week, Hunter says.

How Dumbbells Beat . . . Disease

Modern life leads to a number of fatal or merely painful conditions: heart disease, high blood pressure, diabetes, arthritis. Cancers of the colon, lung, kidney, and rectum have been linked to lack of exercise, surplus weight, or both. Many of these conditions are a direct result of the gradual loss of muscle size, strength, function, and flexibility that comes with the unexercised life. When good muscles go bad, metabolism slows, fat builds, and your body loses its ability to do many everyday activities comfortably. So you don't do them, and disease and disability follow sooner or later.

So how do dumbbells help? They reverse the risk of heart disease, reduce blood pressure, improve glucose tolerance (which lowers the risk of diabetes), stop arthritis, prevent cancer, and increase muscle strength, size, function, and flexibility.

How Dumbbells Beat . . . Depression

Researchers have known for a while that aerobic exercise has a potent effect on anxiety and depression. But the early research on intense weight lifting showed that it seemed to have the opposite effect. In other words, lifters got something like 'roid rage even if they weren't taking steroids. But a 1999 University of Texas study figured out the problem: It's true that lifters are in a worse mood immediately after hard exercise. But that effect disappears quickly, and 45 minutes after lifting, they're in a far better mood than people who haven't lifted. "Ultimately, weight lifting provides the same improvement in mood that follows aerobic exercise," says John B. Bartholomew, Ph.D., the study's author.

How Dumbbells Beat . . . "D'oh!"

When you do intense, challenging exercises, parts of your cerebral cortex reconfigure themselves. The brain doesn't have any room inside your skull to grow bigger, so instead it creates more complex neural junctions. These reconfigured neurons are the key to keeping your brain as chipper as your body. "The more complex the activity, the more the brain responds and the more the brain stays youthful," says Joe Signorile, Ph.D., an exercise researcher at the University of Miami.

Dumbbells, thus, are the ultimate brain-building tool. With barbells or machines, you progress by doing the same exercises with ever-heavier weights, which may not change the neural patterns in your brain. But with dumbbells, the exercises themselves can evolve, employing more complex movements and thus more work for your brain as well as your body—your stronger, leaner, healthier, happier, more energetic body.

BY LOU SCHULER

The Testosterone Advantage Plan™ Workout

Part two of the amazing 9-week program that will change your body—and your life

Traditional weight-control theory has given chunky guys three options: Eat fewer calories, or burn more through exercise, or some combination thereof.

But the majority of the calories you burn throughout the day are controlled by your basal metabolism. These are the calories your body burns whether you're active or not, whether you're sleeping or eating, whether you're thinking about sex or actually having it.

Your body burns about 10 percent of its calories by digesting the food you eat, which is called the thermic effect of feeding. "Thermic" is a great word to remember, because it reminds you that your body is just a skin-wrapped furnace and that the food you eat is the fuel that stokes your furnace.

The other—and most variable—way in which you burn calories is through voluntary activity, which accounts for anywhere from 10 to 30 percent of the energy your body uses each day.

So let's review: Your body has three mechanisms for burning calories. Two of them you don't think about because basal metabolism and the thermic effect of feeding are invisible to you. Yet those two account for 70 to 90 percent of the fuel you burn each day. So it makes sense that the best way to control body weight is to ramp up those two systems. Build muscle and you increase your metabolism by up to 50 calories a day per pound of muscle. Eat more protein and you crank up the thermic effect by as much as one-third.

Now, combine that information with some further findings: Research shows that weight training spurs testosterone production. And certain types of training—particularly compound lifting, which involves several major muscle groups working together—spur it to a dramatic degree. And we've already demonstrated that more T means less fat, less heart disease, and more sex. Not bad, right?

Add to that this fact: While both aerobic exercise and weight training result in metabolic increases immediately afterward, the fat-burning effects of aerobics last only 30 minutes to an hour. The effects of weight training can last up to 48 hours! Bottom line: If you want to lose some weight, pick up some weights.

How To Do the Workout

The following is a composite of the three-phase workout that was designed by Michael Mejia, C.S.C.S., the *Men's Health* exercise consultant, for *The Testosterone Advantage Plan*. (Note: You will get best results from doing the workout in conjunction with the diet on pages 45 to 51.)

Work out three times a week with at least 1 day between workouts.

Phase 1: Do one or two sets of 15 to 20 repetitions of each exercise for 2 weeks.

Phase 2: Do two or three sets of 8 to 12 repetitions of each exercise for 3 weeks.

Phase 3: Do three to five sets of four to six repetitions of each exercise for 4 weeks.

Add your choice of abdominal exercises before or after the workout.

"'You Should See My Dad'"

Around here, we called Cory Schmaldinst our poster boy—and we're not the only ones who noticed his transformation.

Cory on the new him: "I haven't been at my current weight since college. And even then, I never looked like this."

On others' reactions: "People are shocked. They say, 'How long did it take?' I tell them 9 weeks, and they ask me, 'Where do I get this diet?'"

On the intangible results: "It changes you mentally, too. I'm happier with myself. I have energy, and I feel I can do whatever I want."

On the T plan versus his past efforts: "I'd run 3 or 4 days a week, and it wasn't getting me anywhere. I tried Atkins, but you can't keep up with it. This diet is normal eating. It's a program you can stick to."

On his fiancée's reaction: "She definitely likes the way I look. Now, because I'm starting to look better, she's feeling the urge to get back to the gym. . . . Before, [my unhappiness] would affect our relationship. We get along so well now."

On his goals for the future: "I want my kids to say to their friends, 'You should see my dad.' I want to look good and not have problems when I'm 40."

Bottom line: "My life is so much easier. I'm happy with my body and my whole health picture."

Cory Schmaldinst, 26, 6'0"

	BEFORE T PLAN	AFTER T PLAN
Weight	190 lb	172 lb
Waist	36¾"	32"
Bench press	215 lb	245 lb
Chinups	7	"almost 13"

THE EXERCISES

Squat. Place a barbell across your shoulders and step back from the squat rack. Set your feet shoulder-width apart and place your hands just beyond shoulder-width apart on the bar. Bend at the knees and hips, as if you were sitting down in a chair, and lower your body until your thighs are parallel to the floor. Pause, then return to the starting position.

Dumbbell stepup. Grab a pair of dumbbells and stand in front of a bench or step that's 12 to 18 inches high. Step up onto the bench with your right foot and push off with your right heel to lift the rest of your body onto the step. Step down with your left foot first, then your right. Finish the set with your right leg, then repeat the set with your left leg, stepping up with your left and back with your right.

Barbell bench press. Lie on your back on a bench. Grab the bar with your hands just wider than shoulder width. Lift the bar and hold it over your chest. Lower it to your chest, pause, then push it back up.

Seated cable row. Attach a parallel handle to the low cable. Sit on the bench and grab the handle. Keep your torso upright, shoulders back, and arms almost straight in front of you. Pull the handle to your midsection. Pause, then slowly return to the starting position.

Barbell shoulder press. Grab a bar with a grip just wider than shoulder width. Hold it just above your chest. Push the bar up until your arms are fully extended. Don't pause. Slowly lower the bar back to your chest.

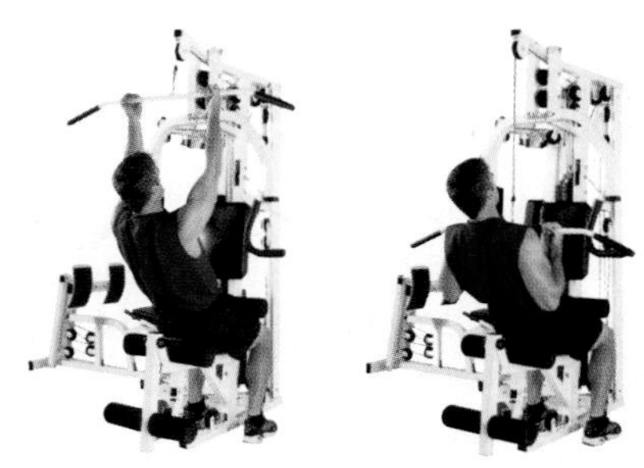

Lat pulldown. Position yourself in a lat-pulldown station and grab the bar with an overhand grip just wider than shoulder width. Pull it down to your chest, pause; slowly return to the starting position.

Lying dumbbell triceps extension. Grab a pair of dumbbells and lie back on a bench. Keep your arms straight and angled toward your head, your palms facing each other. Without moving your upper arms, bend at the elbows and slowly lower the dumbbells as far as you can, raise them to the starting position.

Barbell concentration curl. Grab a barbell with an underhand grip, your hands 4 to 6 inches apart. Sit on the end of a bench leaning your upper body nearly parallel to the floor. Your elbows should touch the insides of your knees. Slowly curl the bar up toward your chin, keeping your upper arms stationary. Pause, then slowly lower it.

Trainer's Forum

with MICHAEL MEJIA

SIX-PACK SECRETS

Q: What's the fastest, easiest way to get rid of belly fat and replace it with a six-pack?

R. H., DIX HILLS, NEW YORK

A: You probably don't want to hear it, but there's no such thing as a fast, easy way to accomplish this. Like it or not, the elusive six-pack so many men covet requires meticulous attention to diet and hours upon hours of diligent training. So, despite what you've seen and heard in those late-night infomercials, there is no magical program or "can't miss" training gizmo that will give you the results you're looking for. Don't waste time whittling yourself away with tons of cardio and thousands of repetitions of abdominal exercises. Lift, concentrating on compound lifts like squats, pullups, and bench presses. And watch every bite you put in your mouth. In 4 to 8 weeks you should see noticeable improvements.

FITNESS

Heart Rate Redux

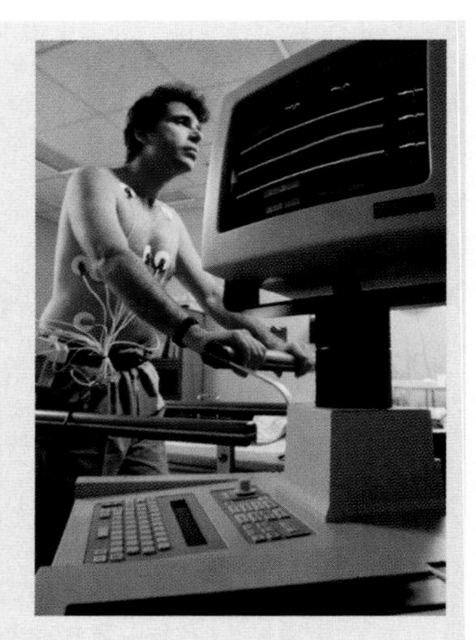

Raising your pulse for a half-hour three times a week (with exercise, not porn) is crucial for heart health. But it's how fast your heart rate drops after the workout that best indicates fitness. Researchers at the Cleveland Clinic found that people whose heart rates slowed by 12 beats or fewer per minute were four times more likely to die in the next 6 years than those with faster recoveries. Speaking of pulses, remember that old formula for maximum heart rate, 220 minus your age? Forget it. That formula often underestimates maximum heart rate, especially of adults over 40, says Hirofumi Tanaka, Ph.D., a researcher at the University of Colorado. The new formula: Multiply your age by 0.7 and subtract that number from 208. (Suggestion: Do this on a calculator before your workout.)

SOUNDS

Muscle Music

Unless you put a "Macarena" tape in the gym stereo, we don't care what music you listen to. But Richard Hart, who produces fitness music, says the right music can help pace your workout. Now listen up.

Running: 120 to 160 beats per minute (bpm), or about the speed of "Run Like Hell" by Pink Floyd

Boxing: 122 to 140 bpm, or about the speed of anything from the *Rocky* soundtrack

Cycling: 130 to 170 bpm, or about the speed of "Panama" by Van Halen

Lifting: 140 to 170 bpm, or about the speed of "Black Dog" by Led Zeppelin (one repetition for every four beats)

Warmup/cooldown: 90 to 110 bpm, or about the speed of "Black Magic Woman" by Santana

UNSTRAPPED

Q: Should I wear one of those lifting belts?

P. D., PROVIDENCE, RHODE ISLAND

A: The problem I have with weight belts is that nowadays it seems like they're more of a fashion accessory than a worthwhile training aid. Besides the traditional brown leather version, you can now get them in more colors than your daughter's Malibu Barbie bikini collection. Even more ridiculous is the fact that most guys wear them cinched around their waist the entire time they're in the gym, whether they need them to perform the exercise or not.

Besides looking silly, the belt can actually cause muscle weakness. The belt acts like an extra set of abdominal and lower-back muscles to stabilize your torso. In theory, the muscles underneath the belt become accustomed to it, so they begin to relax and rely on it. (I say "in theory" because I don't know of any long-term studies showing what happens to lifters who rely on belts.) So the muscles get weaker, and you actually run a greater risk of injury while doing simple things like picking up your kids or hoisting a suitcase.

In my opinion, a belt is seldom, if ever, necessary for the average lifter. You'll be better served by starting with light weights and learning the proper mechanics of each lift without a belt to prop you up or help you lift loads that might otherwise be beyond your capabilities. The one exception is for experienced lifters handling near-maximal weights on squats, deadlifts, and overhead presses. If that applies to you, just be sure to loosen the belt after each set so your core muscles remember how to do their job.

HARD TRUTH

Racket club

Number of days the average health club member worked out at the club in 2000:

90

HARD TRUTH

Certain types of weight training—involving major muscle groups working together—spur testosterone to a dramatic degree

QUICK TIP

Gripping Action

Here's a trick that'll help you set a new max in your deadlift: Try using one overhand and one underhand grip, says Dan Wagman, Ph.D., a certified strength and conditioning specialist and publisher of *Pure Power* magazine. Over time, "You'll lift hundreds of pounds more by training with the alternate grip than if you use a standard overhand grip," Wagman says.

Total-Body Workbook V.2.0

BY LOU SCHULER AND ADAM CAMPBELL
WORKOUTS BY MICHAEL MEJIA, C.S.C.S.

Version 2.0 of the Total-Body Workbook simply and clearly tells you how to develop every muscle group that counts. Designed by Michael Mejia, C.S.C.S., the program will help you develop muscles that show—and go—in just three workouts a week.

V.2.0 is divided into eight phases: Phase 1 works your shoulders, phases 2 and 3 concentrate on your chest and back, 4 and 5 target your legs and butt, 6 stresses your abs and lower back, and 7 and 8 train your arms. Each phase includes programs for beginner, intermediate, and advanced exercisers. If you're new to weight lifting or are returning to it after a long layoff, consider yourself a beginner. An intermediate has been lifting for at least 6 months to a year, has tried several different workout programs, and has seen gains in strength and muscle mass. An advanced lifter has been lifting consistently for more than a year, has seen considerable gains in strength and size, is proficient at squats and several varieties of deadlifts, and can do at least five pullups.

Stick with the Total-Body Workbook, and you'll build the body you want in the time you have. Guaranteed.

PHASE 1: Shoulders

Expecting muscles built for looks to perform well is like gathering your family for a touch-football game and expecting them to run the West Coast offense.

There's a perfect way to build multipurpose muscle, says Michael Mejia. It hinges on one word: *stability*. See, most guys lift weights from the outside in. That is, they start with an idea of what they want their muscles to look like and go from there, pummeling their biceps and pectorals and abs with the most basic exercises. The result: big muscles that look really good from the outside and perform really well in isolation but lack simple balance and coordination. With our plan, you start with the basic exercises most men already know how to do, but as you get comfortable with them, you move on to exercises that challenge your balance and coordination. You still get big, strong muscles, but as they grow bigger and stronger, they also work together better.

This is especially important with the shoulders, which are easily injured. These exercises will help correct that problem and ensure a strong, stable frame.

They'll also provide muscles that will pump up nicely for display purposes, but when it comes time to run a pick-and-roll, toss your kids in the air (for height or distance), or uproot a few saplings to make way for your new backyard putting green, you'll have what it takes.

The Rest of Your Workout

Do the shoulder exercises first in your workout. After that, it's up to you how to fit in exercises for other muscle groups. Most important: Build strength and muscle size with equal effort on both sides of your body. Working the front and neglecting the back is a recipe for injury.

Some suggestions:

BEGINNER

Do a total-body workout two or three times a week. After you finish your shoulder exercises, you can try one set of 8 to 12 repetitions of the following exercises (except where noted).

Lat pulldown
Squat or leg press
Leg curl
Dumbbell chest press
Cable or dumbbell row
Cable triceps extension
Dumbbell biceps curl
Crunch (15 to 20 repetitions)

INTERMEDIATE

Divide your program into two workouts: one for the upper body, one for the lower. Alternate between the two workouts, taking a day off after each. So, you would do the upper-body workout on Monday and Friday of one week and the lower-body workout on Wednesday, then the following week do the lower-body workout on Monday and Friday and the upper-body workout on Wednesday.

Upper-body workout: After doing this shoulder program, choose one exercise each for chest, back, biceps, and triceps. Do two or three sets of the chest and back exercises and one or two sets of the arm exercises.

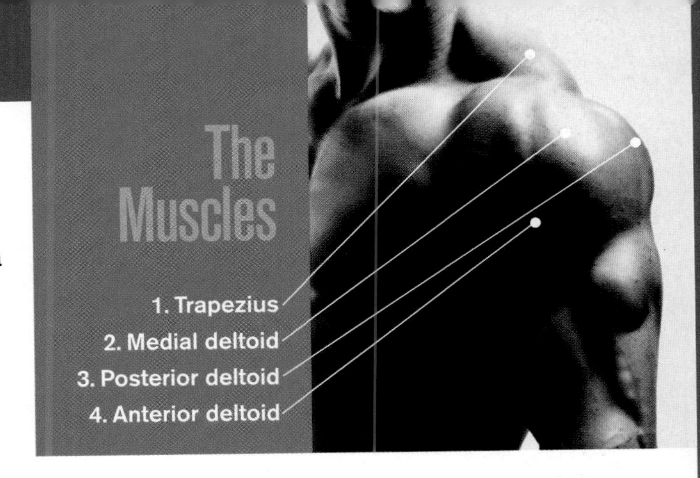

Lower-body workout: Choose one "hip-dominant" exercise, meaning that the main emphasis of the exercise is on the hamstrings and gluteals (examples: stepups and any variety of deadlift). Then choose one "knee-dominant" exercise, meaning the emphasis is on the quadriceps muscles—the front of the thigh. (Squats, leg presses, and lunges qualify.) Do two or three warmup sets and two work sets of each. (Use heavier weights and do fewer repetitions in each warmup set. A work set means you're using the most weight you can for that number of repetitions.) Add your choice of abdominal and calf exercises.

ADVANCED

Divide your workout into four parts. Do each once a week; don't work out more than 2 days in a row.

1. Shoulders and arms
2. Knee-dominant exercises (described above), plus abs and calves
3. Chest and back
4. Hip-dominant exercises (also above), plus abs and calves again

BEGINNER

Do the three beginner exercises for 4 weeks, then switch to the intermediate exercises for 4 weeks. If you want, you can do the advanced exercises for the next 4 weeks after that, or go back and repeat the beginner and intermediate exercises using heavier weights and fewer repetitions.

Week 1: One set of 10 to 12 repetitions of each exercise
Week 2: One or two sets of 10 to 12 reps
Week 3: Two or three sets of 10 to 12 reps
Week 4: Three sets of 10 to 12 reps
Week 5: Two sets of 8 to 10 reps
Week 6: Two or three sets of 8 to 10 reps
Weeks 7 and 8: Three sets of 8 to 10 reps

SEATED ALTERNATING DUMBBELL PRESS

● **Grab a pair of dumbbells and sit on a bench, holding the weights at jaw level, just outside your shoulders. Your palms should face forward.**

● **Starting with your weaker arm (probably your left if you're right handed), lift one dumbbell overhead until your arm is straight. As you lower it, raise the other—that's one repetition. Alternate until you finish the set.**

45-DEGREE SCARECROW

● Set an incline bench to 45 degrees. Holding a pair of light dumbbells, lie chest-down on the bench. Raise your upper arms so they're perpendicular to your torso and parallel to the floor. Bend your elbows 90 degrees, so your forearms hang straight down toward the floor.

● Keeping your elbows, wrists, and upper arms in fixed positions, rotate the weights up and back as far as you can—you want your shoulders to act like hinges, your arms like swinging gates. Pause, then slowly lower the weights.

SNATCH-GRIP SHRUG

● Grab a barbell with an overhand grip that's as wide as comfortably possible. Hold the bar down at arm's length in front of you. Lean forward slightly so the bar is about an inch in front of your thighs.

● Shrug your shoulders as high as you can. Pause, then slowly lower the barbell.

Do the three intermediate exercises for 4 weeks, then switch to the advanced moves for 4 weeks.

Weeks 1 and 2: Two sets of 10 to 12 reps

Weeks 3 and 4: Two or three sets of 8 to 10 reps

Weeks 5 and 6: Two sets of 8 to 10 reps

Weeks 7 and 8: Two or three sets of 6 to 8 reps

HANG CLEAN AND PRESS

- Grab a barbell with an overhand, shoulder-width grip, and hold it in front of your thighs while standing with your knees slightly bent. Your lower back should be in its natural alignment (slightly arched, in other words).
- Shrug your shoulders as you pull the bar up as hard as you can. You should rise up on your toes as you do this.
- When the bar reaches chest level, bend your knees again, rotate your forearms from the elbows, and bend your wrists so they go around the bar as you "catch" the bar on the front of your shoulders (shown).
- Straighten your knees, then press the bar overhead.
- Lower the bar to your shoulders, then rotate your arms and wrists back as you lower the bar to your waist, then finally lower it to your thighs again. Throughout the exercise, the bar should stay as close to your body as possible.

ALTERNATING LATERAL RAISE WITH STATIC HOLD

● Sit holding a pair of dumbbells at your sides, your palms facing in. Lift the dumbbells straight out to your sides.

● Lower and raise one dumbbell, starting with your weaker arm (your left if you're right handed), then lower and raise the other. That's one repetition.

DOUBLE-CABLE EXTERNAL ROTATION

● Attach two stirrup handles to the low cables of a cable-crossover station. Grab the left handle with your right hand and the right handle with your left, and stand in the middle of the station with your elbows bent 90 degrees and the cables crossing over each other in front of your midsection.

● Rotate your forearms up and outward, as if they were two gates swinging out from your upper arms, which act as hinges. Pause, then slowly return your arms to the starting position.

Do the intermediate exercises for 4 weeks, then the advanced exercises for 4 weeks.

Weeks 1 and 2: Two sets of 6 to 8 reps, after a thorough warmup with lighter weights

Weeks 3 and 4: Two or three sets of 4 to 6 reps, after warmup

Weeks 5 and 6: Two sets of 6 to 8 reps

Weeks 7 and 8: Two or three sets of 4 to 6 reps

TWISTING STANDING DUMBBELL SHOULDER PRESS

● **Stand holding a pair of dumbbells just outside your shoulders at jaw level, palms facing in.**

● **Press the dumbbells overhead as you twist to your right. Lower the dumbbells as you twist back to the center, then twist to the left as you press the weights upward again. If you end the set with an odd number of repetitions, start the next set by twisting to the side opposite the one you finished on in the previous set.**

ALTERNATING 45-DEGREE INCLINE SHOULDER PRESS

● Grab a pair of dumbbells and position yourself on your back on a Swiss ball or incline bench so your torso is at a 45-degree angle to the floor. Hold the dumbbells just outside your shoulders at about jaw level, with your palms facing forward. Your forearms should be in line with your torso.

● Lift one dumbbell overhead so the weight is in a line with your torso. As you lower it, lift the other. Alternate until you finish the set. Alternate the arm you start with on each set.

OVERHEAD DUMBBELL SHRUG

● Stand holding a pair of dumbbells overhead, just beyond shoulder-width apart, palms facing forward.

● Shrug your shoulders up as high as you can. Pause, then slowly lower your shoulders.

PHASE 2: Chest & Back (1)

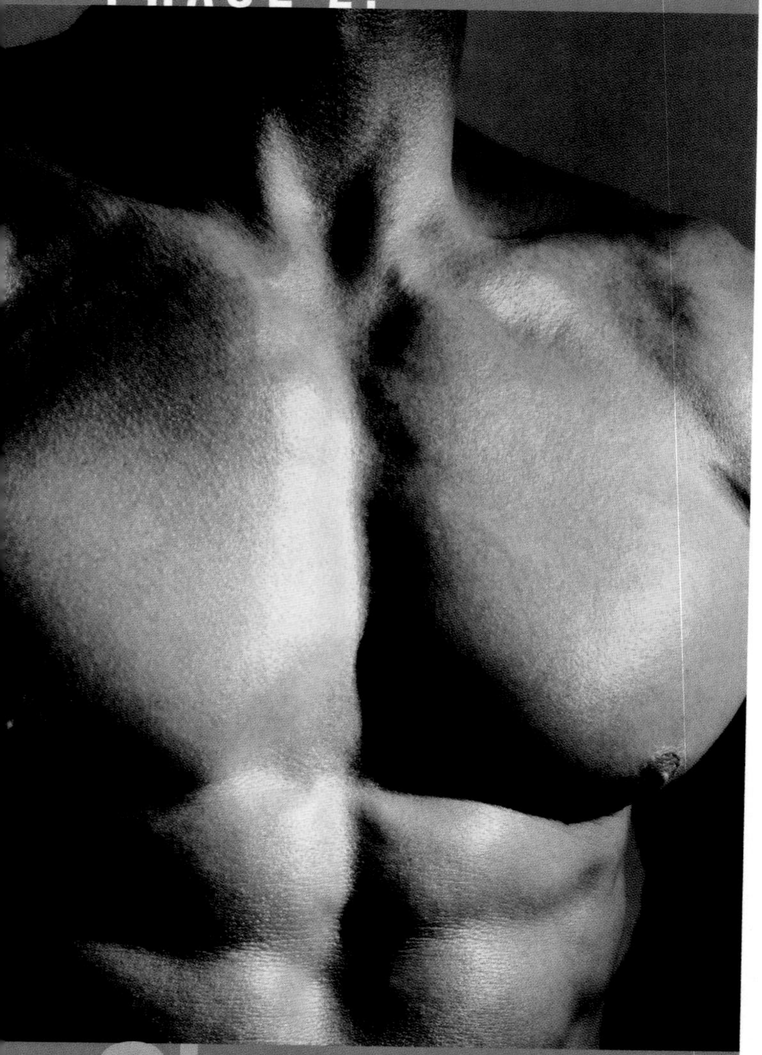

Over the years, you've learned to avoid unstable situations—internships in Iraq and horse-loving girlfriends, for example—because your life is a lot easier that way.

And you probably apply the same thinking to your workouts. That is, you do exercises—such as the standard bench press—with your body in a supported, stable position in order to isolate specific muscle groups. But performing the same exercises while you're in an unstable position—so that you have to balance yourself as you lift—forces the smaller, surrounding muscles to work, too. And that means a more productive workout.

Using instability to your advantage can lead to the best gains you've ever achieved in strength, muscle, and athletic performance, says Michael Mejia. Think about when you first learned to walk. As you advanced from crawling to standing to walking, your body position became less stable. But as a result, you became stronger. That's because your muscles had to perform better in each stage.

In this plan, you'll give your chest and back the same advantage. By changing from stable to less stable positions, you'll not only build the muscles you can see, but you'll also build the underlying stabilizer muscles you've ignored for years. And by training your body in unstable positions, you'll prepare it to be more stable when it counts—like when it's time to get away from that horse-loving girlfriend.

The Rest of Your Workout

Do the chest and back exercises first in your workout—in other words, do the exercises described here in phase 2. After that, it's up to you how to fit in exercises for other muscle groups.

Most important: Build strength and muscle size with equal effort on both sides of your body. Working the front and neglecting the back is a recipe for injury. Some suggestions:

The Muscles

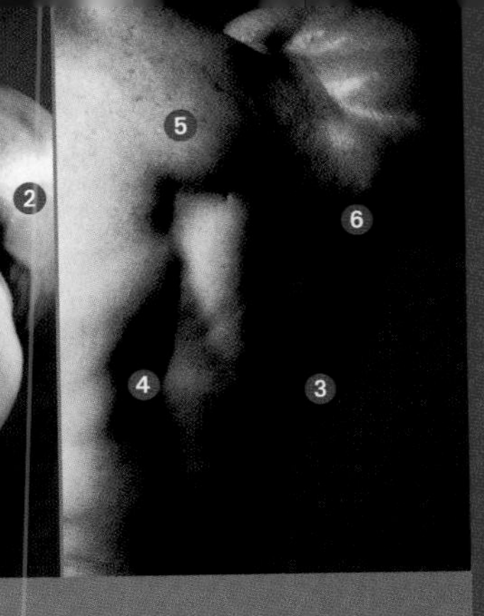

1. Pectoralis major
2. Front deltoid
3. Latissimus dorsi
4. Middle trapezius
5. Upper trapezius
6. Rear deltoids

BEGINNER

Do a total-body workout two or three times a week. After you finish your chest and back exercises, try one set of 8 to 12 repetitions of the following exercises (except where noted).

Squat (or leg press)
Leg curl
Seated alternating dumbbell press
Cable triceps extension
Dumbbell biceps curl
Crunch (15 to 20 repetitions)

INTERMEDIATE

Divide your program into two workouts, one for upper body, one for lower. Alternate between the two, taking a day off after each. So, you'd do the upper-body workout on Monday and Friday of one week and the lower-body workout on Wednesday, then the following week you'd do the lower-body workout on Monday and Friday and the upper-body routine on Wednesday.

Upper-body workout: After doing the chest and back program in this phase, choose one exercise each for shoulders, biceps, and triceps. Do two or three sets of the shoulder exercise and one or two sets of the arm exercises.

Lower-body workout: Choose one "hip-dominant" exercise, meaning the main emphasis of the exercise is on the hamstrings and gluteals (examples include stepups and any variety of deadlift). Then choose one "knee-dominant" exercise, meaning the emphasis is on the quadriceps muscles of the front of the thigh (squats, leg presses, and lunges qualify). Do two or three warmup sets and two work sets. (A work set means you're using the most weight you can for that number of repetitions. The warmup sets should be percentages of that weight—maybe 40, 60, and 80 percent. Do fewer repetitions in each warmup set.) Add your choice of abdominal and calf exercises.

ADVANCED

Divide your workout into four parts. Do each one once a week; don't work out more than 2 days in a row.

1. Chest and back
2. Knee-dominant exercises (described above), plus abs and calves
3. Shoulders and arms
4. Hip-dominant exercises (also above), plus abs and calves again

Do these four beginner exercises for 4 weeks.

Week 1: One set of 10 to 12 repetitions of each exercise

Week 2: One or two sets of 10 to 12 reps

Week 3: Two or three sets of 10 to 12 reps

Week 4: Three sets of 10 to 12 reps

Increase weights each week.

THREE-POINT PUSHUP

● Get into pushup position—your hands set slightly wider than and in line with your shoulders—with your arms straight. Place the ball of your left foot on top of your right heel.

● Keep your back flat, and lower your body until your chest nearly touches the floor. Pause, then push yourself back up to the starting position.

FLAT-BENCH FLY (FEET ELEVATED)

● Grab a pair of dumbbells and lie on your back on a flat bench, with your hips and knees bent 90 degrees and your feet in the air. Hold the dumbbells over your chest with your elbows slightly bent and thumbs turned toward each other.

● Slowly lower the dumbbells down and slightly back until your upper arms are parallel to the floor and in line with your ears. Pause, then lift the dumbbells back to the starting position.

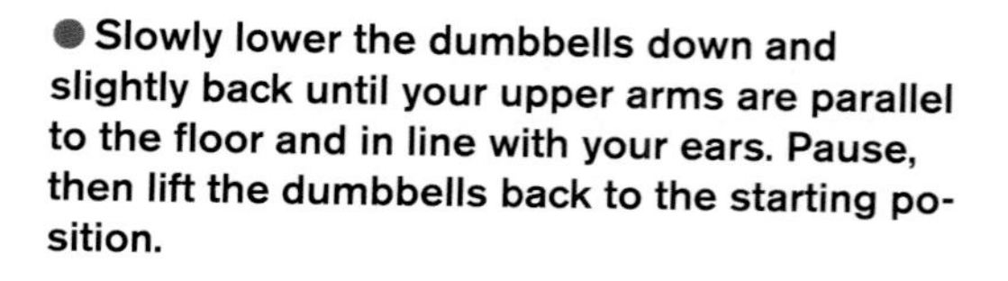

45-DEGREE PRONE DUMBBELL ROW

● Set an incline bench to a 45-degree angle. Grab a pair of dumbbells and lie chest-down against the pad. Let your arms hang straight down from your shoulders and turn your palms so that your thumbs are facing each other.

● Bend your elbows and lift your upper arms as high as you can by squeezing your shoulder blades together. Your upper arms should be almost perpendicular to your body at the top of the move. Your forearms should be pointing toward the floor. Pause, then slowly lower the weights to the starting position.

PRONATED LAT PULLDOWN

● Grab a lat-pulldown bar with a shoulder-width, overhand grip.

● Moving only your arms, pull the bar down to your chest by squeezing your shoulder blades together. Pause, then slowly return to the starting position.

An intermediate should do the six intermediate/advanced exercises shown here for 4 weeks.

Weeks 1 and 2: Two sets of 10 to 12 reps
Weeks 3 and 4: Two or three sets of 8 to 10 reps

If you're an advanced exerciser, do the exercises for 4 weeks, according to the following schedule of sets and reps.

Weeks 1 and 2: Two sets of 6 to 8 reps, after a thorough warmup with lighter weights
Weeks 3 and 4: Two or three sets of 4 to 6 reps, after warmup

SWISS-BALL PUSHUP

- **Get into pushup position—your hands set slightly wider than and in line with your shoulders—but instead of placing your feet on the floor, rest your shins on a Swiss ball. With your arms straight and your back flat, your body should form a straight line from your shoulders to your ankles.**

- **Lower your body until your chest nearly touches the floor. Pause, then push yourself back up to the starting position.**

ALTERNATING DECLINE DUMBBELL PRESS

● Grab a pair of dumbbells and lie on your back on a decline bench. Hold the dumbbells just outside your shoulders, with your arms bent and your palms facing forward.

● Push one dumbbell up and slightly toward your head so that when your arm is extended, the dumbbell is above your chin. As you lower the dumbbell back to your chest, repeat the movement with your other arm. Alternate until you finish the set. Alternate the arm you start with on each set.

LOW-TO-HIGH CABLE FLY

● Attach two stirrup handles to the low cables of a cable-crossover station. Grab the left handle with your left hand and the right handle with your right, and stand upright in a staggered stance in the middle of the station, with your arms outstretched but slightly bent.

● Pull the handles up and together without changing the angle of your elbows, until the handles are even with your eyes. Pause, then return to the starting position.

SNATCH-GRIP BENT-OVER ROW

● Grab a barbell with an overhand grip that's as wide as comfortably possible. Stand with your feet shoulder-width apart and knees slightly bent. Bend at your hips, lowering your torso about 45 degrees, and let the bar hang straight down from your shoulders.

● Pull the bar up to your torso, pause, then slowly lower it.

TOWEL PULLDOWN

● Drape a towel over each handgrip of a lat-pulldown bar. Sit on the bench and grab the ends of each towel so that your palms are facing each other.

● Moving only your arms, pull the bar down below your chin by squeezing your shoulder blades together. Pause, then slowly return to the starting position.

SEATED REAR LATERAL RAISE

● Grab a pair of dumbbells and sit at the end of a bench. Keep your back flat and your elbows slightly bent, and lean forward at the waist as far as you can. Let the dumbbells hang at arm's length, with your thumbs turned toward each other.

● Slowly raise the dumbbells as high as you can without changing the angle of your elbows. Pause, then lower the dumbbells back to the starting position.

PHASE 3:

Chest & Back (2)

If you're like us, you automatically delete any e-mail that has "FWD:FWD:" in the subject line because you're tired of getting the same messages over and over again. Well, imagine how your muscles feel doing the same exercises the same way, workout after workout. Just like your brain, they need something beyond the same old stuff if you want them to get bigger and stronger.

In phase 3, you'll force your muscles to work harder than ever by doing exercises that require you to balance and stabilize your body while lifting a weight. More muscle fibers and nerve endings get involved in each exercise, which means better results. If you're a beginner, this workout will help you build overall strength faster than a routine using traditional versions of these exercises. And if you're an intermediate or advanced lifter, the exercises here will help you see new gains in size and strength.

Oh, and before we forget: Be sure to forward this workout to everyone on your mailing list.

The Rest of Your Workout

Do the chest and back exercises before working other muscle groups. Try to increase the amount of weight you lift in each exercise by roughly 5 to 10 percent each week. You can do the remaining lifts in your workout in any order you wish. Some suggestions:

BEGINNER

Do a total-body workout two or three times a week. After you finish these chest and back exercises, try one set of 8 to 12 repetitions (except where noted) of the following:

Squat (or leg press)
Leg curl
Seated alternating dumbbell press
Cable triceps extension
Dumbbell biceps curl
Crunch (15 to 20 repetitions)

INTERMEDIATE

Divide your program into two workouts, one for upper body, one for lower. Alternate between the two, taking a day off after each. For example, do the upper-body workout on Monday and Friday and the lower-body workout on Wednesday; the following week, do the opposite.

Upper-body workout: After doing these chest and back exercises, choose one exercise each for the shoulders, biceps, and triceps. Do two or three sets of the shoulder exercises and one or two sets of the arm exercises.

Lower-body workout: Choose one "hip-dominant" exercise, meaning it emphasizes the hamstrings and gluteals (examples include stepups and any variety of deadlift). Then choose one "knee-dominant" exercise, meaning it emphasizes the quadriceps muscles of the front of the thigh (squats, leg presses, and lunges qualify). Do two or three warmup sets and two work sets. (A work set means you're using the most weight you can for that number of repetitions. The warmup sets should be percentages of that weight—maybe 40, 60, and 80 percent of the work-set weight. Do fewer repetitions in each warmup set.) Add your choice of abdominal and calf exercises.

ADVANCED

Divide your workout into four parts. Do each one once a week; don't work out more than 2 days in a row.

1. Shoulders and arms
2. Knee-dominant exercises (described above), plus abs and calves
3. Chest and back
4. Hip-dominant exercises (also above), plus abs and calves again

Do the four beginner exercises for 4 weeks.

Weeks 1 and 2: Two sets of 10 to 12 repetitions of each

Weeks 3 and 4: Two or three sets of 8 to 10 reps

BILATERAL CABLE REAR LATERAL RAISE

● Attach two stirrup handles to the low cables of a cable-crossover station. Grab the left handle with your right hand and the right handle with your left, and stand in the middle of the station. Keep your back flat, and bend at the waist and knees until your upper body is parallel to the floor. Your arms should be crossed in front of you and slightly bent.

● Raise your arms until they're parallel to the floor, without changing the angle of your elbows. Pause, then slowly return your arms to the starting position.

SINGLE-ARM ROW (ELBOW OUT)

● Grab a dumbbell in your left hand and place your right hand and right knee on a flat bench. Keep your back flat and your upper body parallel to the floor. Let your left arm hang straight down from your shoulder, and turn your palm so that it's facing your left leg.

● Raise your left upper arm out to the side until it's just past parallel to the floor. Your upper arm should be perpendicular to your body at the top of the move. Your lower arm should be pointing toward the floor. Pause, then slowly lower the weight to the starting position.

WIDE-GRIP BARBELL CHEST PRESS (FEET ELEVATED)

● Lie on your back on a flat bench with your hips bent 90 degrees and feet up in the air. (Keeping your feet elevated forces you to balance on the bench, which calls more muscle fibers into play.) Grab the bar with an overhand grip, your hands a bit farther apart than for a standard bench press, and lift it off the uprights. Hold it over your chin at arm's length.

● Slowly lower the bar until it nearly touches the middle of your chest. Pause, then push the bar back up until your arms are straight and the bar is over your chin again.

DECLINE FLY

● Grab a pair of dumbbells and lie on your back on a decline bench. Hold the dumbbells directly over your lower chest, with your elbows slightly bent and thumbs turned toward each other.

● Slowly lower the dumbbells and bring them slightly back toward your shoulders until your upper arms are parallel with the floor and in line with your ears. Pause, then lift the dumbbells back to the starting position.

INTERMEDIATE/ADVANCED

All of the following six exercises are for intermediate and advanced lifters and should be done for 4 weeks. Note the differences in sets and repetitions for each level.

INTERMEDIATE

Weeks 1 and 2: Two sets of 8 to 10 reps

Weeks 3 and 4: Two or three sets of 6 to 8 reps

ADVANCED

Weeks 1 and 2: Two sets of 6 to 8 reps

Weeks 3 and 4: Two or three sets of 6 to 8 reps, after a thorough warmup with lighter weights

SINGLE-LEG ALTERNATING DUMBBELL ROW

● Grab a pair of dumbbells and stand with your left foot in front of your right. Keep your back flat and bend over at the hips so the dumbbells are hanging at arm's length from your shoulders, palms facing in. Raise your right foot off the floor.

● Raise your left upper arm as high as you can by bending your elbow and squeezing your shoulder blade toward the middle of your back. As you lower it, raise the other—that's one repetition. Alternate until you finish the set. Alternate the foot you raise and the arm you start with on each set.

SWISS-BALL REVERSE PUSHUP

● Secure a bar 3 to 4 feet above the floor. Lie under the bar and grab it with a shoulder-width, overhand grip. Hang at arm's length from the bar with your body straight and your lower legs on a Swiss ball.

● Keep your body rigid and pull your chest to the bar. Pause, then lower yourself back to the starting position.

STAGGERED-GRIP PULLUP

● Grab a pullup bar with an overhand grip. Your right hand should be directly above your right shoulder, and your left hand 6 to 12 inches outside of your left shoulder. Hang at arm's length with your ankles crossed behind you.

● Pull yourself up as high as you can. Pause, then slowly return to the starting position. Alternate hand positions on each set, so your right hand is placed out from the shoulder on the second set.

ALTERNATING SWISS-BALL INCLINE DUMBBELL PRESS

● Grab a pair of dumbbells and position yourself on your back on a Swiss ball so your torso is at a 45-degree angle to the floor. Hold the dumbbells just outside your shoulders at about jaw level, with your palms facing forward.

● Press one dumbbell overhead so the weight is above your chin at the top of the move. As you lower it, press the other. Alternate until you finish the set. Alternate the arm you start with on each set. If you're doing an odd number of sets, start with your weaker arm on the first and third sets.

SANTANA *T*-PUSHUP

● Get into pushup position with your hands on the handles of dumbbells that have been placed shoulder-width apart.

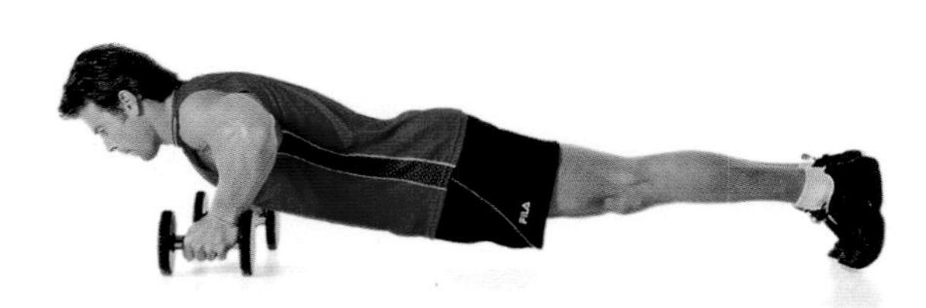

● Do a pushup, and as you come up, rotate your body so that you raise your left arm and the dumbbell straight up over your shoulder and your body forms a *T*. Lower the dumbbell and yourself, and repeat to the other side. If you can, use hexagonal dumbbells the first few times you try this.

BENT-OVER CABLE CROSSOVER

● Attach two stirrup handles to the low cables of a cable-crossover station. Grab the left handle with your left hand and the right handle with your right, and stand in the middle of the station. Keep your back flat and bend at the waist and knees until your upper body is parallel to the floor. Your arms should be outstretched but slightly bent.

● Pull the handles together, without changing the angle of your elbows, until your hands just pass each other. Pause, then return to the starting position.

PHASE 4:

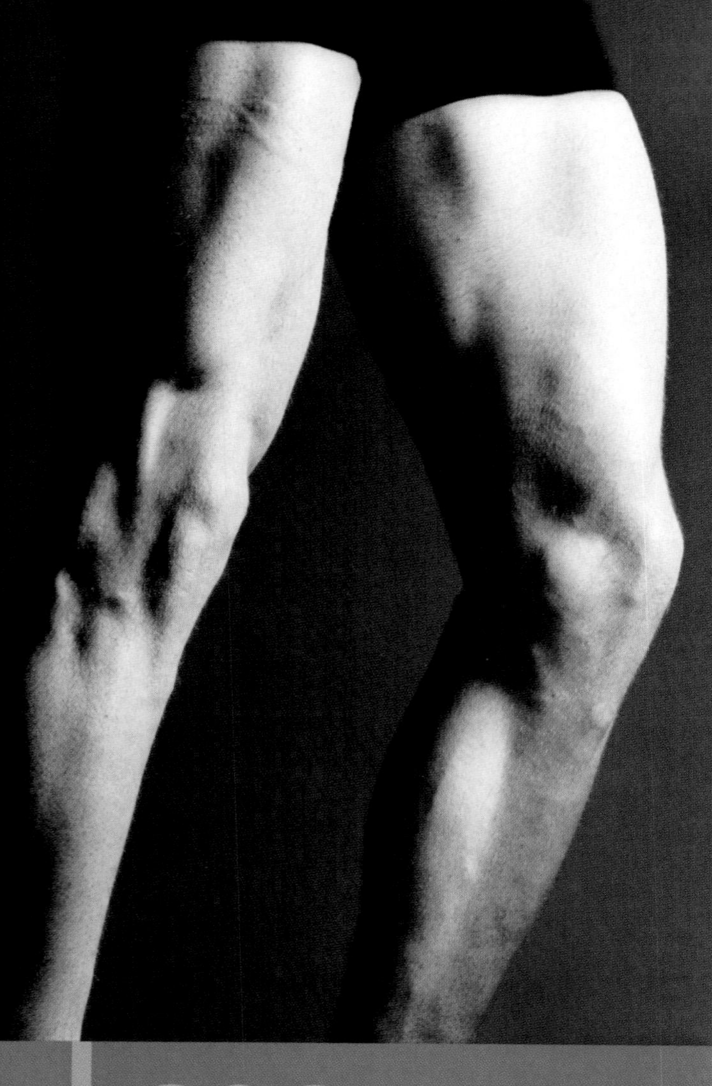

Legs & Glutes (1)

Work out long enough and you're bound to hear a trainer utter this weight-room truism: "You can't shoot a cannon from a rowboat." To which most guys reply, "Huh?"

Say you're a beginner. You walk into the gym with a shopping list: wide shoulders, big biceps, abs like a brick walkway—all the fun stuff you see on the cover of fitness magazines. Getting these things seems like a straightforward proposition, so you press and curl and crunch, and follow that with more pressing, more curling, and more crunching. Then you wonder why you haven't been asked to do a Bowflex commercial.

The problem is, you left out the most important part, says Michael Mejia. Running, jumping, hitting, throwing, and heavy lifting all start with the muscles in your hips, thighs, and lower legs. When those muscles grow bigger and stronger, they allow your torso muscles to grow, which provides the structure for the arm and shoulder muscles you really want. This lower-body workout, the first of two parts, takes your scrawny, shaky foundation and makes it strong and solid enough to support some high-caliber weaponry up top.

So the next time you see a stick-legged guy doing your old press-curl-crunch combo, you can tell him, "You can't fit Clint Eastwood's gun in Roy Rogers's holster." He'll have no idea what you're talking about, but that's not your problem.

The Rest of Your Workout

Do the leg and butt exercises described here before working any other muscle groups. You can do the rest of the lifts in your workout in any order. Try to increase the amount of weight you lift in each exercise by 5 to 10 percent each week.

Most important: Build strength and muscle size with equal effort on both sides of your body. Working the front and neglecting the back is a recipe for injury. Some suggestions:

BEGINNER

Do a total-body workout two or three times a week. After you finish these leg and butt exercises, you can try one set of 8 to 12 repetitions (except where noted) of the following exercises.

Lat pulldown
Dumbbell chest press
Cable or dumbbell row
Seated alternating dumbbell press
Cable triceps extension
Dumbbell biceps curl
Crunch (15 to 20 repetitions)

INTERMEDIATE

Divide your program into two workouts, one for upper body, one for lower. Alternate between the two workouts, taking a day off after each. For example, do the lower-body workout shown here on Monday and Friday and an upper-body workout on Wednesday; the following week, do the opposite.

Upper-body workout: Choose one exercise each for "horizontal pulling" (seated or bent-over row), one for "horizontal pushing" (dumbbell or barbell bench press), one for "vertical pulling" (pullup or lat pulldown), and one for "vertical pushing" (dumbbell or barbell shoulder press). Do two or three warmup sets and two work sets. (A work set means you're using the most weight you can for that number of repetitions. The warmup sets should be percentages of that weight—maybe 40, 60, and 80 percent of the work-set weight. Do fewer repetitions in each warmup set.) You can finish with exercises for your biceps and triceps.

Lower-body workout: Do the exercises described here, followed by abdominal exercises.

ADVANCED

Divide your workout into three parts. Do each part once a week, with a day off between workouts.

1. Vertical pushing and pulling
2. Lower-body exercises, plus abdominals and calves
3. Horizontal pushing and pulling

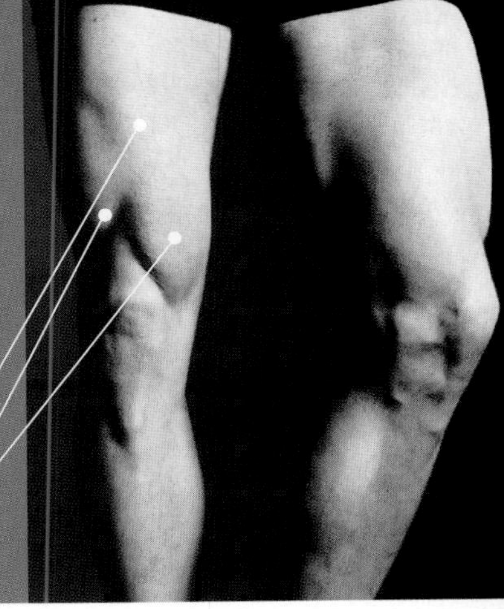

Do the five beginner exercises for 4 weeks.

Weeks 1 and 2: Two sets of 10 to 12 repetitions of each

Weeks 3 and 4: Two or three sets of 8 to 10 reps

DUMBBELL SPLIT SQUAT

● **Grab a pair of dumbbells and hold them at your sides. Stand in a staggered stance with your left foot about 4 feet in front of your right.**

● **Lower your body until your left knee is bent 90 degrees and your right knee nearly touches the floor. Your left lower leg should be perpendicular to the floor, and your torso should remain upright. Push yourself back up to the starting position as quickly as you can. Finish all of your repetitions, then repeat the exercise with your right foot in front of your left.**

LEG PRESS

● Position yourself in a leg-press machine with your back against the pad and your feet about 4 inches apart on the platform.

● Unlock the platform and slowly lower the weight until your knees are bent 90 degrees. Pause, then push the weight back up to the starting position.

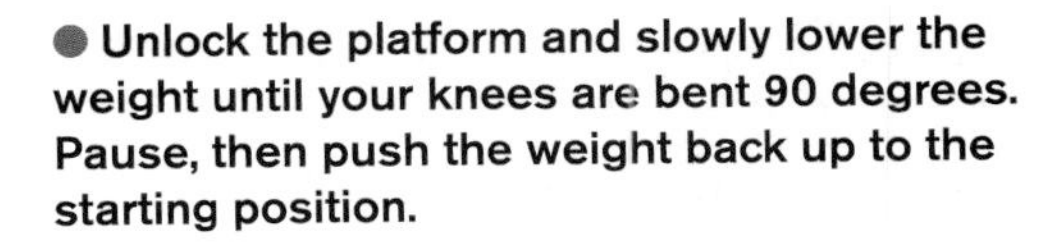

SNATCH-GRIP ROMANIAN DEADLIFT

● Grab a barbell with an overhand grip that's as wide as comfortably possible. Hold the bar down at arm's length in front of you. Your feet should be hip-width apart and your knees slightly bent.

● Keep your lower back slightly arched and bend slowly at the hips as far as you can without losing the arch. Don't change the angle of your knees, and keep the bar close to your body throughout the entire move. Pause, then lift your torso back to the starting position.

LYING LEG CURL

● Lie face down on a leg-curl machine with the pads against your lower legs, above your heels and below your calf muscles.

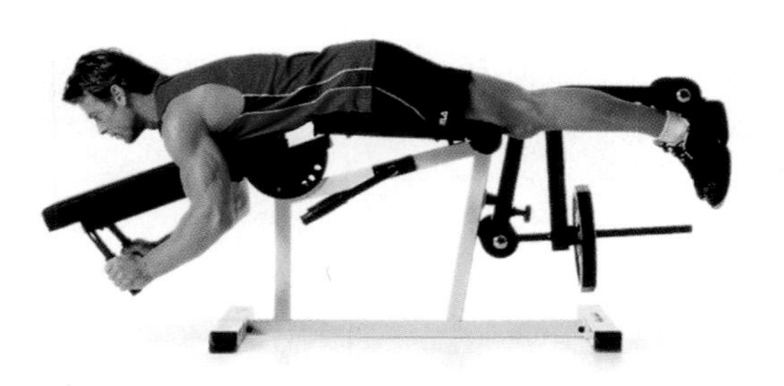

● Without raising your body off the pad, bend your legs at the knees and pull the weight toward you as far as you can. Pause, then slowly return to the starting position.

ALTERNATING SEATED CALF RAISE

● Place a step in front of a bench, grab a pair of dumbbells, and sit down. Set the balls of both feet on the step, and place one dumbbell on each knee. Lower both heels as far as you can without touching the floor.

● Push off the ball of your left foot and lift your left heel as high as you can. As you lower your left heel to the starting position, raise your right heel. Alternate until you finish the set.

All of the following five exercises are for intermediate and advanced lifters and should be done for 4 weeks. Note the differences in sets and repetitions for each level.

INTERMEDIATE

Weeks 1 and 2: Two sets of 8 to 10 reps

Weeks 3 and 4: Two or three sets of 6 to 8 reps

ADVANCED

Weeks 1 and 2: Two sets of 6 to 8 reps, after warmup

Weeks 3 and 4: Two or three sets of 4 to 6 reps, after warmup

BULGARIAN SPLIT SQUAT

- **Hold a barbell with an overhand grip so that it rests comfortably on your upper back (not on your neck) and stand about 3 feet in front of a bench. Place your left foot behind you on the bench so that only your instep is resting on it.**

- **Lower your body until your right knee is bent 90 degrees and your left knee nearly touches the floor. Your right lower leg should be perpendicular to the floor, and your torso should remain upright. Push yourself back to the starting position as quickly as you can. Finish all of your repetitions, then repeat the lift, this time with your right foot resting on the bench while your left leg does the work.**

BARBELL SQUAT

● Hold a barbell with an overhand grip so that it rests comfortably on your upper back (not on your neck). Set your feet shoulder-width apart, and keep your knees slightly bent, back straight, and eyes focused straight ahead.

● Slowly lower your body as if you were sitting back into a chair, keeping your back in its natural alignment and your lower legs nearly perpendicular to the floor. When your thighs are parallel to the floor, pause, and then return to the starting position.

GOOD MORNING

● Start in the same position as for the barbell squat.

● Slowly bend forward at the hips as you lower your chest as far as you can go while maintaining the natural arch in your lower back, or until your upper body is parallel to the floor. Keep your head up and maintain about the same angle of your knees. Lift your upper body back to the starting position.

SINGLE-LEG CURL

● Lie in a leg-curl machine with the pads against your lower legs, above your heels and below your calf muscles.

● Without raising your body off the pad, bend your left leg at the knee and pull the weight toward you as far as you can. Your right leg should remain in the starting position. Pause, then slowly return to the starting position. Finish the set, then repeat with your right leg.

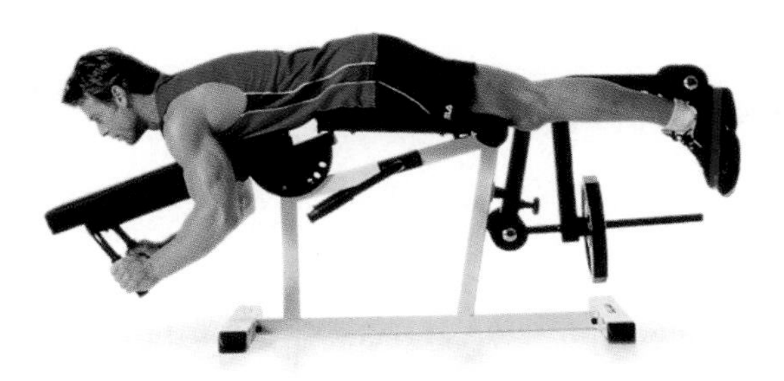

SINGLE-LEG STANDING CALF RAISE

● Grab a dumbbell in your left hand and stand on a step or a block. Put your right hand on something for balance—a wall or a weight stack, for instance. Cross your right foot behind your left ankle and balance yourself on the ball of your left foot.

● Lower your left heel as far as you can, pause, then lift it as high as you can. Finish the set with your left leg, then repeat with your right while holding the dumbbell in your right hand.

PHASE 5:

Legs & Glutes (2)

Most men have a simple philosophy when choosing their lower-body exercises: The more weight plates they can pile on, the better the lift. But choosing your exercises based on the amount of weight you can heft is a lot like timing your 40-yard dash on the moving sidewalk at O'Hare.

That's because the most popular exercises for your lower body—machine exercises like leg presses, leg extensions, and leg curls—allow you to lift heavier weights than their free-weight counterparts. Why? Because they give your body a mechanical advantage. So even though you're able to lift more iron, you're using less muscle. That puts you at a disadvantage when you're trying to maximize your lower-body strength and size, says Mejia.

In this phase of Total-Body Workbook V.2.0, Mejia gives you exercises that force your muscles to work without help from well-designed machinery—the same way they work in sports and real-life activities. You'll hold the weights in different positions—behind your legs, in front of your shoulders, above your head—and prepare your body for virtually any task. What's more, you'll work your muscles more intensely than you have before, which will stimulate them to grow.

When you see the end results of this program, we're guessing you'll have some new favorite exercises.

The Rest of Your Workout

Do the leg and butt exercises described here before working any other muscle groups. You can do the rest of the lifts in your workout in any order. Try to increase the amount of weight you lift in each exercise by 5 to 10 percent each week.

Most important: Build strength and muscle size with equal effort on both sides of your body. Working the front and neglecting the back is a recipe for injury. Some suggestions:

BEGINNER

Do a total-body workout two or three times a week. After you finish these leg and butt exercises, you can try one set of 8 to 12 repetitions (except where noted) of the following exercises.

Lat pulldown
Dumbbell chest press
Cable or dumbbell row
Seated alternating dumbbell press
Cable triceps extension
Dumbbell biceps curl
Crunch (15 to 20 repetitions)

INTERMEDIATE

Divide your program into two workouts, one for upper body, one for lower. Alternate between the two workouts, taking a day off after each. For example, do the lower-body workout shown here on Monday and Friday and an upper-body workout on Wednesday; the following week, do the opposite.

Upper-body workout: Choose one exercise each for "horizontal pulling" (seated or bent-over row), one for "horizontal pushing" (dumbbell or barbell bench press), one for "vertical pulling" (pullup or lat pulldown), and one for "vertical pushing" (dumbbell or barbell shoulder press). Do two or three warmup sets and two work sets. (A work set means you're using the most weight you can for that number of repetitions. The warmup sets should be percentages of that weight—maybe 40, 60, and 80 percent of the work-set weight. Do fewer repetitions in each warmup set.) You can finish with exercises for your biceps and triceps.

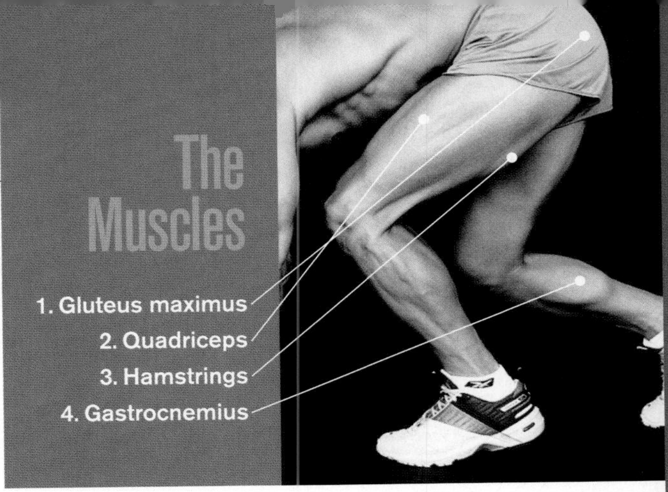

Lower-body workout: Do the exercises described here, followed by abdominal exercises.

ADVANCED

Divide your workout into three parts. Do each part once a week, and take a day off between workouts.

1. Vertical pushing and pulling
2. Lower-body exercises, plus abdominals and calves
3. Horizontal pushing and pulling

The Muscles

1. Gluteus maximus
2. Quadriceps
3. Hamstrings
4. Gastrocnemius

Do the five beginner exercises for 4 weeks.

Weeks 1 and 2: Two sets of 10 to 12 repetitions of each exercise

Weeks 3 and 4: Two or three sets of 8 to 10 reps

MODIFIED FARMER'S WALK

- **Grab a pair of heavy dumbbells and stand holding them at arm's length at your sides.**
- **Stand on the balls of your feet and walk forward until your grip is about to give out.**
- **Put the dumbbells down, rest, and then turn around and repeat, going back to the starting point.**

45-DEGREE TRAVELING LUNGE

● Grab a pair of dumbbells and hold them at your sides. Stand with your feet hip-width apart at one end of your house or gym—you need room to walk forward.

● Step forward with your left leg at a 45-degree angle and lower your body until your right knee almost touches the floor and your left knee is bent 90 degrees. Stand and bring your right foot up next to your left, then repeat with the right leg lunging forward. That's one repetition.

KING DEADLIFT

● Stand with your knees slightly bent and your feet shoulder-width apart. (This is done without weights.) Lift your left foot behind you and bend the knee 90 degrees so your left lower leg is just about parallel to the floor.

● Slowly lower your body until your right thigh is parallel to the floor. Your left leg will rise behind you as a counterbalance, and your torso will bend forward at the hips. Pause, then push your body back to the starting position. Finish all of the repetitions, then repeat, lifting your right leg this time.

SWISS-BALL HIP EXTENSION AND LEG CURL

● Lie on your back on the floor and place your lower legs on a Swiss ball. Put your hands flat on the floor at your sides.

● Push your hips up so that your body forms a straight line from your shoulders to your knees.

● Without pausing, pull your heels toward you and roll the ball as close as possible to your butt. Pause, then reverse the motion—roll the ball back until your body is in a straight line, then lower your back to the floor and repeat.

BARBELL FRONT SQUAT

● Grab a bar with an overhand grip that's just beyond shoulder width and hold it in front of your body, just above your shoulders. Raise your upper arms so they're parallel to the floor and let the bar roll back so it's resting on your fingers, not your palms. Set your feet shoulder-width apart and keep your back straight, knees slightly bent, and eyes focused straight ahead.

● Without changing the position of your arms, lower your body until your thighs are parallel to the floor. Pause, then push yourself back up to the starting position.

All of the following five exercises are for intermediate and advanced lifters and should be done for 4 weeks. Note the differences in sets and repetitions for each level.

INTERMEDIATE

Weeks 1 and 2: Two sets of 8 to 10 reps

Weeks 3 and 4: Two or three sets of 6 to 8 reps

ADVANCED

Weeks 1 and 2: Two sets of 6 to 8 reps, after a thorough warmup with lighter weights

Weeks 3 and 4: Two or three sets of 4 to 6 reps, after warmup

OVERHEAD SQUAT

- With your feet shoulder-width apart, stand holding a barbell with an overhand grip. Press it over your head so your arms are fully extended. The bar should be directly over your shoulders.

- Slowly lower your body as if you were sitting back into a chair, keeping your back in its natural alignment. When your thighs are parallel to the floor, pause, then return to the starting position.

BARBELL HACK SQUAT

● Stand holding a barbell at arm's length behind your back, using an overhand grip. Set your feet shoulder-width apart and place each heel on a 25-pound weight plate.

● Slowly lower your body as if you were sitting back into a chair, keeping your back in its natural alignment. When your thighs are parallel to the floor, pause, then return to the starting position.

SINGLE-LEG SWISS-BALL HIP EXTENSION AND LEG CURL

● Lie on your back on the floor; place your right lower leg on a Swiss ball and your left leg in the air, perpendicular to your body. Put your hands flat on the floor at your sides.

● Push your hips up so that your body forms a straight line from your shoulders to your knees.

● Without pausing, pull your right heel toward you and roll the ball as close as possible to your butt. Pause, then reverse the movement and return to the starting position. Finish the repetitions and repeat with your left leg.

DUMBBELL CALF JUMP

● Stand with your feet hip-width apart. Grab a pair of dumbbells and hold them at your sides at arm's length.

● Dip your knees so they're bent about 45 degrees and jump as high as you can. Point your toes toward the floor when you jump. Allow your knees to bend 45 degrees when you land, then immediately jump again.

SINGLE-LEG BACK EXTENSION

● Position yourself in a back-extension station. Hook one foot under the leg anchor and leave the other foot resting on top. Cross your arms over your chest.

● Lower your upper body, allowing your lower back to round, until it's just short of perpendicular to the floor. Raise your upper body until it's slightly above parallel to the floor. At this point you should have a slight arch in your back, and your shoulder blades should be pulled together in back. Finish the set, then repeat with your other foot under the leg anchor.

PHASE 6:

Abs

Your abdominal muscles are a lot like a skilled group of employees. The harder they work, the better they make you look. And vice versa.

That's because you use your abs in virtually every movement that matters: Lifting. Running. Jumping. Reproducing. (It takes a lot of midsection stability to stand over that copy machine. Especially when it's printing on both sides of the page.) So the stronger they are, the harder and longer you'll be able to play.

This 8-week ab-building program works your entire midsection—not just the six-pack muscle (rectus abdominis, for you Latin lovers), but also your obliques (at the sides of your waist) and your lower back. So whether you're bending, twisting, or leaping, these exercises ensure that you and your abs will perform better and last longer.

And, on the off chance that you need to remove your shirt before bending, twisting, or leaping, your hardworking, multitasking abdominal muscles will make that a painless experience, too.

The Rest of Your Workout

Do the abdominal exercises first in your workout. After that, it's up to you how to fit in exercises for other muscle groups. Here are some suggestions.

BEGINNER

Do a total-body workout two or three times a week. After you finish your abdominal exercises, you can try one set of 8 to 12 repetitions of the following exercises:

Lat pulldown
Squat or leg press
Leg curl
Dumbbell chest press
Cable or dumbbell row
Cable triceps extension
Dumbbell biceps curl

INTERMEDIATE

Divide your program into two workouts, one for your upper body and one for your lower body. Perform your abdominal exercises on the day you do your lower-body workout. Alternate between the two workouts, taking a day off after each. So, you would do the upper-body workout on Monday and Friday one week and the lower-body workout on Wednesday, then the following week do the lower-body workout on Monday and Friday and the upper-body workout on Wednesday.

Upper-body workout: Choose one exercise each for chest, back, biceps, and triceps. Do two or three sets of the chest and back exercises and one or two sets of the exercises for the arms.

Lower-body workout: After doing the abdominal program in this phase, choose one "hip-dominant" lift—an exercise that emphasizes the hamstrings and gluteals (examples include stepups and deadlifts). Then choose one "knee-dominant" exercise, meaning the emphasis is on the quadriceps muscles of the front of the thigh (squats, leg presses, and lunges qualify). Do two or three warmup sets and two work sets. (A work set means you're using the most weight you can for that number of repetitions. The warmup sets should be percentages of that weight—maybe 40, 60, and 80 percent. Do fewer repetitions in each warmup set.) Add your choice of calf exercises.

The Muscles

1. Rectus abdominis
2. External oblique

ADVANCED

Divide your workout into four parts. Do each one once a week; don't work out more than 2 days in a row.

1. Shoulders and arms
2. Abdominal and knee-dominant exercises (described above), plus calves
3. Chest and back
4. Abdominal and hip-dominant exercises (also above), plus calves again

Do the following four beginner exercises for 4 weeks, followed by the intermediate exercises on pages 138 and 139 for weeks 5 through 8.

Weeks 1 and 2: Two sets of 10 to 12 repetitions of each exercise except the bridge

Weeks 3 and 4: Two or three sets of 12 to 15 reps

Weeks 5 through 8: Do the intermediate program

BRIDGE

● Start to get into a pushup position, but bend your elbows and rest your weight on your forearms instead of your hands. Your body should form a straight line from your shoulders to your ankles.

● Pull your abdominals in; imagine you're trying to move your belly button back to your spine. Hold this for 20 to 30 seconds, breathing steadily. Release, then repeat for another 20 to 30 seconds. That equals two complete sets. As you build endurance, you can do one 60-second set instead of two shorter ones.

RUSSIAN TWIST

● Sit on the floor with your knees bent and your feet flat. Hold your arms straight out in front of your chest with your palms facing down. Lean back so your torso is at a 45-degree angle to the floor.

● Twist to the left as far as you can, pause, then reverse your movement and twist all the way back to the right as far as you can. As you get stronger, hold a light weight in your hands as you do the movement.

TOWEL CRUNCH

● Sit on the floor with your knees bent and your feet flat on the floor. Set a rolled-up towel under the arch of your lower back and lie back so your head rests on the floor. Place your fingers behind your ears.

● Raise your head and shoulders and crunch your rib cage toward your pelvis. Pause, then slowly return to the starting position.

BACK EXTENSION

● Position yourself in a back-extension station and hook your feet under the leg anchor. Hold your arms straight out in front of you. Your body should form a straight line from your hands to your hips. Lower your torso, allowing your lower back to round, until it's just short of perpendicular to the floor.

● Raise your upper body until it's slightly above parallel to the floor. At this point you should have a slight arch in your back and your shoulder blades should be pulled together in back. Pause, then repeat.

An intermediate should do the exercises shown here for 4 weeks, then the advanced exercises on pages 140 and 141 for weeks 5 through 8.

Weeks 1 and 2: Two sets of 4 to 6 reps

Weeks 3 and 4: Two or three sets of 6 to 8 reps

Weeks 5 and 6: Two sets of 3 to 5 reps

Weeks 7 and 8: Two or three sets of 5 to 8 reps

TWO-POINT BRIDGE

- **Get into the standard pushup position.**
- **Lift your right hand and your left leg off the floor at the same time. Hold for 3 to 5 seconds. That's one repetition. Return to the starting position, then repeat, lifting your left hand and your right leg this time. Continue to alternate until you've completed all of your repetitions. Make sure you do an equal number with each hand and leg.**

SWISS-BALL CRUNCH

- **Lie on your back on a Swiss ball with your hands behind your ears.**
- **Raise your head and shoulders and crunch your rib cage toward your pelvis. Pause and slowly return to the starting position.**

SWISS-BALL JACKKNIFE

● Get into pushup position—your hands set slightly wider than and in line with your shoulders—but instead of placing your feet on the floor, rest your shins on a Swiss ball. With your arms straight and your back flat, your body should form a straight line from your shoulders to your ankles.

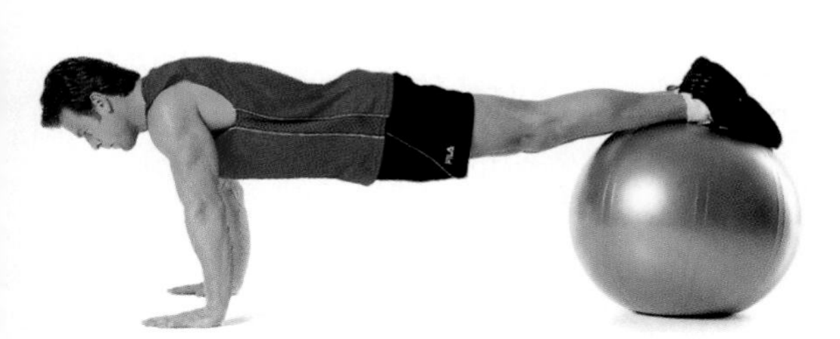

● Roll the Swiss ball toward your chest by raising your hips and rounding your back as you pull the ball forward with your feet. Pause, then return the ball to the starting position by lowering your hips and rolling it backward.

LOW-TO-HIGH REVERSE WOODCHOPPER

● Attach a stirrup handle to a low cable pulley, grab it with both hands, and stand with your right side facing the cable station and your feet shoulder-width apart. Bend over and hold the handle with both hands just outside your right calf muscle. Your shoulders will be rotated toward the cable machine. Straighten your arms and keep them straight throughout the entire movement.

● Pull the handle up and across your torso as you straighten your body and twist your shoulders to the left. Your right arm ends up in front of your face, and the handle is at the same height as your ear. Pause, then slowly return to the starting position. Finish the repetitions on this side, then switch sides to complete the set.

ADVANCED

Do the four intermediate exercises on pages 138 and 139 for 4 weeks, then switch to the following advanced exercises for weeks 5 through 8.

Weeks 1 and 2: Two sets of 6 to 8 reps
Weeks 3 and 4: Two or three sets of 8 to 10 reps
Weeks 5 and 6: Two sets of 6 to 8 reps
Weeks 7 and 8: Two or three sets of 8 to 10 reps

HANGING LEG RAISE

● Grasp a chinup bar with an overhand grip and hang from it at arm's length, with your knees slightly bent. If you have elbow straps—Ab-OrigiOnals, for example—hang from them.

● Without bending your legs any more, lift your knees as close to your chest as possible by rounding your back and curling your hips toward your rib cage. Pause, then slowly lower your legs to the starting position.

OBLIQUE HANGING LEG RAISE

● Grasp a chinup bar with an overhand grip and hang from it at arm's length, with your knees slightly bent. If you have elbow straps—Ab-OrigiOnals, for instance—hang from them. Then raise your legs until your knees are bent 90 degrees.

● Keep your knees bent and lift your left hip toward your left armpit until your lower legs are parallel to the floor. Pause, then return to the starting position and lift your right hip toward your right armpit. That's one repetition.

LONG-ARM CIRCLE CRUNCH

● Lie on your back on a Swiss ball with arms extended straight above your head—in line with your ears—and your thumbs crossed so that they interlock.

● Raise your head and shoulders and crunch your rib cage toward your right hip, then continue contracting your abdominals to move your torso counterclockwise till you're crunching upward, then left, then down, so that your upper body moves in a circle. Each circle you complete is one repetition.

TWISTING BACK EXTENSION

● Position yourself in a back-extension station and hook your feet under the leg anchor. Place your fingers behind your ears. Lower your upper body, allowing your lower back to round, until it's just short of perpendicular to the floor.

● Raise and twist your upper body until it's slightly above parallel to the floor and facing left. Pause, then lower your torso and repeat, this time twisting to the right. That's one repetition.

PHASE 7: Arms (1)

Experience has taught us this little-known muscle-training secret: If you build the rest of your body, your arms will grow by default. That's because they're involved in virtually every exercise you do. You'll never see a guy with wide shoulders, a meaty chest, a V-shaped back . . . and puny arms. On the other hand, you'll see plenty of guys who spend an hour a week on their arms and look as if they hardly work out at all. The lesson: Spend the majority of your workout time on your big muscles, and the smaller muscles—like your biceps and triceps—will take care of themselves.

However, there are times when your arms should be the center of attention—and not just when you're updating your tattoo collection. Say you've been following our program from the beginning. You've spent time working your shoulders, chest and back, lower body, and abs. You're bigger, stronger, and leaner, and probably better at every physical activity you attempt. But now your arms may actually be holding you back, for reasons that have nothing to do with the fact your ex-girlfriend's name is still engraved on your left biceps.

The next 8 weeks are going to be all about arms. In each of the following 4-week programs designed by Michael Mejia, you'll do exercises that work your biceps and triceps hard, in ways they've never been challenged before.

You should notice the difference in obvious and subtle ways. You'll get stronger in exercises like the bench press and pullup because your arms will provide better assistance. And when you finally get your new girlfriend's name tattooed on your arm, well, you'll be able to use bigger letters.

The Rest of Your Workout

Do the arm exercises first in your workout. After that, it's up to you how to fit in exercises for other muscle groups. Here are some suggestions.

BEGINNER

Do a total-body workout two or three times a week. Here's a sample: Do one set of 8 to 12 repetitions of the following exercises after you finish your arm exercises.

Lat pulldown
Squat or leg press
Leg curl
Dumbbell chest press
Cable or dumbbell row
Crunch

INTERMEDIATE

Divide your program into two workouts, one for your upper body and one for your lower body. Perform your arm exercises on the day you do your upper-body workout. Alternate between the two workouts, taking a day off after each. So, for example, you might do the upper-body workout on Monday and Friday one week and the lower-body workout on Wednesday, then the following week do the lower-body workout on Monday and Friday and the upper-body workout on Wednesday.

Upper-body workout: After doing the arm program in this phase, choose one exercise each for your chest, back, and shoulders. Do two or three sets of the chest and back exercises and one or two sets of the exercises for your shoulders.

Lower-body workout: Choose one "hip-dominant" lift—an exercise that emphasizes the hamstrings and gluteals (examples include stepups and deadlifts). Then choose one "knee-dominant" exercise, meaning the emphasis is on the quadriceps muscles of the front of the thigh (squats, leg presses, and lunges qualify). Do two or three warmup sets and two work sets. (A work set means you're using the most weight you can for that number of repetitions. The warmup sets should be percentages of that weight—maybe 40, 60, and 80 percent. Do fewer repetitions in each warmup set.) Add your choice of abdominal and calf exercises.

ADVANCED

Divide your workout into four parts. Do each one once a week; don't work out more than 2 days in a row.

1. Arms and shoulders
2. Knee-dominant exercises (described above), plus abdominals and calves
3. Chest and back
4. Hip-dominant exercises (also above), plus abdominals and calves again

Do the four beginner exercises for 4 weeks.

Weeks 1 and 2: One or two sets of 10 to 12 repetitions of each exercise

Weeks 3 and 4: Two or three sets of 10 to 12 reps

OVERHEAD TRICEPS EXTENSION

- **Grab an EZ-curl bar with a shoulder-width, overhand grip. Hold the bar at arm's length over your head.**

- **Lower the bar behind your head without moving your upper arms until your lower arms are just past parallel to the floor. Pause, then return the bar to the starting position by straightening your arms.**

LYING DUMBBELL TRICEPS EXTENSION

- **Grab a pair of dumbbells and lie on your back on a flat bench. Hold the dumbbells over and slightly behind your head with straight arms, your palms facing each other. Your upper arms should be angled back so they're next to your ears.**

- **Lower the dumbbells without moving your upper arms until your lower arms are nearly perpendicular to the floor. Pause, then lift the dumbbells back to the starting position by straightening your arms.**

STANDING HAMMER CURL

● Grab a pair of dumbbells and stand with your feet hip-width apart. Let your arms hang straight down from your shoulders and turn your palms so they're facing each other.

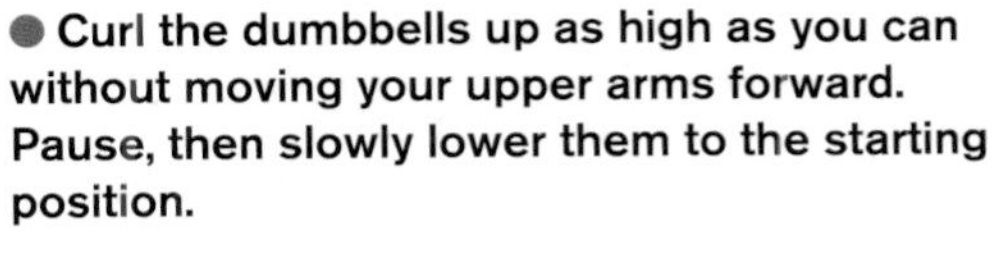

● Curl the dumbbells up as high as you can without moving your upper arms forward. Pause, then slowly lower them to the starting position.

SEATED PREACHER CURL

● Grab an EZ-curl bar with an underhand grip. Rest your upper arms on the sloping pad of the preacher bench and hold the bar at arm's length in front of you, with your elbows bent about 5 degrees.

● Lift the bar as high as you can without moving your upper arms off the pad. Pause, then slowly lower the bar to the starting position.

All of the following four exercises are for intermediate and advanced lifters and should be done for 4 weeks. Note the differences in sets and repetitions for each level.

INTERMEDIATE

Weeks 1 and 2: Two sets of 8 to 10 reps

Weeks 3 and 4: Two or three sets of 6 to 8 reps

ADVANCED

Weeks 1 and 2: Two sets of 6 to 8 reps, after a thorough warmup with lighter weights

Weeks 3 and 4: Two or three sets of 4 to 6 reps, after warmup

DUMBBELL OVERHEAD TRICEPS EXTENSION WITH FEET ELEVATED

- Grab a pair of dumbbells and sit at the end of a bench with your back straight. Hold the dumbbells at arm's length above your head, your palms facing each other. Lift your feet off the ground a few inches by raising your thighs slightly.

- Lower the dumbbells behind your head without moving your upper arms until your lower arms are just past parallel to the floor. Pause, then return the dumbbells to the starting position by straightening your arms.

BODY-WEIGHT TRICEPS EXTENSION

- Set the barbell supports of a squat rack about 3 to 4 feet above the floor, and place a bar across them. Grab the bar with an overhand grip, your hands about 6 to 8 inches apart. Still holding the bar, back up until your arms are straight, your body nearly forms a line from your head to your ankles, and you're standing on the balls of your feet. Your hands should be in line with your head.

- Lower your head toward the bar by bending your elbows until your head nearly touches the bar. Pause, then push yourself back up to the starting position by straightening your arms.

SINGLE-ARM UNSUPPORTED CONCENTRATION CURL

● Grab a dumbbell with your left hand and stand with your feet shoulder-width apart. Keep your back flat and bend at your hips and knees until your upper body is almost parallel to the ground. Let your left arm hang straight down from your shoulder and place your right hand on your right thigh.

● Curl the dumbbell toward your chin as high as you can without moving your upper arm. Pause, then slowly return to the starting position. Finish the repetitions with your left arm, then switch to your right to complete the set.

INCLINE ZOTTMAN CURL

● Set an incline bench at about a 60-degree angle and grab a pair of dumbbells. Lie on your back on the incline bench and let the dumbbells hang at arm's length straight from your shoulders, your palms facing forward.

● Curl the weights up as high as you can without moving your upper arms forward.

● At the top of the curl, rotate your wrists downward so your palms face the floor. Slowly lower them in that position.

● At the bottom of the curl, turn your palms forward again to start the next repetition.

PHASE 8:

Arms (2)

Video games aren't usually associated with fitness. But you could probably learn something about building muscle from that old Atari 2600 in your basement. Like most video game systems, it lets you start with easier versions of a game when you're a beginner and adds tougher levels of play later on. The reason: You need to keep challenging yourself in order to improve.

The same holds true for your muscles. They adapt to your exercise routine by growing, which in turn makes your workout easier. But the longer you use the same exercises the same way, the less your muscles are forced to progress. And that means you get diminishing returns on your workout investment.

In this phase of Total-Body Workbook V.2.0, we're going to make all of the standard arm exercises guys normally use more difficult. Think of it as playing a video game on the "expert" level for the first time. You have to rise to the occasion. Follow this plan and your muscles will do the same.

The Rest of Your Workout

Do the arm exercises first in your workout. After that, it's up to you how to fit in exercises for other muscle groups. Here are some suggestions.

BEGINNER

Do a total-body workout two or three times a week. Here's a sample: Do one set of 8 to 12 repetitions of the following exercises after you finish your arm exercises.

Lat pulldown
Squat or leg press
Leg curl
Dumbbell chest press
Cable or dumbbell row
Crunch

INTERMEDIATE

Divide your program into two workouts, one for your upper body and one for your lower body. Perform your arm exercises on the day you do your upper-body workout. Alternate between the two workouts, taking a day off after each. So, for example, you might do the upper-body workout on Monday and Friday one week and the lower-body workout on Wednesday, then the following week do the lower-body workout on Monday and Friday and the upper-body workout on Wednesday.

Upper-body workout: After doing the arm program in this phase, choose one exercise each for your chest, back, and shoulders. Do two or three sets of the chest and back exercises and one or two sets of the exercises for your shoulders.

Lower-body workout: Choose one "hip-dominant" lift—an exercise that emphasizes the hamstrings and gluteals (examples include stepups and deadlifts). Then choose one "knee-dominant" exercise, meaning the emphasis is on the quadriceps muscles of the front of the thigh (squats, leg presses, and lunges qualify). Do two or three warmup sets and two work sets. (A work set means you're using the most weight you can for that number of repetitions. The warmup sets should be percentages of that weight—maybe 40, 60, and 80 percent. Do fewer repetitions in each warmup set.) Add your choice of abdominal and calf exercises.

The Muscles

1. Triceps
2. Brachialis
3. Biceps
4. Brachioradialis

ADVANCED

Divide your workout into four parts. Do each one once a week; don't work out more than 2 days in a row.

1. Arms and shoulders
2. Knee-dominant exercises (described above), plus abdominals and calves
3. Chest and back
4. Hip-dominant exercises (also above), plus abdominals and calves again

Do the four beginner exercises for 4 weeks.

Weeks 1 and 2: Two sets of 10 to 12 repetitions of each exercise

Weeks 3 and 4: Two or three sets of 8 to 10 reps

DIP

● Grab the parallel bars on a dip station and lift yourself so that your arms are fully extended. Bend your knees and cross your feet behind you.

● Slowly lower your body by bending your elbows until your upper arms are parallel to the floor. Pause, then push yourself back up to the starting position.

CLOSE-GRIP CHINUP

● Grab the chinup bar with an underhand grip—your hands about 6 inches apart—and hang with your feet crossed behind you.

● Pull yourself up as high as you can. Pause, then slowly return to the starting position.

DOUBLE-CABLE TRICEPS EXTENSION

● Attach a single-arm handle to the high pulley on each side of a cable station. Grab the left handle with your right hand and the right handle with your left hand. Stand with your feet shoulder-width apart and your knees slightly bent. Hold the handles near your chin, with your arms crossed.

● Without moving your upper arms, slowly pull the handles away from your body until your arms are straight. Pause, then slowly return to the starting position.

DUMBBELL BICEPS CURL WITH A STATIC HOLD

● Grab a pair of dumbbells with an underhand grip and hold them at arm's length in front of your waist. Raise your lower left arm so that your elbow is bent 90 degrees and hold it there.

● Curl the dumbbell in your right hand toward your chest as far as you can without moving your upper right arm. Pause, then slowly lower the weight to the starting position. Continue holding your left arm at 90 degrees while you perform all of your repetitions with your right arm, then switch arms, performing the static hold with your right arm and curling with your left arm.

All of the following four exercises are for intermediate and advanced lifters and should be done for 4 weeks. Note the differences in sets and repetitions for each level.

INTERMEDIATE

Weeks 1 and 2: Two sets of 8 to 10 reps

Weeks 3 and 4: Two or three sets of 6 to 8 reps

ADVANCED

Weeks 1 and 2: Two sets of 6 to 8 reps, after a thorough warmup with lighter weights

Weeks 3 and 4: Two or three sets of 4 to 6 reps, after warmup

SWISS-BALL CLOSE-GRIP PUSHUP

- **Place your hands 6 to 8 inches apart on a Swiss ball and your feet on a bench, in pushup position. Your body should form a straight line from your shoulders to your ankles.**

- **Lower your body by bending your elbows until your upper arms are parallel to the floor. Pause, then push yourself back up to the starting position.**

45-DEGREE PRONE REVERSE CURL

● Set an incline bench to a 45-degree angle. Grab a pair of dumbbells with an overhand grip, and sit with your chest against the pad, letting your arms hang straight down from your shoulders.

● Curl the weights as high as you can without moving your upper arms. Pause, then slowly return to the starting position.

SWISS-BALL ALTERNATING DUMBBELL EXTENSION

● Grab a pair of dumbbells and position yourself on your back on a Swiss ball so that your body forms a straight line from your chest to your knees. Hold the dumbbells over your forehead with straight arms, your palms facing each other. Without moving your upper arms, lower the weights until your lower arms are just below parallel to the floor.

● Hold the right dumbbell in the lowered position as you raise the left dumbbell back up by straightening your arm. Lower the left dumbbell, keep it in that position, then raise the right dumbbell. Continue to alternate until you perform the prescribed number of repetitions with each arm.

SWISS-BALL PREACHER CURL

● Grab an EZ-curl bar with an underhand grip. Kneel behind a Swiss ball and rest your upper arms on the ball, your body weight resting back toward your heels. Hold the bar at arm's length in front of you, with your elbows bent about 5 degrees.

● Curl the weights up as high as you can without moving your upper arms off the Swiss ball, or until the bar is about 6 inches away from your biceps. Pause, then slowly lower the bar to the starting position.

SCAPJACKS

● Attach a single-arm handle to the high pulley of a cable station and pull it down with your right hand until your elbow is bent 90 degrees. Then, grab a dumbbell with your left hand and hold it at arm's length at your side, with your palm facing out.

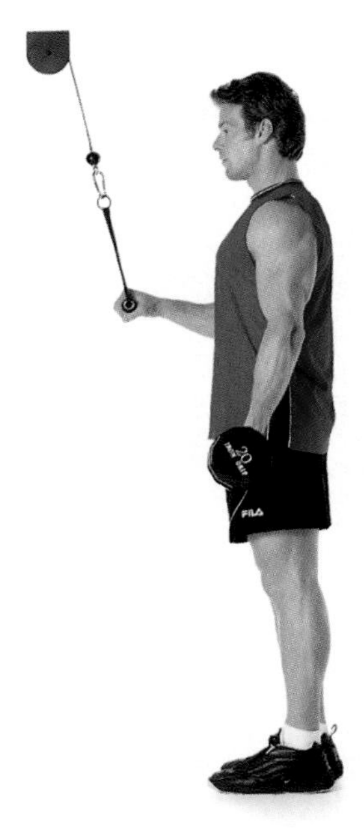

● Pull the handle down to your side with your right hand while you curl the dumbbell toward your chest with your left hand. Pause, then return to the starting position.

PLAY
HARD

PART FOUR

No matter what sport you play, it's essential that you seize the moment—and the momentum. Unless you've done some serious physical and mental preparation, you'll be at the mercy of opponents who have mastered the arts of psyching you out and finishing you off.

We've picked the brains of some of the world's best professional and Olympic athletes to see what gives them their edge. Take their advice with you to the basketball court, softball field, or anyplace else where you play to win.

MH•QUIZ

How Do You Rate?

This is the reality of being male: It's in your genetic coding to want to know how you measure up to the next guy. It's why we like arm wrestling and boxing and golf. And why most women don't.

But, unless you compete in sports that test individual accomplishment, it's hard to figure out how you're doing compared to other guys. So, we enlisted top exercise physiologists, trainers, and coaches to help us devise 9 tests to measure your strength, speed, aerobic and anaerobic capacity, balance, and flexibility—all key indicators of fitness. And all key indicators of such feats as being able to steal a base, grab a rebound, hit a 300-yard tee shot, and haul your wife's luggage through three airport terminals.

Take these tests to find out where you stand.

1 BENCH PRESS

Use a bench-press machine and keep your feet flat on the floor during the entire lift. To get your score, divide the heaviest weight you can lift one time by your body weight.

- ☐ Less than 1.0: Weak
- ☐ 1.0 to 1.49: Ordinary
- ☐ 1.5 or more: You rule on the bench

2 1.5-MILE RUN

Run 1½ miles on a flat path as fast as you can.

- ☐ 12 minutes or more: Slow
- ☐ 10 to 12 minutes: Ordinary
- ☐ 10 minutes or less: Endurance excellence

3 VERTICAL JUMP

You'll need a small bag of chalk to do this test. Chalk your fingers and stand flat footed next to a wall. Place your chalked hand as high as possible on the wall and mark it with your fingertips. Then, without taking a step, dip your knees, swing your arms up, and jump as high as you can, again marking the wall with your fingertips. The distance between the two marks is your vertical-jump height.

- ☐ 20 inches or less: Grounded
- ☐ 20 to 26 inches: Ordinary
- ☐ Higher than 26 inches: High flyer

4 LEG PRESS

Assume the position in the leg-press machine. Lower the weight until your knees are bent 90 degrees, then push the weight back up. To get your score, divide the highest amount of weight you can lift one time by your body weight.

- ☐ Less than 1.8: A shaky foundation
- ☐ 1.8 to 2.2: Ordinary
- ☐ More than 2.2: Serious strength

5 700-YARD SWIM

Swim as far as you can in 12 minutes. Your total distance in yards is your score.

- ☐ Less than 500 yards: You're sunk
- ☐ 500 to 700 yards: Ordinary
- ☐ More than 700 yards: Aquatic excellence

6 PUSHUPS

Lower your body until your upper arms are parallel to the floor, then push yourself up. Repeat as many times as you can.

- ☐ 25 or fewer: Weak
- ☐ 26 to 39: Ordinary
- ☐ 40 or more: Strong and tough

7 300-YARD DASH

Run as fast as you can between two lines spaced 25 yards apart. Do six round-trips, for a total of 300 yards.

- ☐ More than 70 seconds: Slow
- ☐ 60 to 70 seconds: Ordinary
- ☐ Less than 60 seconds: Fast and agile

8 SIT AND REACH

Place a yardstick on the floor and put a foot-long piece of masking tape across the 15-inch mark. Sit down with your legs out in front of you and your heels at the edge of the tape, one on each side of the yardstick. Put one hand on top of the other and reach forward on the yardstick as far as you can by bending at your hips. Your score is the number your fingertips touch.

- ☐ Less than 15 inches: Stiff
- ☐ 15 to 17 inches: Ordinary
- ☐ More than 17 inches: Fantastic flexibility

9 KNEELING BASKETBALL TOSS

Kneel on the court, just behind the baseline. Throw the basketball overhand as far as you can. The top of the key at the far end of the court is 73 feet.

- ☐ Less than 60 feet: Lousy arm
- ☐ 60 to 74 feet: Ordinary
- ☐ More than 74 feet: Cannon fire

IMPROVE YOUR SCORE

1. The key to strengthening any muscle is lifting fast, says Louie Simmons, strength coach to five of the world's top bench pressers. Follow Simmons's plan for 4 weeks to improve your own bench-press performance.

Using a weight that's about 40 percent of what you can lift one time, do nine sets of three repetitions, with 60 seconds' rest between sets. Lower and raise the bar as fast as possible, and alternate your grip every three sets, so that your hands are 16, then 20, then 24 inches apart.

Three days later, perform three sets of flat, incline, or decline barbell bench presses (alternate varieties each week) with the heaviest weight you can lift six times.

2. To build aerobic capacity, you need to run far. But you also need to run fast, says Barrie Shepley, C.S.C.S., Canadian Olympic triathlon coach and president of Personal Best Health and Performance. Follow Shepley's plan for 6 to 10 weeks and you'll increase your endurance about 30 percent.

Perform a 40- to 60-minute run on Saturday at a pace just slow enough that you never feel winded. (Walk if you need to.)

On Tuesday, do four to six half-mile intervals at your goal

Actual Results (Like Yours) May Vary

The ideal scores for optimal fitness are based on reference ranges for 20- to 29-year-old men. Note: Get a physical exam before you take these tests if you're over 40 or have two or more of the following risk factors for heart disease: You're overweight, you're sedentary, you smoke, or you have high blood pressure or high cholesterol.

pace for the mile-and-a-half run. (If your goal is 10 minutes, run each interval in 3 minutes, 20 seconds.) Rest for the same amount of time as each interval takes.

On Thursday, perform four to six uphill runs at a moderate pace, with each lasting about 90 seconds, and take about 2 minutes' rest after each interval. After your last interval, jog for 10 to 15 minutes at an easy pace.

3. To leap higher, you have to practice explosive jumps, says Craig Ballantyne, C.S.C.S., a strength coach in Toronto.

Stand on a box or step that's about 12 inches high. Step off the box, and as soon as your feet hit the floor, jump as high as you can. Repeat five times.

Do four more sets, resting 30 seconds between sets.

4. Try this technique, called diminished-rest interval training. You'll improve your leg-press performance by 10 to 20 percent in 3 weeks, says Alwyn Cosgrove, C.S.C.S., a personal trainer and the owner of Cosgrove Fitness and Sports Training Systems in Santa Clarita, California.

Using a weight that's about 95 percent of the amount you lifted in the test, perform 10 sets of one repetition, resting 80 seconds after each set.

Do this workout twice a week, each time reducing the rest period between sets by 10 seconds. When your rest period is down to 30 seconds, retake the test and increase the weight.

5. According to the American Swim Coaches Association, only two out of 100 Americans swim well enough to complete a quarter of a mile without stopping. That's usually because they have poor form, says Terry Laughlin, author of *Swimming Made Easy*. Follow this rule: Keep your head aligned with your body (the way you hold it when you're not in the water) the entire time you're swimming. When you breathe, roll your entire body—as if you were breathing with your belly button—without changing the position of your head. You'll float better and use less energy. And that means you'll be able to swim farther.

6. Try this program from Charles Staley, a strength coach in Las Vegas. It will get your upper-body endurance to fit-man level in 12 workouts.

Perform sets of half the number of pushups that you completed in the test—resting 60 seconds between sets—until you've done a total of 40 pushups. (For example, if you did 12 pushups in the test, you'll do seven sets of six pushups.)

Each workout (do it every 4 days), deduct 5 seconds from the rest interval. After 12 workouts, you'll be able to do 40 pushups without rest.

7. Train with sprint intervals three times a week, says Mike Gough, C.S.C.S., a strength and conditioning coach in Ottawa, Ontario. Sprint at 85 percent of your full effort for 1 minute. Then run at a lower intensity—about 40 percent of your full effort—for the next minute. Continue to alternate between intensities for 20 minutes. Try this workout on a hill to get even better.

8. Your muscles can be stretched more effectively when they're completely relaxed, says Joel Ninos, P.T., C.S.C.S., a physical therapist in Allentown, Pennsylvania. Try this stretching technique, called hold-relax, to increase your flexibility: Place your right leg on a bench or a desk that's between knee- and waist-high. Keep your leg straight and lean forward as far as comfortably possible by bending at your hips. Continue leaning forward as you bend your knee slightly and gently push your heel into the bench for 10 seconds. Then relax and straighten your leg. Now you'll be able to lean forward farther than when you started. Hold this new position for 20 to 30 seconds. Repeat three more times, leaning forward a bit more each time.

9. The single-arm clean and press will improve both upper-body speed and strength, says Ballantyne. Grab a dumbbell with an overhand grip and hold it in your left hand so that it hangs down at arm's length in front of you. Stand with your feet shoulder-width apart and your knees slightly bent. Explosively pull the dumbbell straight up by dipping your knees, then straightening up as you shrug your shoulder. As you pull upward, rotate the weight in an arc over your upper arm until the dumbbell rests on the top of your shoulder. Your upper arm should be parallel to the floor, and your knees slightly bent again. Dip at your knees and push the weight above your shoulder until your arm is straight. Return to the starting position and repeat with your right arm.

Do this move 2 days a week, with 3 days of rest in between. Perform three sets of four repetitions with a heavy weight in one workout, and eights sets of one repetition with a lighter weight—about 30 percent of the heaviest weight you can lift one time—in the other.

—ADAM CAMPBELL WITH ETHAN BOLDT

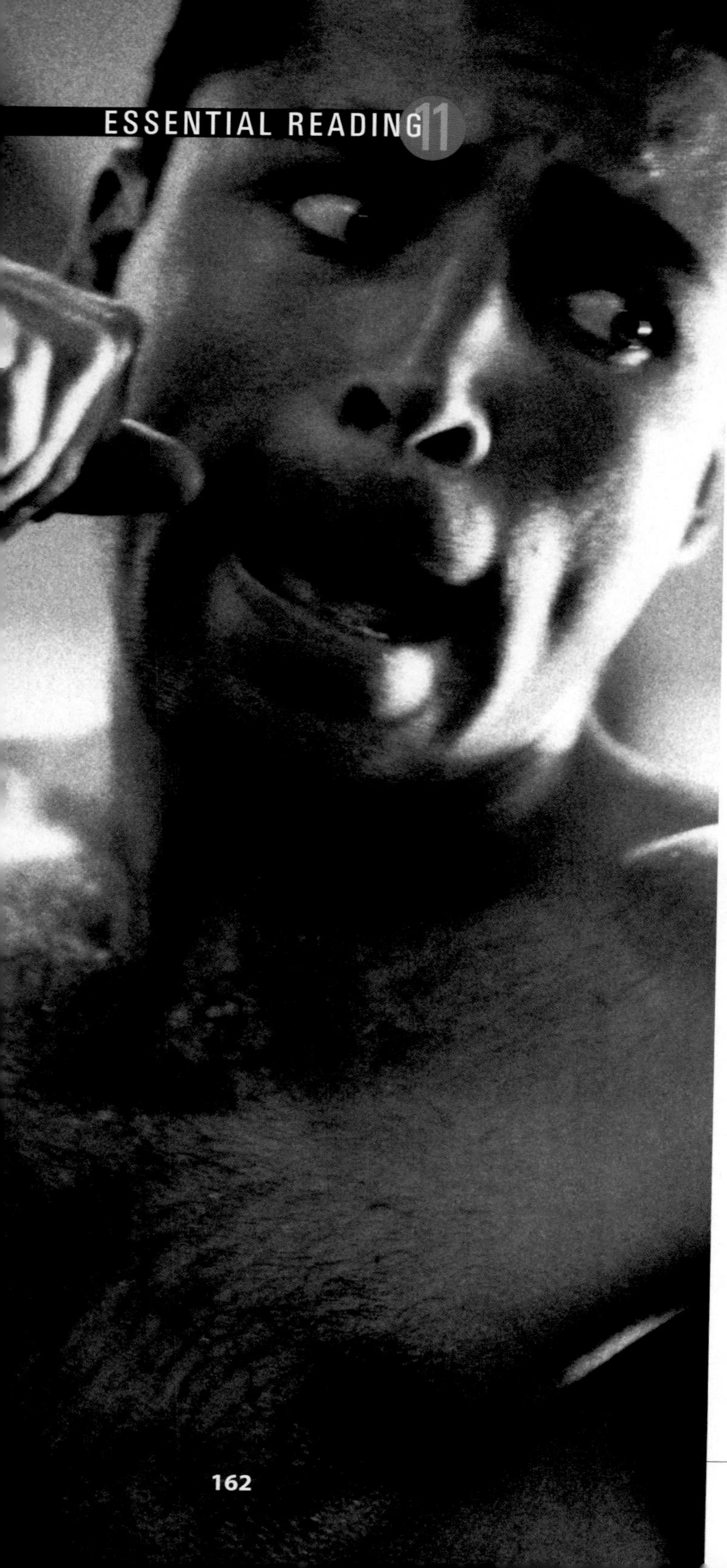

Walk Away a Winner

Nine secrets that separate champs from chumps—in sports and in life

Entering the final round of their 1990 title bout in Las Vegas, the undefeated junior welterweight Meldrick Taylor owned a sizable lead over the legendary Julio Cesar Chavez. All Taylor had to do was survive another 3 minutes in the ring with Chavez and he'd have the biggest win of his life. For the next 2 minutes and 58 seconds, Taylor allowed Chavez to land one punch after another, a barrage of punishing blows to the body and the face. He'd grab and cover up, secure that time was on his side.

It was a grave miscalculation. Two seconds from the final bell, the referee stopped the fight. Chavez won by technical knockout in the 12th round, adding Taylor's title belt to his own. In the most dramatic fashion possible, Taylor had allowed a beaten opponent to resurrect himself and triumph.

It happens all the time to the pros, and to the hackers, too. "If you're serving to close out a match, the man across the net isn't nervous—you're the one who's nervous," says Patrick Rafter, a two-time U.S. Open men's singles champion. Of course, closing the door on a talented opponent isn't always as easy as Rafter makes it look. Some top pros still haven't figured it out. Think of those guys who had the talent but never got the ring: Patrick Ewing, Barry Bonds, Dan Marino.

Real winners know when to go for the jugular. "There are certain points in a game when you just have that feeling," says Peyton Manning, the Indianapolis Colts' All-Pro quarterback. "You see the defense on the ropes. So you go back to the huddle and you say, 'We score right here and this game might just be over.' Do that and you can break a team's will."

Understanding how to finish off an opponent is crucial to your success in sports, in business, even in the ruthless jungle of sexual relations. *Men's Health* asked Manning, Rafter, the New Jersey Nets' Jason Kidd, and six other successful athletes for their secrets.

❶ Don't Be Afraid to Win

For some competitors, the only thing worse than losing is winning. "Until they've won

something big, I think most people are scared of it," says the golfer Karrie Webb, who has won four LPGA majors. "They're out of their comfort zone because they're not accustomed to that situation. It makes sense. Especially in tournament golf, you're going to finish second, third, and even 20th more than you're going to win."

The boxer Oscar de la Hoya had won five world titles and was going for a record sixth earlier this year. "Because of the history involved, I was actually scared of winning," he admits. "What I did was start thinking of how prepared I was for the fight, both mentally and physically. I had done so much before the fight, and now I was just a few minutes away from having it all pay off. I reminded myself that in 5 or 10 years, a career is all over. Here was the opportunity to accomplish something, so I did."

The good news is, the more you win, the easier it gets. "Winning can become a habit, just as losing can become a habit," says hockey's Mike Modano, who led the Dallas Stars to the 1999 Stanley Cup. The best teams on which Modano has played in his 13-year NHL career not only wanted to win, they convinced themselves they deserved to, night after night.

"We had an air of confidence from October on," Modano says of the '98 to '99 Stars. "If we were ahead going into the third period, we just knew that we were not going to lose."

TOUGH TALK

"Nobody is hurt. Hurt is in the mind. If you can walk, you can run."

VINCE LOMBARDI

2 Be Afraid to Lose

"My biggest fear is finishing second," says the auto racer Michael Andretti, career leader in Championship Auto Racing Teams (CART) victories with 42. "That drives me. There are guys out there who can put in a quicker lap than I can. They put their cars on the [starting] grid near the front every time, but they can't turn it into wins." Andretti, who grew up absorbing the competitive intensity of his famous father, Mario, says he can't stand failing at anything, not tennis or board games or racing. "If you really want to win," he says, "you have to feel that way."

Whenever your fear of losing starts to paralyze you, make it motivate you instead. "It keeps me focused," says Parker Bohn III, a bowler who won 18 PBA events in the 1990s, second only to Walter Ray Williams's 25. "In my sport, one bad shot in a given frame can cost me roughly 35 pins. It can cost me the tournament. Worry about that. Let it drive you."

Try it. Arrive at your next sales call thinking you'll lose your job if you don't make a sale. You won't, of course—and if you do, that's not a job you wanted, anyway. But the air of urgency you project just might give you the edge you need.

3 Seize the Opening

You don't have to be a psych major to know when momentum has swung your way. Losers use that advantage to take a break from the intensity, and the next thing they know, the advantage is gone. Winners see it as an opportunity to put their opponent away for good.

"If we're up 1-0 or 2-0 after two periods, we'll say, 'Let's play this game like it's 0-0 and not get soft,'" says Modano. "If we're up 3-0, that's different. Then it's, 'Now's our chance. Let's put this team out of its misery.'"

One man I know picked exactly the wrong time to back off a woman he was after. She was ending a relationship with a steady boyfriend and was looking for security in any form. "She's confused," he said. "I just want to give her some time."

Before he knew it, she had met someone new, and his window of opportunity had slammed shut.

❹ Place Negative Thoughts in His Mind

If you carry yourself as if you expect to win, your opponent will expect to lose. "Never give the other team the sense that it might be able to come back," says the Nets' Jason Kidd, subject of the single most lopsided trade of the 2001–2002 NBA season. "Do that and you're liable to have a whole team coming at you full steam. Do everything you can to make them feel like the game is over, and there's nothing they can do. A lot of times, they believe it."

At the same time, if your opponent looks as though he's ready to lose, take that as a sign that you should win. "Try to feed on the negative body language," says Modano. "The shoulders start drooping, and that's when you realize you have them."

You don't want to be known as the office trash talker, even when it comes to friendly wagers on the golf course. But a discreet "That's okay; it's just not your day" when your rival's ball hits the sand can work wonders.

❺ Embarrass Your Opponent

You can apologize later, after the game. "Kick them when they're down," advises Manning. Football teams are often criticized for running up scores, but Manning believes that anyone who carps doesn't understand the nature of competition. Help your opponent save face and you're helping him back into the game.

"Even before I played in the NFL, I tried to go for the throat," Manning says. "I feel no remorse about trying to score on every play until the game is over."

Keeping the pressure on, in sports or in business, sends the message that you're serious about the competition. It also shows your opponent that you know how to win.

6 Never Look Ahead

We've all imagined ourselves accepting congratulations, the championship trophy in our hands. The 15th green is not the place to do that.

"People start thinking about what winning is going to mean for them, and they forget they have to finish out the match," Webb says. "Whether I'm being chased by number 150 on the money list or by Annika Sorenstam, I've learned not to take anything for granted. Now, I don't think I've won the tournament until I've actually won it."

If you're mentally spending the money you'll earn from that new account as you walk in the door to pitch it, or undressing her in your mind during the introductions, you're mistaking foolishness for confidence. Seal the deal, then enjoy the spoils.

"Don't get overconfident," warns jockey Laffit Pincay Jr., who has won more races than anyone in the history of his sport. "I say that because it has happened to me. I've been ahead and lost races because I got caught from behind. That doesn't happen too often anymore because I've learned not to think that I've won a race until I've actually crossed the line."

7 Play a Game within a Game

A simple mental exercise works for Kidd, whose passing artistry is revered throughout the NBA. "Once you have a lead, try to increase it," Kidd says. "Look at the clock. Say you're up 10—you try to get up by 15 by a certain time. Set that as a goal. Maybe you won't make it and you'll still only be up by 10, but it reminds you to keep playing hard."

TOUGH TALK

"Defeat is worse than death, because you have to live with defeat."

BILL MUSSELMAN

Manning is all too aware of what defensive linemen sound like when they're protecting a shutout in the waning moments of a game they've won long ago. "Even though the outcome isn't in doubt anymore, if we score, they're going to be really angry at themselves," he says. "I've seen it in their eyes. That's the way they stay focused."

Think of ways to quantify your performance at work. How many memos did you act on today? In the past hour? Keep trying to top the total of the day before. You can't set a record if you don't know the score.

8 Be in Better Shape

Part of being able to finish off a game or a match is to have the strength left to do it. "When I'm in front, I'm very tough to beat," says Pincay. "I win a lot of races down the stretch, and the reason is that I'm in the best shape. And because I know that I'm not going to run out of strength, that gives me confidence. The other jockeys know it, too, which helps me. Even the horses realize it. They can tell when a jockey is tired."

"When your physical side drops down, your mental side definitely goes with it," Andretti says. "That' s why you have to be in good shape. Don't let that be the thing that beats you."

Think of this the next time you're at the gym. Just when you're ready to call it a workout, put in one more set of reps, or another 5 minutes on the exercise bike. The knowledge that you can push, and survive, makes you stronger than the man who's already in the shower.

9 Do the Unexpected

Rafter believes one of the best ways to nail a coffin shut is to make your opponent react to something different at the last minute. Yes, that contradicts the common advice to keep doing what got you there, but sometimes a new twist is exactly what you need to finish off an opponent. "A new serve to close out a match, even if one particular serve has been working well before," says Rafter. "A different strategy at a crucial point. Read your opponent. Figure out what he's looking for. Then do something else."

Whatever you do, stay relaxed. Win or lose, it isn't the end of the world—and it won't help you to treat it like it is. "If someone's better than you that day or that week, there's really nothing you can do about it," Webb says. "So just put yourself in the position to do your best. Realize that if you're good enough to be in front, you're good enough to win. And then keep it up."

BY ETHAN BOLDT

A Drill a Minute

Whatever your sport, we've got a workout for you

The first sign of spring is when David Wells, the Yankees pitcher, grunts across a Florida lawn like a manatee out of water. The difference between you and David Wells? Millions of dollars and a winter full of workouts. He has the former. You have the latter. The thing you have in common? In spring, neither one of you is ready to play.

Even ballplayers who work out year-round don't go south in the spring just to be near Space Mountain. They go because they know that making the transition from gym to turf isn't as simple as stepping outside. You need ways to move your indoor-trained muscles out into the real world.

"You need to build a bridge between the weight room and the sport you participate in," says Alwyn Cosgrove, C.S.C.S., a personal trainer and the owner of Cosgrove Fitness and Sports Training Systems in Santa Clarita, California. That means adjusting your strength and cardiovascular workouts so they include running drills and power moves along with sport-specific weight lifting. Do that and you'll be not only fit, but fit to play.

The 6-Week Plan

Two days a week—Monday and Thursday—you'll do the weight-lifting workout described in the "Strength Training" section on pages 169 and 170. On Tuesday and Friday you'll do the

speed drills described in the "Cardiovascular Training" section on page 170. On the weekends you'll practice your sport, using the principles described—where else?—in "Practicing Your Sport," starting on page 171.

During the first week, try the exercises at what feels like 75 percent of your full effort, then work at 85 to 90 percent the second week. If you're sore, do the third week at a little less than full speed. Then open the throttle. "After 2 or 3 weeks, you'll jump higher and move faster," says Marcus C. C. W. Elliott, M.D., a sports-medicine and conditioning specialist. "You'll be able to do twice as much as you were doing a few weeks before." Just be sure to increase your weights in the gym (keeping a notebook helps) and go harder in the running drills each week.

After 6 weeks of training, you'll be able to play with more speed, power, and stamina. Add an arm like Wells's and a belly for ballast, and you'll feel like a million.

Strength Training

These exercises don't just build muscle; they teach your body to move explosively, too. Keep repetitions low—five to eight at most. "You don't repeat the same action 12 times in a row when you play sports," Cosgrove points out. Perform three sets of each, and rest for 2 to 3 minutes between sets. (You may need to rest for up to 5 minutes after the squat/vertical jump combination.)

One note of caution: These exercises are for guys who've been lifting consistently for at least a few months. If you're just starting out, or if you've fallen out of the exercise habit, begin with the usual strengthening exercises—leg press, bench press, lat pulldown, crunch, and so on—until you're back on track.

Squat and vertical jump

Works all the lower-body muscles. Improves lower-body strength and power for rebounding, spiking, and snagging line drives.

Do the squats as shown above, then set the bar down and do the same number of vertical jumps. Start from a half-squat position and leap as high as you can, tucking your knees into your chest on the way up, straightening your legs on the way down. Land on the balls of your feet, and go right back up.

High pull

Works all the back and lower-body muscles, and the biceps. Improves upper-body power for driving the lane, blocking spikes, and returning serves.

Start with a light weight. The bar alone will be enough for most guys who haven't done this before. The object is to pull the bar upward as explosively as possible, and that takes some getting used to.

Woodcutter

Works all the abdominal muscles. Improves midsection power for driving golf balls, hitting softballs, and blasting forehands.

Twist only at the waist. Your arm should stay fixed throughout the movement; you want to use it like a hook. Do the same number of repetitions on each side.

Incline dumbbell press and pushup

Works the chest, front shoulders, triceps, forearms, and hands. Improves chest strength and builds explosive upper-body power for cross-court passing, fighting off rebounders, and just plain fighting—these are the muscles you use for jabs and crosses.

As soon as you're finished with the presses, get into pushup position on a padded surface. Lower your chest to the floor, then push yourself back up explosively. Land and push off again as quickly as possible.

Crossover stepup

Works the inner and outer thighs and the outer glutes. Improves the strength of lateral movements in basketball, soccer, hockey, and tennis.

Step up forcefully, but step down slowly—reversing the motion shown here—to protect your knees. Repeat to the other side. To start, try it using just your body weight, then hold light dumbbells when you're ready.

Cardiovascular Training

To prepare for sports running, you need to work at higher speeds but shorter distances and durations, says Jim Wharton, exercise physiologist and coauthor of *The Whartons' Strength Book*.

Start drill

Improves timing and takeoff speed for stealing bases and charging the net.

Grab a shoe, a baseball glove, whatever. Throw the object into the air. When it hits the ground, take off and sprint for 8 to 10 steps. Do 8 to 10 starts.

Sprint-and-float drill

Improves your ability to change speeds for running fast breaks, taking extra bases, and blowing past defensive backs on long pass routes.

Sprint for 25 yards, then "float"—run at a fast jog—for the same distance. Start with one set of 7 to 10 sprint/float combos. Work up to 50 yards for each sprint and each float. Then go to two sets.

Practicing Your Sport

You can smack hundreds of golf balls, toss up innumerable three-pointers, and still not improve much. If you're going to give up precious time to practice, you ought to be able to do better than that. Here are some ways to use your practice time more effectively.

Softball. To really unload on a softball, you have to learn back-leg drive, says Mike "Big Cat" Macenko, a household name in slow-pitch softball. Macenko, who hit 844 home runs in a single 350-game season, recommends this batting-cage drill.

Stand in the batter's box with your weight entirely on the ball of your back foot. Only the tip of your front foot should touch the ground [A]. As you start your swing, step forward and shift your weight to your front foot [B]. It should feel like stepping off a seesaw, Macenko says. "You'll be able to feel the difference in the way the ball jumps off the bat" at impact.

Also practice hitting to the opposite field. If you're right handed, try hitting to right, and vice versa. You might catch a fielder napping. Step with your front foot in the direction you want the ball to go.

Tennis. Don't be in a rush to play a match, says Brian Gottfried, a senior competitor and an instructor to many players on the ATP tour. Instead, talk your partner into spending half your court time working on these drills.

- ▶Play "short court." You and your partner stand on the service lines and hit back and forth. This exercise develops better control of your racket head.

- ▶Hit to target areas. Try to hit crosscourt shots—forehands and backhands—to specific points on the court. You'll know you're a stud when you can consistently hit your spots.

- ▶Target your service area. Divide the service area into three sections—left, center, and right—and practice hitting serves to each of them.

Basketball. "You see a lot of fast breaks in rec leagues," says Frank DiLeo, assistant men's basketball coach at the University of Iowa. But most recreational players won't be able to sprint up and down the court more than two or three times without spewing Gatorade. "You want to be able to outhustle and outrun those guys," DiLeo says. Here's the drill.

PEAK performance

Never Miss a Grounder

Practice snagging grounders using a smaller glove than you normally use and a baseball instead of a softball, suggests Mike Candrea, softball coach for the University of Arizona. Go to a pet store and buy one of those spiked rubber balls for dogs, then practice catching bad hops. "The key to grabbing grounders is to charge hard and overplay the ball to the glove-hand side," says Candrea. Commit yourself and play either the big hop or the short hop—not the in-between.

Run the length of the court, dribbling the ball with your right hand, and make a right-handed layup. Turn around and run back, this time dribbling with your left, and make a left-handed layup. Run back again, and this time pull up short of the basket and pop a short jumper from the right side. Run back, stop, and pop from the left. Keep going until exhaustion stops you. Then practice shooting. He who shoots best while tired will win.

Golf. "If you hit a golf ball a quarter of an inch off the center of the club face, you can lose 20 yards in both distance and direction," says T. J. Tomasi, director of the Player's School at PGA National in Palm Beach Gardens, Florida. Yet many amateur players never hit the ball with the center of the club face—the sweet spot.

The following simple drill, Tomasi says, will change your golf game forever. Tee up a ball just slightly above the grass. Grab your 7-iron and choke up on it so you can take only half-swings. Try to hit the ball 30 to 40 yards. You should quickly get into the groove with this stroke, hitting the ball with the center of the club each time. "The impact will feel like butter," Tomasi says. "No torquing or turning." Gradually lengthen your swing, then try hitting with different clubs. Whenever you feel the jarring impact of an off-center hit, go back to practicing this drill until you regain your stroke.

Volleyball. "Volleyball is so multifaceted, you can't get away with one particular skill and expect to be good," says Chuck Moore, assistant men's volleyball coach at the University of Southern California. "You have to play the front row, play the back row, pass, and block."

So if you have neither the time to master all those skills nor a team to practice with, how do you get better? "The thing that ties every skill together is the footwork—getting to the ball—whether you're setting or spiking or blocking," Moore says.

TOUGH TALK

"Don't look back. Someone might be gaining on you."
LEROY (SATCHEL) PAIGE

Try this, and do it as rapidly as you can: Start with your feet hip-width apart, with your hands at your sides. Lift your left foot in front of you, touch it with your right hand, and lower it to the floor. Lift your right foot, touch it with your left hand, and lower it. Then touch your left foot behind you with your right hand, and your right foot behind you with your left hand.

"You'll feel uncoordinated when you try it," Moore says, "but it's unbelievable how much your foot speed will improve."

Go for 20 seconds at a time, and repeat for a total of three to five sets.

Fly Guy: Morton's middle helps him make the cut.

All-Star Abs

Build abdominal muscles that will help you play hard—on the field or off

Abs are money.

There's evidence everywhere. A molded midsection is pure cash flow for anyone who has to remove his shirt in his line of work. Would the name "Pitt" be anything more than a signal to roll on some deodorant, save for an ab-flexing scene in *Thelma and Louise*?

The bankability reaches beyond aesthetics. If you're an athlete, abs are your body's big-play muscles. Your legs and arms may do the grunt work, but it's your abdominals that put you on SportsCenter.

So we asked professional athletes and actors to show us the abdominal exercises that help them earn a living.

BY ADAM CAMPBELL, C.S.C.S.

You already know this stuff works. You've seen the results on ESPN and in the local cineplex. Now it's time to see how a set of pro abs will look on you.

Speed Shift

The man: Johnnie Morton, wide receiver, Kansas City Chiefs

The move: standing abdominal twist

Sometimes catching a football involves moving your upper body one way while your lower body goes the other. To pull it off, Morton needs balance and superhuman control of his midsection muscles—qualities that will help in any sport that requires quick changes in direction, like baseball, basketball, tennis, soccer, or hockey.

How you do it: Hold a medicine ball or weight plate with both hands out in front of your chest, your arms slightly bent. Without moving your legs, rotate your torso 90 degrees to the right. (Don't go any farther—that would be too tough on your lower back.) Pause, then rotate back 180 degrees so you're facing left. Pause and rotate right to the starting position. That's one repetition. Work up to three sets of 20 or more repetitions, beginning and ending each set with the weight in the middle. "This gives me a good burn and helps me develop stamina as well as strength," Morton says.

Fix Your Alignment

The man: Pierce Brosnan, actor

The move: towel stretch

When he's playing James Bond, Brosnan makes everything look as easy as the women he beds. But in reality, his stunts would create devastating lower-back problems if he didn't prepare. One of the best ways to keep that area healthy is to stretch the hip-flexor muscles on the front of the pelvis. Overly tight hip flexors can pull the lower back into a swayback alignment, leaving it one awkward landing away from serious injury. Greg Isaacs, an L.A.-based trainer, has Brosnan do this move each time they train together.

How you do it: Lie on your stomach. Bend your right knee and wrap a towel around your right shin. Tighten your ab muscles, then relax your hips and press them into the floor. Use the towel to pull your right lower leg toward your butt. Hold for 15 to 20 seconds, and do four or five with each leg.

Get Strong, Go Deep

The man: Brady Anderson, outfielder, Cleveland Indians

Brady's Bunch: A six-pack helps deep six your opponents.

The move: V-sit

Anderson needs his abs for more than the revenue they generate in his nutritional-supplement ads. A strong midsection is important for both hitting and throwing a baseball, and in any other sport that demands quick bursts of power. At the top of Anderson's exercise lineup is the V-sit, which works the upper- and lower-abdominal regions simultaneously. To get the most out of his time, Anderson uses a medicine ball.

How you do it: Lie on your back and hold a medicine ball at arm's length behind your head. Lift the ball and your legs simultaneously, trying to touch ball to feet, until your body forms a V.

Double Your Results

The man: Christian Slater, actor

The move: the "George" crunch

Slater's L.A.-based trainer, Michael George, has him do 10 minutes of abdominal work each time they train. And although they rotate the exercises, this move is a favorite. It's George's invention (which you probably guessed) and builds oblique and upper-abdominal muscles at the same time.

How you do it: Lie on your back with your knees bent and your feet flat on the floor. Put your left hand on your head so that your fingers are just touching behind your left ear, and place your right hand on your abs. Straighten your left leg and hold it about an inch off the floor. Then bring your left elbow toward your right knee by raising your head and shoulders off the floor. Do two sets of 15 to 25 repetitions on each side.

Extend Yourself

The man: Dain Blanton, Olympic gold medalist in beach volleyball

The move: cross-legged crunch

A beach volleyball player never knows where the next serve or spike is going to take him. But he knows his abs have to get him there. He uses them to bend, twist, and extend his

Stay the Course

It's not enough to reach the starting gate. The winner is the man who lasts the longest, not the one who's up and running first. So even though midsection strength is great, overall stamina matters, too. We asked some top performers how they manage to keep revving while others have already called it a night.

Jeff Gordon, NASCAR Driver

"I believe the rowing-machine exercise I do benefits my driving the most. It's a great cardiovascular workout that benefits the whole body, including your lower back—a problem area for drivers," he says. He rows whenever he can between traveling.

Dan Majerle,
Guard/Forward, Miami Heat

"Because I've had several surgeries, I try to limit the pounding on my back. So I do a lot of bike work in the off-season. It's a great way to keep my wind and build my legs up without pounding," says Majerle. He "spins" for 45 minutes, 4 or 5 days a week.

Desmond Howard,
Wide Receiver, Detroit Lions

This former Heisman Trophy winner and Super Bowl MVP has to have speed endurance—the ability to go full throttle, play after play, for all four quarters of a game. So he runs sprints "on any type of elevation—hills, stairs, or even an incline on a treadmill."

Sean Michaels, Adult Film Star

The secret to Michaels's staying power is high-repetition training. "Because I have to stay in certain positions, as well as thrust, for long periods of time, it's important for me to have a lot of muscular endurance in my legs and hips," he says. Michaels typically does four sets of 25 repetitions of squats with no weight.

Henry Rollins, Musician

Rollins performs intensely and uses his workouts to prepare for it. Often, at the end of a workout, he forces himself to do 50 additional repetitions in 5 minutes. He'll pick a weight that's about 50 percent of his maximum, and gut out 50 repetitions. He might start with a set of 15, rest 30 seconds, do 10 more, rest a few seconds, do the next 10, and so on. "Almost no matter what happens to me, it's never tougher than my workout," he says.

Beach Blanton Bingo: Constant variety makes a greater Dain.

body into position for a return. So Blanton tries to shift his legs and torso into different positions each workout in an effort to give the midsection muscles new and different challenges.

How you do it: Lie on your back on the floor, your lower legs crossed on the floor. Hold your hands behind your ears and pull your elbows back as far as possible. Now crunch your head and shoulders up off the floor and hold the contraction, then slowly lower yourself. Do three sets of 10 to 15 repetitions.

Make 'em Last

The man: Tiki Barber, running back, New York Giants

The move: cycling crunch

A running back, like an obstetrician, has to spend a lot of time in a crouch. But unlike the OB, a running back has to spend every second on the field prepared to hit as well as be hit. This requires not only midsection strength but also stamina, which is why Barber does cycling crunches. These force him to contract his abdominals—as he would if he knew Ray Lewis had him in his sights—while keeping his legs moving. Any athlete who needs a low center of gravity—for guarding in basketball, working the baseline in tennis, scooping up throws at first base—will benefit from cycling crunches.

How you do it: Lie on your back and bend your knees and hips 90 degrees so your feet are in the air. Place your fingertips behind

The Ab Originals

BY KURT BRUNGARDT

A well-done crunch is a thing of beauty. Feet flat on the floor, hands behind the ears, slow and steady movements up and down. Nothing rushed, no movement wasted.

Of course, you don't see this poetic motion very often. Few people do the basic crunch anymore.

Which makes this as good a time as any to remind you of the basics of abdominal exercise. After you master the simplest exercises, the advanced ones become far more beneficial.

The following three exercises form the crux of the 6-week core program in my book, *Essential Abs*. Do one set of each move for the first 2 weeks, working up to 18 slow, perfect repetitions of each.

Then add more exercises to your ab routine, but continue to do one set of each of these after finishing the new ones. You'll become really good at the basic moves because you'll have to do them with ever greater levels of exhaustion.

Try your new routine three times a week for 6 weeks. By then you will have mastered the three beginner exercises—and be good and ready to move on, too.

Crunch

Lie on your back with your knees bent, your feet flat on the floor, and your hands behind your ears. Use your upper abs to raise your rib cage toward your pelvis and lift your shoulder blades off the floor. Then slowly lower your shoulders back to the starting position.

Performance Tips

- ▶Make sure your shoulder blades come off the floor each time. Don't just move your head and neck.
- ▶Pause at the top of the movement after you've exhaled.

Reverse Crunch

Lie on your back with your head and neck relaxed and your hands on the floor near your butt. Use your lower-abdominal muscles to raise your hips off the floor and toward your rib cage. Then slowly lower your hips back to the starting position. As they lightly touch the floor, repeat.

Performance Tips

- ▶Don't quickly rock up and down. You'd be using momentum to aid you in the exercise, taking work away from your lower abs.
- ▶Keep constant tension on your abs—don't rest between repetitions.
- ▶Use your hands for balance. Don't use them to push your hips off the floor.
- ▶Keep your head and neck relaxed.

Crossover Crunch

Lie on your back with your knees up and your feet on the floor. Cross your left leg over your right knee. Put your right hand behind your head, with your elbow extended to the side. Place your left hand on your right side.

Raise your right shoulder and cross it toward your left knee. Then slowly lower your shoulder back to the starting position. When you finish all of your repetitions on your right side, repeat on your left side.

Performance Tips

- ▶Make sure your entire torso twists up and toward your knee. Don't move just your elbow or shoulder.
- ▶Feel the squeeze in your obliques—the muscles on the sides of your abdominals—on the side you're working.

your ears and perform an abdominal crunch by lifting your head and shoulders off the floor. At the same time, lift your right leg to your chest. Lower your torso to the floor as you straighten your right leg, keeping it a few inches off the floor. Crunch again, this time lifting your left leg to your chest. Do three sets of 20 repetitions.

Balance Your Back, Abs, and Glutes

The man: Scottie Pippen, guard, Portland Trail Blazers

The move: shoulder bridge

You can't have good abs if your lower back is out of whack. Pippen, who has a history of back problems, picked up this exercise from Tim Grover, owner of Attack Athletics in

PEAK performance

Hang 'em High

A tight spiral pass is nice. But a big, thumping punt gets everyone's attention. Darren Bennett knows. He played Australian-rules football for 12 years before joining the San Diego Chargers at age 30. Now he's an NFL star who routinely punts 50-yarders with 5 seconds of hang time. With practice, he says, any of us can launch a 4-second boomer. And in the backyard, it's height, not distance, that matters.

1. The "mold." It doesn't matter how you hold the ball, as long as your arms are extended, you "mold" your hands into the same position each time, and you angle the ball's nose 10 to 15 degrees down. (Bennett's mold is a hand on each side.)

2. The steps. Take your left hand (if you're right footed) off the ball and use that arm for balance. Take a quick jab-step forward with your left foot, a full step with the right, and a plant-step with your left.

3. The drop. As you make your plant-step, drop the ball, with no spin or change in angle. A good angle leads to a good spiral, which leads to extra hang time.

4. The kick. As you drop the ball, swing your kicking foot straight up and through the ball, making sure the bridge of your foot connects with the ball under the second lace. Extend your leg as much as you can on the follow-through. It's like a golf swing, Bennett says. "Power doesn't matter, only form and extension."

Most common mistakes. Trying to kick the ball too hard, and swinging the kicking foot sideways to create a spiral. The mold, not the kick, creates the spiral. And if you shank it, "just say, 'The wind took my drop,'" Bennett says. "It sounds professional, and it's what I usually tell my coaches."

Chicago. The beauty of this bridge is that it strengthens your abs, lower back, and gluteals simultaneously. "That's where all your balance, stability, and power come from," Grover says.

How you do it: Lie on your back with your legs bent and your feet flat on the floor. Push up with your hips so your weight rests on your shoulders. Your body should form a straight line from your knees to your shoulders. Hold this position for 20 seconds, and gradually work your way up to 1 minute. (Pippen does it for 5 minutes.) Advanced version: Straighten one leg and hold it up in the air while you do the exercise. Start with your weaker leg in the air, and give equal time to both sides.

TOUGH TALK

"There's only one way to succeed in anything, and that is to give it everything. I do, and I demand that my players do."

VINCE LOMBARDI

BUILD YOUR EDGE

Q: I'm a competitive runner. Should I do any strength training at all, or will that just make me bigger and slower?

K. K., MIDDLETOWN, OHIO

A: Building muscle depends mostly on calories. In order to get bigger, you consistently need to consume more calories than you expend. So, don't worry—you probably won't get bigger considering the amount of running you need to do to remain competitive in your sport. No matter how sound a training program you're on, if you can't support your efforts in the gym with enough calories, you're not going to gain an ounce of muscle.

A regular strength-training program can also offer dramatic improvements to your running performance. Here's how. Strength training helps your nervous system improve the process by which it causes muscle fibers to contract. A muscle that contracts more quickly and forcefully will better propel you down the road, giving you a decided advantage over your nonlifting opponent. Strength training also increases your muscles' tolerance of metabolic fatigue. So when that deep burn starts to set in toward the end of a grueling race, you'll be able to push through and finish, while others fall by the wayside.

PERFECT FORM

Kick Habit

Of course you don't play soccer, but your kid does. When the ball comes your way during practice, don't use your hands (gauche) or head (ouch) to send it back. Keep it under control by one-timing it with this quick kick. The Major League Soccer star Brian McBride calls it the side volley. We call it major points with the hot moms standing on the sidelines.

Get set. Plant your nonkicking foot and turn your torso in the direction you want the ball to go. Bring your kicking leg back and raise it parallel to the ground, your knee bent and facing forward.

Make contact. Kick the top half of the ball with the laces of your shoes or your instep. Don't use your toes, which will send the ball directly onto Route 33. You hit it, you chase it.

Follow through. As you make contact, rotate your torso, dipping your front shoulder to help angle the kick downward. Savor the awestruck stares from the kids.

HOOP DREAMS

Q: I've been lifting a while and I'm in pretty good "gym shape"—I'm lean and pretty strong. Some buddies want me to play in their regular basketball game once a week. I haven't picked up a basketball in 10 years. What kind of prep work should I do? I don't want to suck or get hurt.

L. R., DENTON, TEXAS

A: Playing basketball requires you to move differently than you do in the gym. Unlike the slow, controlled pace you use when lifting weights, basketball demands lots of explosive bursts and sudden changes of direction, as well as larger ranges of motion.

You'll need to make your muscles and connective tissues ready for these changes. Begin with stretches like these two.

Groin stretch: Sit on the floor and place the soles of your feet together. Keeping your back as straight as possible, grab your insteps and use your elbows to press your knees toward the floor.

Calf stretch: Stand facing a wall and lean your arms against it, positioning them about shoulder-width apart. Move one foot 3 to 4 feet away from the wall. Keeping that leg straight and the heel in contact with the floor, bend your opposite knee and lean toward the wall.

Then, incorporate power-based lifts like hang cleans and push presses into your workout. And to mimic movements you'll make on the court, run all out for 5 to 10 yards and then rapidly shuffle 5 yards to the right or left. Or run hard for 5 to 15 yards and then quickly leap into the air.

HARD TRUTH

Spinning wheels

Percent that participation in stationary cycling decreased in the United States between 1999 and 2000:

7

SOURCE: American Sports Data, Inc.

Lastly, don't expect to be your neighborhood's answer to Kobe right off the bench.

PRACTICE

Turn Up the Heat

Research on performing under pressure may help us all, in sports and in life. In a study at Michigan State University, 54 novice golfers practiced putting—some under normal conditions, some while being distracted, and some while being videotaped and expecting a golf pro to review their form. In a putting contest for money, the videotaped group did best. So if you practice under pressure, you'll perform better when it counts. Work on free throws as though the game were on the line; rehearse your presentation as if the boss were listening. Slight distractions may help, though, when it's time to perform for real. Try counting backward or humming to stay calm. (Don't try this during an oral presentation.) "The worst thing to do [under pressure] is to tell yourself to really concentrate because it's important," says study coauthor Sian Beilock.

CHALLENGE YOURSELF

PART FIVE

Some guys are their own harshest critics. We don't think anyone should beat himself up. But we do recommend striving to best yourself. Add another weight plate to your barbell; jog a new, longer route; play left field instead of right.

Becoming your own toughest opponent can help renew your competitive spirit. So turn the page to learn new ways to test yourself. Soon you'll be more ready than ever to take on the other guys.

MH • QUIZ

Are You in a Rut?

Think you've had a rough week? It can't be worse than this: A few years ago a 75-year-old Virginia man fell through his outhouse floor and was sludge-bound for 3 days before being rescued by a postal worker. His experience gives new meaning to the phrase "down in the dumps."

If you're feeling trapped in your own mental sludge, don't wait for the U.S. Postal Service to pull you from the muck. Research shows that physical challenges trigger the release of endorphins and other brain chemicals that lift your mood.

Answer the questions below to identify your rut. The challenges that follow will help bust you out.

1 How happy are you in your current job?

- ☐ It's great.
- ☐ I need a new one.
- ☐ Job? Yeah, I've been trying to get one of those.

2 How do you spend your Sundays?

- ☐ Waking up from drunken stupor
- ☐ Watching NFL, NHL, NBA, or the PGA
- ☐ Waking up from drunken stupor and then watching NFL, NHL, NBA, or the PGA

3 What have you changed about your workout in the past few weeks?

- ☐ I put on clean gym shorts.
- ☐ I've been exercising in the morning instead of after work.
- ☐ Why would I want to change it?

4 Where do you go to meet women?

- ☐ A bar
- ☐ The gym
- ☐ The local quilting club

5 Got a light?

- ☐ Faster than you can say "Zippo"
- ☐ Been trying to quit
- ☐ Don't smoke

6 During sex, what position are you most likely to be in?

- ☐ Man on top
- ☐ Doggie
- ☐ There's more than one?

WHAT YOUR ANSWERS SAY ABOUT YOU

1. Half of all Americans are dissatisfied with their jobs. A resume blitz might seem like the obvious answer here, but in reality many guys are in no position to job hop. Instead call a travel agent and book an adventure vacation. A week of, say, whitewater rafting, canoeing, or rock climbing will invigorate your mind and body and give you a sense of accomplishment you may not get from your job. Plus, it'll keep on giving. "Down the road, you're going to be sitting in a conference room, and that trip's going to pop into your mind and you're going to relive it," says Jerry Mallett, president and CEO of the Adventure Travel Society in Salida, Colorado.

2. Whatever sport you've been glued to, we challenge you to get out there and play it—with other people. A review of 113 exercise-adherence studies published in the *Journal of Sport and Exercise Psychology* shows you're more likely to stick with exercise if you don't go it alone. The key, believes Jim Annesi, Ph.D., an exercise psychologist with the YMCA of Metropolitan Atlanta, is to feel that you're part of a group. But do it for the challenge, not for the postgame brewskies. While the numbing effect of beer may make you feel good in the short term, alcohol is a depressant and will just dig your rut deeper.

3. To break out of a workout rut, try these variations: 1) Do different exercises that work the same muscle groups. The basic barbell curl, for example, has dozens of variations. We bet you haven't tried half of them. 2) For lifts that are tough to vary, like the bench press, try a "wave" system of reps: 7, 5, 3, 7, 5, 3, where you use at least 5 pounds more on the second wave than on the first. 3) Cut the rest interval between lifts. 4) Change the order of your exercises from week to week. 5) Dedicate specific days to individual muscles.

4. If you've resorted to quilting, you'll never get your blood moving. Our solution? Take a hike. "A singles hike is a great way to meet women," says Leah Furman, coauthor of *The Everything Dating Book*. "It's a comfortable zone where you can meet and talk and get to know one another." And you'll meet someone who shares your interest in staying active and being fit. For a schedule of singles hikes near you, log onto www.sierraclub.org/singles/ or call (415) 977-5500.

5. If you smoke, quit. This one-word challenge is the toughest we'll give you here, but we're not going to let you off easy. Smoking puts you at risk for numerous health conditions, including heart disease, stroke, certain cancers, even impotence. If you'd like to snuff out that butt for good, add exercise to your quitting strategy. Studies show that quitters who exercise have milder withdrawal symptoms and fewer mood swings than nonexercisers. "Plus, it can help prevent the weight gain that often occurs when people quit smoking," says Douglas E. Jorenby, Ph.D., associate professor of medicine at the University of Wisconsin Medical School's Center for Tobacco Research and Intervention.

6. The average guy does it missionary style most often. But who wants to settle for average sex? The perfect fix? Nude partner yoga! "After just 10 or 15 minutes of practicing partner yoga, your body can move more freely, is more sensitized, and your pleasure is heightened," says Cain Carroll, certified yoga instructor and coauthor of *Partner Yoga*.

Try the "Standing Straddle" from his book. Relax your body. Then, stand back to back with your feet about 3 feet apart. Grasp each other's hands. Inhale, then exhale and slowly bend forward at your hips while pressing your legs and buttocks firmly together. Keeping your back flat, continue to bend forward as far as you can comfortably. Grab your partner's legs just under the knee. Relax, breathe, and let gravity gently pull you farther into the stretch. Hold the pose for about 30 to 60 seconds, and release.

Then, try another kind of straddle. And release.

—DEANNA PORTZ

BY ED PAVELKA

Four Exercise Bets You Can Win

Want to get fit?
Put some money on it.
Here are four exercise wagers you can cash in on

Competition is the glue of male friendship. You might be a responsible adult with life insurance and a midsize sedan, but if you're like most guys, you'll try just about anything a buddy dares you to do. This instinct explains such venerable male institutions as the pie-eating contest, the hog-calling competition, and the whole *Survivor* thing.

Fortunately, there is a way to use this power for good, not evil. Challenging another guy to a head-to-head competition at the gym, track, or pool can be a great way to breathe some life into a tired exercise program. Give yourself a few weeks to train for the event, and whether you're betting a case of beer or your firstborn child, your wager will motivate you to train harder and achieve more.

Here, we offer you four manly fitness bets to test your strength, speed, and endurance—each with its own training program to ensure that you prevail. Now go find a sucker.

Benching for Bucks

The sting: Find someone who's a match for you in terms of strength. To account for differences in size, challenge him to see who can do

Go for the gold: You'll be fitter and richer, and he'll be left in a puddle of sweat.

the most repetitions bench pressing 75 percent of body weight.

The skill: Give yourself a month to prepare, but before you even begin to train, make sure you're both using good form. Either guy loses if his hips rise from the bench. Have a spotter for each end of the bar.

The workout: Assuming you're already lifting weights three times a week, stick with your regular workout, but add the following exercises immediately after your normal lifting routine. After only 4 weeks, this should pay off with as many as three extra repetitions on Bet Day, says Harvey Newton, C.S.C.S., executive director of the National Strength and Conditioning Association.

▶***Mondays:*** Do three sets of negative bench presses at the end of your regular workout. This requires two or three spotters, because you need to use 110 percent of the maximum weight you can bench for one rep. Have them hoist the bar to full extension for you, then remain at the ready as you lower it very slowly (take a maximum of 6 seconds) to your chest. Repeat, letting your spotters do most of the work going up but accepting the full load coming down. Try for four repetitions the first week, six the second, then cut back to five for the third. (Tapering off in the final week lets you save your strength for the competition.)

▶***Wednesdays:*** Do your normal bench-press routine.

▶***Fridays:*** After your regular lifting routine, squeeze out some partial bench presses. You'll use your Monday weight—110 percent of the maximum weight you can bench for one repetition—but this time you won't need spotters. Put the bar in a power rack with the pins positioned to hold it at about two-thirds of an arm's length. Do three sets of three to six repetitions, pressing the weight until your arms are fully extended (you'll need to move the bar only a few inches), then lowering it to the starting position. These "partials" build your finishing strength, helping you complete repetitions even when your muscles are nearing exhaustion.

During the final week leading up to the bet, go back to your regular lifting routine, minus the negative presses and partials. As-

Get the Advantage: Benching

Get situated. Before taking the bar, get into proper bench-press position: shoulders back, chest forward, upper back slightly arched. This shortens the distance you must move the bar. Your lower back should retain its natural curve.

Use a wide grip. This also reduces the distance you have to move the bar.

Breathe strategically. Inhale as you lower the bar—this expands your chest, lessening the distance you have to move the bar. Exhale during the push.

Follow the arc. After initially pressing straight up, let the bar arc several inches back toward your head as you complete the rep. Don't fight this natural trajectory.

Don't lose steam. To help squeeze out those final winning repetitions, lower the bar more quickly, then immediately apply upward power. Never bounce the bar off your chest.

suming the competition is on a Friday, Newton recommends using no more than 80 percent of normal weight during Monday's workout, and no more than 60 percent on Wednesday.

Dashing for Dollars

The sting: Because he beats you deep in touch football, your buddy is certain that he has more speed. You challenge him to a 100-yard dash.

Get the Advantage: Sprinting

Warm up. Run a mile at an easy pace, then stretch.

Psych him out. Next, do two or three of the "Flying 50s" at 90 percent effort. "Sprinters always do better after a couple of heats," coach Roy Benson says.

Start fast. Begin with your right foot on the line and your left foot just behind, knees flexed. Hold your right arm low and behind. On "Go!" throw your right hand forward and take a big step with your left foot. Instant lead.

Use your arms. To lengthen your stride, bring your arms way up on the backswing with your elbows bent at a 90-degree angle. Keep your arms close to your body as you swing them forward, letting your hands rise to shoulder level.

Don't overstride. If you're reaching so far that your heels hit first, it's like braking with each footfall. "Stay up on the balls of your feet and run like you're pawing the ground," Benson says.

Tighten up. As you approach full speed, tighten stride rate without decreasing length by tightening your elbow angle as you swing your arms in front of you. This quickens your arm action, automatically increasing the rate your feet strike the ground.

Stay loose. As you run, form a circle with each thumb and index finger. This keeps your hands relaxed, which helps prevent tension in your arms and shoulders—and that helps you run with proper form.

Run through the line. Don't lose your bet by easing up several steps too soon.

The skill: Sprinting speed is a simple equation, says Roy Benson, owner of Running Ltd., an Atlanta coaching service. It's a matter of stride length times stride frequency. But because most guys can pick 'em up and lay 'em down at about the same frequency, Benson says you will run faster by lengthening your stride.

The workout: To prepare for a sprinting contest, replace two of your regular runs each week with Benson's speed workouts. Don't do them back to back, though: They should be separated by at least 2 days of rest or regular running.

Do your normal running on other days. Don't get carried away and add sprints—you'll need to give your body enough recovery time between speed workouts.

TOUGH TALK

"A man surprised is half beaten."

THOMAS FULLER

WORKOUT #1: "SPEED ENDURANCE" TRAINING

You'll need a 100-yard course for this drill. Run it at a local track or football field; or, if none is available, approximate the distance by stepping off 100 full strides.

▶***Warmup:*** Spend 15 to 20 minutes jogging and stretching so your muscles feel warm and loose. Make sure the warmup includes a few lunges to stretch your hip flexors and groin muscles.

▶***The drill:*** Run the course at 75 to 80 percent of full speed. Practice proper sprinting form (see "Get the Advantage: Sprinting," on the previous page), exaggerating your knee lift and heel kick. Walk back to the start. Do six repeats in week one, eight repeats in week two, 10 repeats in week three, and 12 repeats in week four. Cut back to six repeats in Bet Week.

WORKOUT #2: "FLYING 50S"

This workout helps you feel comfortable running at full speed.

▶***Warmup:*** Same as Workout #1.

▶***The drill:*** Begin 20 yards behind the starting line and use that distance to accelerate to full speed, then run as fast as you can for the next 50 yards. Walk back and regain comfortable breathing before going again. Do two repetitions the first week, four the second week, six in week three, and eight in week four. Skip this workout altogether during Bet Week.

Profitable Pullups

The sting: The beefy guy at the health club can handle a few more pounds than you in every lift, so he's certain he can do more pullups, too. But the bigger they are, the more they'll probably have to pay to settle this bet. Lighter guys have the benefit of less weight to support and hoist.

The skill: Most men can't even hang from a chinning bar for as long as 2 minutes, notes Tory Allman, general manager of Frog's: An Athletic Club, in Solana Beach, California. With gravity pulling down and blood rushing from the arms, your grip quickly fatigues. The trick is to complete the most repetitions possible while you have strength in your hands and biceps—the weak links in this exercise.

The workout: With this month-long training program, Allman says you can expect to do an extra three to five pullups on Bet Day. You should also stick to regular aerobic workouts—any excess body fat you can drop will give you an advantage.

Do these exercises three times a week, immediately following your regular weight-lifting workout:

PULLUPS

▶***Warmup:*** Start with one set of regular pullups using good form. (See "Get the Advantage: Pullups.") Your chin should clear the bar with each repetition; leaning your head back and raising your chin is cheating. Stop when you sense that the next one is going to be tough.

▶***More pullups:*** Do up to five sets of pullups, going to failure in each set. (Stop when you can't get your chin up to bar level.) Rest for at least 30 seconds between sets, or as long as it takes for your breathing and heart rate to return to normal.

▶***Advanced version:*** If you're able to do eight or more regular pullups per set, Allman suggests replacing them with weighted pullups. Using a chain, attach a 5-, 10-, or 20-pound weight plate (depending on your strength) to a weight belt, and fasten the belt around your waist. Do five to seven sets, going to failure in each set.

Caution: Although biceps are key to pullups, skip biceps curls during your regular weight-lifting workout this month—you'll risk overtraining these relatively small muscles. Don't worry about losing definition in your biceps; you'll work them hard enough with pullups.

LAT PULLDOWNS

Sit at a lat pulldown machine and fasten the strap around your waist. Grab the bar with a wide overhand grip. Pull the bar to the front

Get the Advantage: Pullups

Use the right grip. Underhand grip, hands shoulder-width apart. This gives your biceps their maximum mechanical advantage.

Lean backward slightly. This recruits the bigger, stronger back muscles, taking some responsibility from the biceps.

Breathe right. Exhale while pulling up, inhale as you let yourself down.

Finish smoothly. Let yourself down quickly but without snapping your shoulder or elbow joints.

of your chest. Do as many repetitions as possible, up to five sets, going to failure in each set. Rest for at least 30 seconds between sets. If you're fairly strong, Allman recommends using 60 percent of your body weight the first week, 70 percent the second, and 80 percent the third and fourth. Aim for 10 repetitions per set using good form. If you can't do 10, drop down to a lighter weight.

BET WEEK

Do your final full training session 3 days before the showdown. One day before, do an easy workout, using only 60 percent of your usual weight for each exercise. Skip the pullups.

Get the Advantage: Swimming

Keep 'em close. For a meaningful advantage, wear a tight-fitting racing suit, not your baggy trunks. If you have a lot of hair, wear a swim cap.

Open up. A few moments before the race, do five big, slow arm circles, combined with deep breaths. This helps expand your chest and fill your lungs.

Take big strokes. Push off forcefully and glide like a torpedo. Then begin an underwater breaststroke just below the surface, using a sweeping frog kick in sync with strong arm pulls. "Don't rush," Bolster cautions. "Glide as far as you can after each stroke."

Blow bubbles. Exhaling a little at a time helps expel carbon dioxide and reduce the panicky sense that you're going to explode.

Underwater Wagering

The sting: You're at the pool. The local version of Jacques Cousteau is ripe for a soaking. You bet him that you can swim farther underwater on just one breath.

The skill: The unexpected key to winning this bet is relaxation, according to Jim Bolster, head swimming coach at Columbia University. "Speed isn't the idea," he says. "In fact, you should try to be leisurely and efficient" to get the most from your last gulp of air.

The workout: Each time you hit the pool, practice the following techniques to improve your breath control and manage the anxiety that comes from low oxygen levels. Be sure to do them at least twice a week. And even if you're a strong swimmer, do them only when there's a lifeguard on duty, or at least other good swimmers present. Stupid people have drowned doing this stuff; so be careful with your training and you'll survive to win the bet.

Sit and breathe: Timing yourself with a wristwatch, sit on the bottom of the shallow end for 15 seconds, then come up and breathe normally for 15 seconds. Repeat, but this time stay down for 30 seconds, then come up and catch your breath for 30 seconds. Keep going, adding an extra 10 seconds to your underwater and recovery phases until you hit your limit.

Underwater swims: Swim an underwater breaststroke as far as you can on a single breath, practicing the contest techniques below. After each swim, take as much time as you need to catch your breath. Repeat six to eight times.

Turn practice: Starting about 10 yards away from the wall, swim underwater to the wall and practice making a quick, tight pivot and pushoff. Don't thrash or break the surface.

Pushoffs: This exercise develops explosive leg power, helping you gain distance on the start and get more momentum out of your turns. In the shallow end, crouch underwater with your arms extended overhead, biceps pressing against your ears, hands overlapping. Spring straight up, then immediately crouch and spring again. Repeat for 1 minute. Rest for 30 seconds, then repeat the drill for another minute.

Throughout these drills, pay attention to what you're thinking about when you're underwater. Bolster says some swimmers stay more relaxed and are able to remain submerged longer when they think about something else. Others do better by focusing on the task. Experiment to see what works better for you.

A Year of Fitness Goals

Conquering these monthly physical tests will make this year your fittest, fastest, most confident one yet. Think you can handle it?

BY MARTIN DUGARD

Isaac Newton must have been a cross-trainer. Sure, it's easy to see how he got the gravity idea from a falling apple. But how about all those other scientific laws governing motion?

We think he must have been out jogging after a couple of hours of calculus when he developed that most basic principle of motion, which led to our understanding of momentum—you know, from 11th-grade physics: "A body in motion stays in motion. . . . A body at rest, well, it forms butt marks in the sofa cushions."

As you face another year of struggling to find the time and momentum to stay in shape, we thought we'd help keep your body in motion with a little challenge. Actually, 12 little challenges. Each month we lay down a new physical test, a dare, if you will. Something like "add 20 pounds to your maximum bench press," or "swim a mile." Then we offer a workout that will help you reach that goal within 30 days. New month, new challenge.

"Without a doubt, the best way to maintain interest in a fitness program over an extended length of time is to diversify your workout," says Herman Falsetti, M.D., an

Irvine, California cardiologist who has worked as a training consultant to Olympic cyclists.

And that's the terrific thing about the program below: You'll never get bored. Each monthly goal builds on the last, so, by the end of the year, you'll probably be in better shape than ever. And isn't that how you want to ring in the next New Year?

JANUARY CHALLENGE

Start a Running and Weight-Training Program

For the benefit of those who haven't broken a sweat since the air conditioner blew last August, we'll begin slowly. Starting in January and moving through February, you're going to create a foundation of fitness upon which to build. (But first, be sure to get your doctor's

How to Do It

Bench press. Lie on your back on a bench with your feet flat on the floor. Hold the barbell at arm's length above you with your hands a few inches wider than your shoulders. Lower the bar to your chest, then push it up to arm's length.

Military press. Stand facing a squat rack with a barbell resting on it at shoulder height. With feet shoulder-width apart and hands a little wider than that, lift the bar and rest it at the top of your chest, just below shoulder height. Slowly press it overhead.

Front squat. Stand facing a barbell on the squat rack, legs shoulder-width apart and feet pointing straight. Cross your arms in front of you, palms facing in. With your hands about 10 inches apart, step in and lift the bar so it rests across your chest. Keeping your back straight and head up, squat until your upper thighs are almost parallel to the floor. Pause and straighten up.

Triceps extension. Lie on your back on a bench, with your head resting on it. Hold a barbell with a narrow grip (about 6 inches wide), palms facing up. Extend your arms so the bar is above you. This is the starting position. Now slowly bend your elbows, bringing the bar toward your forehead. Press it up, following the same path.

Calf raise. Grasp a bar and rest it on the back of your shoulders. Your feet should be about 12 inches apart, toes pointing straight ahead. Now slowly push up on your toes, raising your heels as far as you can. At the top, pause a second, then slowly lower your heels.

Biceps curl. Hold a barbell with palms up, hands about 18 inches apart. Keeping your elbows at your sides, curl the bar until forearms touch biceps. Then slowly lower the bar.

Upright row. Stand and hold the barbell with your hands 3 to 4 inches apart, palms down. Allow the bar to rest against your thighs. Now pull it straight up until it nearly touches your chin. Keeping the bar close to your body, pause, then lower it to your thighs.

Crunches. Lie on your back with your legs bent at a 90-degree angle, feet flat on the floor. Touching your ears lightly with your fingertips, curl up until your shoulders rise 4 to 6 inches off the floor. Do 15 to 20 repetitions.

okay to start this or any conditioning program.)

Aerobic conditioning. The best way to get fit fast is to mix walking into an easy jogging workout, according to Budd Coates, a four-time Olympic marathon trials qualifier. "Novice runners make two mistakes," he explains. "First, they tend to think in mile increments instead of in minutes of running, and second, they try to run too fast."

Coates has designed a program that avoids these pitfalls. Don't worry about overlapping with the February and March challenges. This plan fits nicely into the workouts designed for those months.

Each week, do your run/walk workouts on Monday, Wednesday, Friday, and Saturday, taking the other days off. The idea is to gradually build the number of minutes you run: For example, you start out by running 2 minutes and walking 4, and doing that four more times. Here's the whole plan:

WEEK	MIN RUN	MIN WALKED	REPS
1	2	4	5
2	3	3	5
3	5	2.5	4
4	7	3	3
5	8	2	3
6	9	2	2*
7	9	1	3
8	13	2	2
9	14	1	2
10	30		

* Finish by running another 8 minutes.

Strength conditioning. The goal here is to build some muscle mass and increase strength without spending a lot of time in the gym. You'll lift 3 days a week for only 30 minutes a session. How? By doing just one set of each lift.

"The research suggests that one good set of resistance exercise is as effective as two or three sets for producing significant strength gains," says Wayne L. Westcott, Ph.D., fitness/research director at the South Shore YMCA in Quincy, Massachusetts.

Do one set of 8 to 12 repetitions of each exercise, using 75 percent of your maximum resistance. In other words, if you can bench-press 100 pounds once, do your set with just 75 pounds on the bar. Follow the workout in "How to Do It" on the opposite page.

FEBRUARY CHALLENGE

Jump Rope for 15 Minutes without Stopping

If you've never jumped rope before, you may think it's easy—schoolyard stuff. But it's one of the true tests of aerobic endurance. First thing to do is get a jump rope that fits. According to champion rope jumper Ken Solis, M.D., author of *Ropics*, you test a rope for fit by standing on its middle and checking to see that the handles reach almost to your armpits.

How to jump: Stand on a mat or wooden floor with your feet together in front of the rope. Your hands should be just below your waist, your elbows close to your sides. The trick is to use only your wrists and forearms to swing the rope over your head and down in front of you. Try it. As the rope falls in front of you, jump an inch off the floor so it can pass under. Land on the balls of your feet.

Jump for time: Once you've got the rhythm, practice endurance, but start slowly. Jumping rope brings your heart rate up very quickly. If you haven't already gotten an okay from your doctor to embark on a vigorous plan of exercise, do so before continuing.

For the first week, try to jump rope for about 2 minutes without missing. Focus on technique: Stay on the balls of your feet so your calves absorb the impact, rather than your shins and knees. Work in about 10 minutes of rope jumping a couple of times a week. Once you can jump 2 minutes without stopping, build to 5, then 10, then 15. And keep up with your lifting and running.

MARCH CHALLENGE

Increase the Weight You Can Bench-Press by 20 Pounds

Building the strength to bench-press a lot of weight requires a different lifting style than the one that builds chest size. "Treat the bench press as an exercise for your triceps instead of your chest," says Dave Tate, C.S.C.S., a strength coach and champion power lifter in Columbus, Ohio. That's because the most effective way to move weight off your chest is to tuck your elbows close to your sides and push the bar straight up from your lower chest. That technique also shortens the range of motion of your arms by 10 inches, which enables you to heft heavier weights.

In this program, you'll train for the bench press twice a week, using a different method each workout. For your first session, you'll use lighter weights and work on speed. In the second, you'll use the heaviest weights possible and focus on the final two-thirds of the lift. The speed workout teaches your muscles to blow through their sticking point, the position at which they give out when you're lifting a weight that's just beyond your max. The heavy-weight workout builds the strength to push the bar the last few inches. Schedule at least 3 days between these two workouts.

Workout 1 (Speed)

Perform nine sets of three repetitions of the bench press with a weight that's about half what you can lift one time. Press the weight as fast as possible each time. Try to complete each three-repetition set in $3^1/_2$ seconds or less. Rest 45 seconds after each set, and alternate your grip every three sets—so your hands are about 16, then 20, then 24 inches apart.

After you've finished the nine sets of bench presses, do two triceps exercises, and then finish up with exercises for your upper back, shoulders, and forearms. Here's a sample workout.

- Close-grip bench press (work up to one heavy set of five repetitions)
- Lying triceps extension (three sets of eight repetitions)
- Bent-over row (five sets of five repetitions)
- Shoulder press (three sets of eight repetitions)
- Reverse curl (one set of 10 repetitions)

Workout 2 (Maximum Weight)

Choose one of the three chest exercises listed in the following exercise menu. (Switch to a different one every 2 weeks.) Start by lifting the empty bar for three repetitions as a warmup. Rest 45 seconds. Add 20 to 40 pounds and do another three repetitions. Continue this way until a three-repetition set feels difficult. Then add weight, but do only one repetition instead of three, and increase your rest between sets to 2 minutes. Work up to the weight you can lift only one time. Keep track of this record, and try to break it during each maximum-weight workout.

Complete your workout with five sets of 10 repetitions of the following exercises.

- ▶ Dumbbell triceps press
- ▶ Triceps pushdown
- ▶ Dumbbell bent-over row
- ▶ Front raise

Exercise Menu

Incorporate one of these three variations during Workout 2.

▶ ***Board press:*** Use a pair of 12-inch-long two-by-fours. Stack one on top of the other on your chest, and rest the bar on the boards momentarily before you push it back to the starting position.

TOUGH TALK

"At the beginning of the year, I was lucky to survive 15 minutes of cardio and a half-mile run. Now I am at the point where I have recently registered to run in my first 10-K."

JOE REPOSA, *MEN'S HEALTH* BELLY-OFF CLUB MEMBER, ON LOSING 52 POUNDS

▶ ***Floor press:*** Lie on the floor instead of on a bench and hold a barbell in your hands. Pause in each repetition before you push the bar to the starting position.

▶ ***Pin press:*** Place a bench inside a power rack. Then set the safety pins just below where you think your sticking point is. Rest the bar on the pins. Lie on the bench, press the bar up, and then slowly lower it onto the pins. Pause a second and repeat.

Tate says the you should expect to increase your maximum bench press by 20 to 50 pounds in 8 weeks on this program.

APRIL CHALLENGE

Play a Game of Full-Court Basketball Each Week

Thanks to the jogging and rope jumping you've been doing, you should be able to make it through a full-court game without sucking wind. If you can't rustle up enough friends for a weekly game, go to the health club, the local YMCA, or a playground to find a game.

To improve your quickness, lateral movement, and jumping ability, we suggest a couple of exercises. The obstacle jump: Place a shoe box on the ground and stand with your feet together next to it. Now jump sideways across the box. As soon as you touch down, jump back. Jump as high as you can. Do two sets of five, resting between sets. Each week this month, add five repetitions. This is one of the best drills for building leg power.

The second exercise is the classic box drill: Mark off a 15-by-15-foot box on the playground blacktop. Starting in the bottom left corner of the box, sprint to the top left corner and tap the corner with your left hand. Sidestep to the right corner, keeping your feet spread. Touch down with your right hand, then backpedal to the bottom right corner and touch it with your right hand. Finally, shuffle laterally to the bottom left corner. Repeat in the opposite direction.

The best thing to do to improve your technique is to play a lot, says Tom Danley, who has run basketball camps in southern California for more than 20 years. "Keep your game as simple as possible," he says. "Execution breaks down when you try to get too fancy."

TOUGH TALK

"Well, we knocked the bastard off!"

EDMUND HILLARY, ON CONQUERING MOUNT EVEREST

MAY CHALLENGE

Run Your First 10-K

Thirty days isn't enough time for the average Joe to prepare for this 6.2-mile race, especially if the course has hills. But if you followed January's running program and played basketball once a week, you're ready. Increase your running to 5 days a week, following this 4-week schedule.

Week 1

▶***Sunday:*** Run for 30 to 45 minutes at an easy pace that's slow enough so you can carry on a conversation with a partner.

▶***Monday:*** Rest.

▶***Tuesday:*** Run easily for 10 minutes to warm up. Next, quicken your pace for 5 minutes, then jog for 5 minutes, speed up for another 5, then slow down a bit for 5 minutes. Finally, cool down with 10 minutes of easy jogging.

▶***Wednesday and Thursday:*** Run easily for 15 to 30 minutes.

▶***Friday:*** Take a 10-minute warmup jog. Then run up a 100- to 200-yard hill at a modest pace five times, and at your race pace five times, recovering with a slow jog on the way down. Finish with a 10-minute cooldown.

▶***Saturday:*** Rest.

Weeks 2 and 3

▶Repeat the week-1 workout, but increase your Sunday runs by 15 minutes each week, picking up your pace slightly.

Week 4 (race week)

▶***Sunday:*** Run for 45 to 60 minutes at an easy pace.

▶***Monday:*** Rest.

▶***Tuesday:*** Warm up for 10 minutes. Alternate 2 minutes of race-pace running with 3 minutes of easy jogging for three cycles. Cool down for 10 minutes.

▶***Wednesday:*** Rest.

▶***Thursday and Friday:*** 15 to 30 minutes of easy running.

▶***Saturday:*** Rest or jog easily for 10 minutes to keep your legs loose.

▶***Sunday:*** Race day.

Some Tips on Racing Smart

Above all, don't start out too fast. The idea is to cover the distance, not finish in the top 10. If you're gasping for breath, it's okay to walk awhile; many runners do in a race this long. You can always pick up your pace as you approach the finish. Okay, you only have 200 yards to go and you're feeling strong. Start your kick. To eke more speed out of your body, try this trick: Pick a runner 20 yards in front of you and hunt him down like a greyhound after a rabbit. Blow past him to the finish line. Once you cross, grab a victory water and walk for 5 or 10 minutes.

JUNE CHALLENGE

Learn the Eskimo Roll in a Kayak

To the uninitiated, whitewater kayaking is the stuff of National Geographic videos: rugged men in plastic boats bobbing and weaving down the boulder-strewn Colorado, going head-to-head with Old Man River himself. Before you can watusi with the whitecaps, you have to learn that crucial tool of self-preservation, the Eskimo roll.

This is the method by which a capsized kayaker rolls his vessel upright by quickly rotating, or snapping, his hips. It seems a sure way to drown until you learn what goes on beneath the water.

The best place to learn is at a kayaking clinic given by a river-running club or at a commercial kayaking school. To find local contacts, ask at a paddling shop or call the American Whitewater Affiliation, (866) 262-8429. Your class will probably take place in a swimming pool, and the school will provide loaner equipment and spotters. This way you can experience the scariest moment in the sport without leaving a lot of slightly used equipment to your survivors.

Sit in your kayak with your feet forward and pressed against foot braces. Make sure your spray skirt is pulled snug over the cockpit to keep the water out. Holding your paddle with two hands, shoulder-width apart, place the paddle shaft along one side of the kayak. At the same time, bend forward as far as you can, with your face touching the deck of the kayak. This is the position you want to be in underwater, not only because it protects your face from rocks but also because it places your paddle where it can help you.

The dunk: From this position, take a deep breath, then lean to the paddle side to capsize the boat. (It won't happen this way on the river, of course, but this is a good way to practice.)

The paddle sweep: You're upside down now, and there's water up your nose. It stings. But don't think about it. Concentrate on bending forward and reaching with your arms until you can push the paddle blades and shaft above the surface. Rotate the paddle so it's perpendicular to the bottom of the boat, and mostly above the surface of the water.

The hip-snap: Forget your natural urge to get your head above water as soon as you can. Instead, quickly twist, or snap, your hips to bring the boat back under you. At the same time, pull down on the paddle blade farther from the boat, to get more leverage for your hips. Bear in mind that your hips are doing the major work. Keep your head low—i.e., underwater—until the boat swings upright. Lifting your head too soon will tip you back under.

It may take several practice sessions before you get a reliable roll. But once you have it, you'll never forget it.

JULY CHALLENGE

Knock Five Strokes Off Your Golf Game

If you're very lucky, you get in one or two games of golf each week. Most of us don't, and yet we expect to play skillfully at the company tourney. It doesn't work that way, unless you're an undiscovered John Daly.

But there are simple exercises and drills you can do at home, at the driving range, and on the course that can help you knock strokes off your game, says golf instructor Jim McLean, author of *The Putter's Pocket Companion.*

At home: Putt in your living room a couple of nights a week. You don't need a green and a cup; just practice keeping your clubface aimed correctly. To do this, stick a length of masking tape to the rug and putt balls along the line. If the ball follows the line, you know your clubface is steady. Next, hit 25 putts into a bedpost that's about 3 feet away. Concentrate on freezing your knees and accelerating the putter toward the target.

On the driving range: Pretend you're on the golf course. This means mimicking everything you do when you swing on the course. After every ball you hit, change clubs and aim at a different target. "Some players have a range game, and they can't take anything to the course," says McLean. This drill helps you simulate course play in practice.

Before you play: Practice putting and chipping before you go to the driving range. "Most people warm up in the opposite order," says McLean. "They go from the practice green straight to tee-off, and they're cold and tight—it's been 20 minutes since they've driven a ball." Instead, start at the practice green, using 25 percent of your preplay time to work on long and short putts and chipping. Then go to the driving range just before teeing off.

During play: "Tension kills the golf swing," says McLean. "You have to relax your shoulders and arms." To loosen up: Twist your trunk a few times with the club resting across your shoulders, lift the club far over your head to stretch your shoulders and arms, and take practice swings, working from small ones to full swings.

AUGUST CHALLENGE

Swim a Mile

Assuming you haven't forgotten how to swim, this program will turn you into a tuna in 30 days.

Find a 25-yard lap pool; swim one length and count your strokes. "If you take more than 20 arm strokes, you should improve your stroke efficiency first," says Terry Laughlin, director of Total Immersion national swimming camps for adults, based in Goshen, New York. "For novices, swimming is at least 80 percent proper mechanics."

The keys are keeping your hips and legs from dragging, and lengthening your stroke. "Try leaning on your chest more so that it feels as if you're swimming downhill," Laughlin says. "That'll keep your hips and legs near the surface so you'll be more streamlined."

Two tricks for lengthening your stroke: 1) As each arm enters the water, reach—just as you would for something on a high shelf—before starting your pull; 2) roll your hips from side to side with each stroke.

The workout. Swim one or two lengths, practicing the moves mentioned above, then rest. Repeat for 30 to 40 minutes three times a week. When you can swim 100 yards in 80 strokes or fewer, start building sets of 100-yard repeats, resting for 15 to 30 seconds between 100-yard swims. Once you can swim about 18 of these, attempt a mile swim. That's 1,760 yards or 71 laps in a 25-yard pool. To beat the boredom of lap swimming, swim your mile in a lake, with a buddy rowing a boat ahead of you for safety. For more information on Total Immersion workshops or a video on proper stroke technique, call (800) 609-7946.

SEPTEMBER CHALLENGE

Cycle a Metric Century

September is National Century Month, when cyclists across the country hit the road in organized, one-day rides of 100 miles. While that's a tall order to prepare for in 1 month, most of these rides have shorter options, and one of the most popular for beginning cyclists is the 100-kilometer (62-mile) metric century. To find a century ride near you, inquire at your local bike shop.

The training schedule below was prepared by the editors of *Bicycling* magazine. It's a proven program that has helped thousands of cyclists just like you meet the challenge.

	MON (Easy)*	TUE (Pace)**	WED (Brisk)***	THU	FRI (Pace)	SAT (Pace)	SUN (Pace)	Mileage****
Week 1	6	10	12	Off	10	30	9	77
Week 2	7	11	13	Off	11	34	10	86
Week 3	8	13	15	Off	13	38	11	98
Week 4	8	14	17	Off	14	42	13	108
Week 5	8	14	17	Off	10	5 (easy)	Century	116

* "Easy" means a leisurely ride.

** "Pace" means matching the speed you hope to maintain during the metric century. (Depending on how hilly the course is, you can expect a 62-mile century to take you between 4 and 6 hours, so plan your pace accordingly.)

*** "Brisk" means riding at least 2 or 3 miles per hour faster than your century speed.

**** It's important to ride at least 5 days per week. If you skip a day, make sure it's not a Saturday, your long mileage day. Covering greater distances each weekend is key. If weather or something else derails your Saturday ride, use Sunday as the long day.

OCTOBER CHALLENGE

Compete in a Short-Course Triathlon

Never considered yourself Ironman material? Hell, you've been swimming, running, and cycling for months. Now's the time to put it all together. A short-course triathlon gives a casual athlete the opportunity to do just that. Generally, short-course events consist of a 1-K swim, 30-K bicycle race, and 5-K run. For information about short-course triathlons near you, call USA Triathlon, the sport's U.S. governing body, at (719) 597-9090.

Triathlon training is a delicate blend of workouts and rest. "You don't want to overtrain," warns two-time Ironman winner Scott Tinley. Men who overtrain tend to feel lethargic during the race, he says. In fact, you're better off going into a race slightly undertrained. "It won't hurt you unless you're really unprepared," he says.

It's important to practice the individual disciplines separately each week. Never combine them in one workout, says Tinley. Here's a sample schedule. Exercise for at least 45 minutes each day. Monday, run; Tuesday, cycle; Wednesday, rest; Thursday, swim; Friday, practice your weakest event; Saturday, your choice; Sunday, rest. Be sure to rest twice a week.

The day before the triathlon, stay off your feet, and increase your intake of fluids. On race day, eat a light breakfast and drink a couple of glasses of water. You'll want to drink water throughout the race. The order of events is: swim, bike, run. But if you forget, follow the guy ahead of you. The biggest mistake first-time racers make is "getting too excited and going out too hard," says Tinley. "In your first triathlon, all you're trying to do is finish. So go out easy." And smile for the cheering crowds. After all, this is supposed to be fun—even if it hurts like hell.

NOVEMBER CHALLENGE

Go a Few Rounds with a Heavy Bag

A boxing workout is a terrific cross-training tool because it exercises the whole body. Punching a heavy bag works the shoulders, arms, chest, abdominals, and legs, says boxing instructor Tony Fluke, a former sparring partner for Thomas "Hit Man" Hearns. It's also an extremely rigorous cardiovascular workout. To further boost the aerobic component of this workout, do your exercises in 3-minute bursts with 1-minute rests in between to simulate the rounds in a boxing match.

Week 1: Warm up by jogging a mile. Then do two sets of 20 crunches and 20 pushups. Next, work on your stamina and arm strength by jumping rope in 3-minute rounds. Do two sets.

Now take some time to practice proper boxing form. Stand in front of a mirror. If left handed, stand with your right foot slightly forward. Do the opposite if you're right handed. Position your fists about 2 inches apart, with your knuckles facing the ceiling. Your forearms should form a 45-degree angle in front of your chest. From this position, practice some shadowboxing. As you throw a punch, push off your back leg and twist your torso. "Make short punches. Never extend your arm completely and snap the elbow," says Fluke. Doing so can strain ligaments.

Weeks 2 and 3: Start each workout as you

did in week 1. Then move to the speed bag to build hand-eye coordination, rhythm, and stamina. Assume your boxing stance far enough from the bag that you can touch it with your arm almost extended. Start with two rights and two lefts, punching slowly at first. The bag should hit the wood three times before you throw the next punch. With practice, you'll develop a rhythm and increase speed.

Next, try the heavy bag. Start with some easy jabs to get a feel for it. Then work on some straight punches and hooks. Do a 3-minute round using each punch.

Week 4: Increase sessions with the jump rope, speed bag, and heavy bag by one to three rounds. Work combination punches into your heavy-bag routine.

If you want to try your luck in the ring, consider joining a boxing gym or getting some personal training from an instructor to pick up the technical skills.

DECEMBER CHALLENGE

Learn to Juggle

Every man should be able to juggle, if only to impress women and amuse children at family reunions. So give your body a break after a year of hard exercise. Relax and exercise your hand-eye coordination. As a side benefit, juggling is a superb stress reducer.

First get three weighted juggling balls or beanbags (nothing that will bounce). Now find a spot to practice. Standing in front of a bed is a smart idea; you won't have to stoop to pick up dropped balls.

Imagine an X that crosses the upper half of your body, with the intersection just above chin level. You'll want to follow this X pattern as you throw the balls. Aim for a point above your opposite shoulder and throw strongly enough to reach above forehead height.

Begin practice with only one ball. Toss it back and forth between your hands. Try to make the ball follow the same gentle curve each time. Keep your hands at waist level and relaxed. Don't reach to catch the ball; let it fall into your hand. Let your wrists do the work.

Next, try the two-ball pattern. Put a ball in each palm. Toss one from the left hand. Just as it reaches its peak and begins to drop, toss the other from the right. Catch ball one with the right hand. Catch ball two with your left. Freeze. Check position. Do it again. Once you feel comfortable with this toss, try to keep it going for a few minutes.

The three-ball cascade adds one more step. Start with two balls in one hand and toss one of those to start. As that ball reaches your opposite shoulder point, toss ball two from your other hand, leaving that hand free to catch the first ball.

Remember, the next ball you toss is always one underneath the ball in the air. As ball two descends, toss the third ball and catch ball two. Freeze and check your position after each three-toss cycle. After you get the hang of it, try adding more tosses. To find expert help, call the International Jugglers Association, (413) 367-2401, for a juggling club in your area. With practice, you'll be juggling turkey legs and carving knives by New Year's Day.

At last, your 12 challenges are finished. Now head for the Gulf Coast of Florida for a little fishing. You deserve a rest.

Jack LaLanne and He Can Still

Is 85 Years Old Kick Your Butt

Isn't it time you learned how to match the old man, muscle for muscle?

BY JOE KITA

No poser: Jack's bod is still nearly as chiseled as the sculpture he modeled for a half-century ago. Kita's "needs work."

I almost puked in Jack LaLanne's bedroom. All over his flowery bedspread, right on his plush carpet, in plain view of his sweet wife, Elaine, who was finishing her makeup.

But I'm getting ahead of myself.

It's not yet 7:00 A.M., and I'm trying to match Jack in his everyday series of gut-busting good-morning exercises. Never mind that's he's 85 and I'm 40. The old man is snarling, cussing, and methodically humbling me.

"This is not pussy stuff, boy," he barks, as I hang from a chinup bar in his sprawling California home. "Come on, make it hurt! Once more! Harder! Outta my way, kid. Watch this."

And he grabs the bar, locks his knees, and proceeds to swing his legs slowly forward and up until his toes nearly touch the ceiling. Then he does it again and again and again. While doing so, he taunts his muscles as if they were street thugs surrounding him in an alley.

"C'mon, you bastards!" he yells. "See, you gotta talk to 'em. These muscles are saying, 'I can't do it anymore.' The hell you can't! I won't feed you! You sons of bitches work for me, Jack LaLanne! These muscles are my servants."

Push up the intensity: Jack believes in "vigorous, violent, daily, systematic exercise to the point of muscle failure." Kita obviously doesn't.

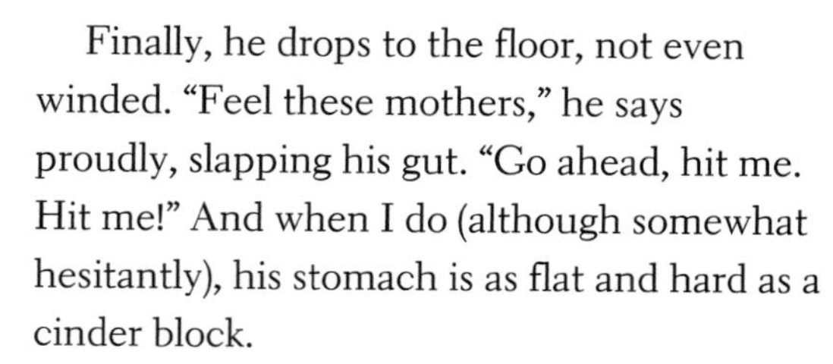

Finally, he drops to the floor, not even winded. "Feel these mothers," he says proudly, slapping his gut. "Go ahead, hit me. Hit me!" And when I do (although somewhat hesitantly), his stomach is as flat and hard as a cinder block.

"Now come over here. I'm going to show you something I invented. It's called the Hindu jump." Jack pushes me down into a squat, then orders me to spring up as high as I can. "Drop your butt almost to the floor! Now jump high, higher!" After a series of these, he has me do splits—bend both legs 90 degrees, dip down, then quickly alternate. Finally, he raises his arm to chest level and tells me to march in place, goading me to touch my knees to his hand.

"I do six sets of these three exercises," he growls, when I collapse after one.

That's when I feel like I'm going to be sick.

The Making of a Legend

Jack LaLanne is to inactivity what Jonas Salk was to polio: its scourge, its antidote. LaLanne's TV exercise show debuted in 1951. Dressed in his trademark one-piece jumpsuit and ballet slippers, the former Mr. Professional America charmed housewives everywhere.

Using nothing more than an ordinary kitchen chair, he'd get them bending and panting and perspiring. He'd talk candidly about their inner thighs, buttocks, and bustlines. He'd even sing to them when he was done. This daily 30-minute affair left aproned America flushed in more ways than one.

And in case any husbands considered him a namby-pamby, he performed incredible

Jack's Killer Exercises

Jackknife. Keep your legs, spine, and arms straight. Exhale as you reach. Hold the *V* as long as you can and, like Jack, keep smiling. Tip: Gain some extra momentum by starting with your arms stretched out on the floor behind your head.

Hindu jump/split/march. A three-part exercise. Do each segment for 30 seconds, rest, then start again (if you can).

1. Squat deeply with feet shoulder-width apart, then jump as high as possible.

2. Bend your front leg 90 degrees and bend the back one while dipping down as if into a split. Alternate right and left.

3. March in place, lifting each knee chest-high.

Dumbbell circle. While sitting on a bench or chair, grasp a 10- to 15-pound dumbbell in each hand. With palms facing each other and elbows bent, make big, slow circles in front of you.

Toe raises to ceiling. While holding on to a chinup bar or *L* seat, put your legs together, lock your knees, and slowly swing them forward and upward. Touch your toes to the ceiling. If that's too hard, bring your thighs to your chest, then straighten out your legs and lift them up from there.

Scissors (prone). Lie on your side, stabilize yourself with your arms, then straighten your legs and lift them off the ground. Swing them back and forth—the higher and wider the better. Go fast, then slow. Roll over and do the other side. A great toner for your middle.

Scissors (sitting). Grip the seat of an armless chair, straighten your legs, lift them as high as you can, then quickly and continuously cross them over each other.

Dumbbell swing. Spread your legs shoulder-width apart and bend at the waist until your back is horizontal. Use both hands to pick up a dumbbell. Keeping your knees flexed and spine straight, slowly swing it back between your legs and then up as high as you can. When your muscles start screaming, remember that Jack used to do this with 140 pounds. (If you have a bad back, avoid this exercise.)

Splayed-fingertip pushup. Lie facedown on the floor and make your body resemble an *X*, legs and arms extended into wide *V*s. Then do pushups while balancing on just your fingertips and toes.

Never Get Wrinkles!

Tone your facial muscles by doing these repeatedly each morning.

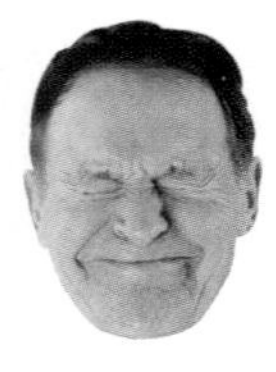

feats of strength, such as doing 1,033 pushups in 23 minutes and swimming the 6½-mile length of the Golden Gate channel, towing a 2,500-pound cabin cruiser.

No stunt was more audacious, though, than his offer of a $10,000 bounty to anyone who could keep pace with him through his morning workout. Although lots of guys took the challenge, no one ever collected—not even Arnold Schwarzenegger. Though Jack no longer publicly offers such a reward, I've convinced him to let me try. After all, how fit can a guy be at 85?

His publicist, Brenda, had been coy, divulging only that his workout consists of an hour in the gym with weights, followed by another hour in the pool. Also, she added, "He starts at 4:00 or 5:00 A.M."

With only a month to prepare, I panicked and began an intensive training program. It's amazing the focus that money brings. But the more I researched LaLanne as part of my preparation, the more his legend grew, the more maniacal he seemed, and the more intimidated I became. Entirely self-taught, he had been a skinny weakling who built up his body, then apparently never let it go to pot. On his 70th birthday, he towed 70 boats bearing a total of 70 people 1½ miles while handcuffed and shackled. When a car accident banged up his knees, he had a chinup bar installed over his hospital bed the day after surgery. His typical breakfast has long consisted of 400 different supplements, for a while chased with fresh bull's blood. He has even compared himself to Jesus—a preacher of rebirth, an invincible being, a miracle worker.

But this recent quote is what scared me most: "I believe in vigorous, violent, daily, systematic exercise to the point of muscle failure." Evidently, this has been Jack's credo since he was 15. In the same article that featured that comment, he claimed never to have missed a workout, and presented a 49-inch chest, 27-inch waist, and 17-inch biceps as proof that he wasn't lying.

So it's with trepidation that I sidestep barking dogs and barbell topiary to ring Jack's doorbell at 6:45 A.M. The evening before, when I'd called to confirm, he'd said he would push back his workout until 7:00 so I could sleep in. Brenda had also taken some last-minute pity on me, recommending I bring a wet suit since the pool water was a crisp 55°F.

"You're early," Jack snaps as he opens the door and squints at me, my photographer, and our two assistants. "You brought a damn army! Elaine!"

And with only a perfunctory greeting, he hustles us into his bedroom and immediately begins to exercise—hard. At such proximity, the legend is still impressively large, but I'm encouraged by some dents in the armor. There are small holes in Jack's blue velour jumpsuit. I have to speak loudly in order for him to hear me. He alludes to a recent shoulder injury. He's just $5^{1}/_{2}$ feet tall. And he can't instantly recall the names of his two watchdogs, Nicki and Princess.

He seems like the quintessential grandpa—cute, absentminded, and delightfully ornery—until you notice those impressive muscles and his remarkable flexibility. He boasts that a recent computer analysis pegged his physiological age at 29. Indeed, with his brown hair and bright eyes, he looks no more than 55.

As he grunts out 10-repetition sets of various crunches, Jack warms into his stage persona. When it's my turn to duplicate what's been done, he's pumped up and ready to go on. "Contract everything as hard as you can!" he raves. "C'mon!"

I keep pace on this part of the challenge, then follow him into the bathroom, where there's a small device that looks as if it came from the 1940s. Called the Mini-Gym, it resembles a bathroom scale, except that the needle specifies not weight but rather the amount of force generated when we pull on a foot-long handle. We take turns standing on the thing, doing overhead presses, bent-over rows, and pullup presses. When he finishes his set, he starts singing, "To dream the impossible dream. . . ." Although these exercises hurt like hell, I notice I'm yanking more forcefully than Jack. Despite his bravado, maybe he'll crack.

But any hope I had of pocketing the cash quickly disintegrates when he touches his toes to the ceiling and has me do those Hindu jumps.

I had lasted all of 20 minutes. "See why I had that $10,000 challenge?" asks Jack, as I fight nausea. "That's it for the warmup. Let's go to the gym."

The Competition Continues

Jack actually has two gyms in his home: one that's a daily workout room and another that's a sort of museum. The latter is stuffed with memorabilia, but most notably the exercise devices he invented and used in his original Oakland health club in 1936.

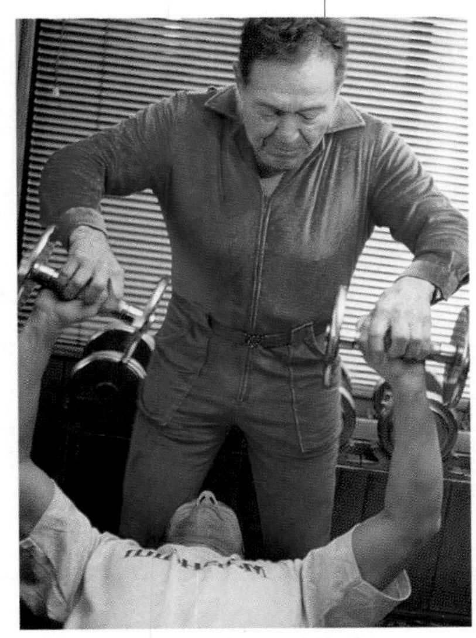

Feeling like a dumbbell: On every exercise, Jack lifts 50 more pounds than Kita does. "Hold on, kid," he yells. "That's too heavy for you."

Jack's gym and certain niches of his home have a mad-scientist feel to them. He's constantly pointing to various contraptions. "You can do over 200 exercises with that one," he says with a pitchman's fervor. "You want to market it? It'll make you a million."

Such inventiveness is fueled by an almost manic desire for new challenges. "Fitness starts between your ears," Jack says, poking himself there. "Your muscles—what the hell do they know? Nothing. It's brains. If you had to eat carrots the rest of your life, you'd go nuts. It's variety, see? That's why I change my workout every 30 days, and that's why when I had my gym, I'd invent new pieces of equipment to keep my students' interest up."

By now, we're well into the second third of the workout, and even though his $10,000 is secure, Jack isn't letting up. Lat pulldowns, seated rows—on every exercise he lifts at least 50 more pounds than I do. Inevitably, he does his set, watches me struggling with mine, then yells, "Hold on, kid, that's too heavy for you!" It's thoroughly humbling.

What's worse, while I'm sweating under the iron, Jack is coming on to my wife, whom I'd introduced as an anonymous note-taking assistant. "You're looking great. . . . You have a good butt. . . . I thought you'd be topless." Fortunately, these comments aren't dropped in a lecherous way but in the style of a guy who's brimming with life and lust. Elaine, who's 74 and still carries the nickname Tight Buns, is used to it. She and Jack have been married for nearly 50 years.

"You getting any help from Viagra?" I ask.

"Are you kidding?" he scoffs. "I wake up every morning with an erection a cat can't scratch. Let me tell you something, kid. I never think of age. Never, ever. And I never think of dying. I think of living. Any stupid ass can die. That's the easiest thing there is. But living, boy, you have to work at it."

And Jack does. His diligence with his exercise and especially his diet is obsessive. "If man makes it, I don't eat it," he says. "And I don't eat anything that comes from a cow—butter, cream, milk. I'm no suckling calf."

Breakfast, his biggest meal of the day, is a blended concoction of juice, wheat germ, brewer's yeast, bone meal, protein powder, and handfuls of vitamins and minerals. He drinks it after his workout, when he's too thirsty to mind the awful taste. Lunch is three to five pieces of fruit, vegetable soup, and four egg whites. Dinner is a salad, plus fresh fish and brown rice.

"Look at my Corvette, a '98—one of the finest sports cars I've ever had. Would I put water in the gas tank? Well, think about the crap people put in their bodies—white flour, sugar, all this processed food. It's just like using water for fuel."

With that, he tells me it's time to get wet.

Staying Afloat, Staying Alive

"Strangers in the Night" is playing softly in the pool yard when I step outside dressed in my new wet suit. Jack is already in the adjacent hot tub, suspiciously devoid of any insulation except swim trunks.

I toe the icy water, then follow orders. He drill-sergeants me through another series of bizarre exercises. While I float on my stomach and grip the side of the pool, he has me kick without bending my knees. Then he throws me a pair of neoprene mitts (another invention) and has me do arm exercises against the increased water resistance. Finally, he waves toward a white strap and says, "Put that on."

It's the crudest device yet. It looks like a seat belt that's been ripped from an old Buick. It's attached to a thick rope that's bolted to the side of the pool. "Buckle it around your waist and start butterflying," says Jack. My thrashing prompts Nicki and Princess to start barking. They sense that someone's in trouble.

After just a few minutes, I thank God for the extra buoyancy of my wet suit. "How does it feel?" he taunts. "I did that for an hour when I was training for my boat pulls."

The genius behind Jack's training style is

The loves of his life: Swimming, strutting, and, yes, sex. Wife Elaine, 74, is nicknamed Tight Buns.

intensity. Every exercise is done as hard as possible. If you're going to make the effort to work out, then go all out.

Completeness is Jack's other credo. He claims he works every one of the 640 muscles in his body every day. This includes goofy facial contortions and picking up marbles with his toes.

After the challenge is finished and all 640 of my muscles are sufficiently aggravated, Jack leads me up the stairs into his "little escape." I brace for another torture chamber. But there's a deck with a marvelous view, an aquarium with tropical fish that Jack talks to, a big-screen TV, and a leather recliner that swallows him when he sinks into it. For the first time today, he is motionless.

I have been thoroughly impressed by this man—his ability, his spirit, his gutter wisdom. It wouldn't be hyperbole to use the word *hero*. But watching him here, I start to have another feeling. It's sadness (or dare I say pity?), because I can tell that he's clinging. When I tried to put a tape measure around his famous physique, he balked, conceding that his chest is a less-impressive 46, waist 31, and biceps 15 only because he's no longer competing. But I think he's exaggerating. He doesn't want the world to see that he's slipped, that Jack LaLanne isn't invincible, that ultimately death will ruin his image. Sitting here, he seems tired, and not from the exercise.

For all he has accomplished, at this moment he seems forgotten and remarkably hidden away. Although he still lectures and produces videos, most people are surprised to learn he's still alive.

For baby boomers who are doing everything possible to ensure that they'll never die, it seems ironic that we've overlooked the poster boy. He's the man in the blue velour jumpsuit. He is me. He is you. If we're smart. If we take care of ourselves.

Not that we won't die. Not that we won't age. Just that we can do both with vibrancy, grace, and dignity. That's the last exercise in Jack's show, the one he's teaching us now.

"Man alive, wake up!" he shouts. "You're half dead."

HANDS-ON EXPERIENCE

Q: I started rock climbing and bouldering and really enjoy it. But my hands are too weak for me to get really good. What can I do?

H. G., TACOMA, WASHINGTON

A: There are tons of great, albeit slightly unconventional, ways to strengthen your climbing grip. For instance, you can perform standard exercises like bench presses, curls, and rows with what's known as a "fat" bar. This specialized bar, which measures more than twice as thick as a standard Olympic bar, challenges your hand muscles while providing the usual stimulus for the primary muscles you're training. If you don't have access to a fat bar, you can make your own simply by wrapping a bath towel around a standard Olympic bar.

You can also use towels to increase the grip component of other challenging exercises such as pullups and cable rows. For pullups, drape two towels over the bar, about shoulder-width apart, and grab both ends of a towel in each hand. For cable rows, thread a towel through the cable handle and grab the ends.

Finally, try pinching some weight plates. Place two 10-pound plates together and hold them between four fingers and your thumb for as long as possible. By the time you get up to using the 45s, you'll be climbing Kilamanjaro.

OUTDOORS

Hike Up Your Effort

If you're planning a trek of 10 miles a day on steep terrain this summer—and you hope to enjoy it—you have to condition your body. Otherwise, you'll end up a sore, miserable, broken man. Trust us. We've done it without training. In new boots. It was ugly.

Here's the right way to go, from the editors of *Backpacker* magazine.

- **Make either running, swimming, or cycling the foundation of your pretrip program. Keep your workouts at a moderate intensity to mimic backpacking. Remember: It's hiking, not sprinting.**
- **Strengthen your legs, back, and torso with a routine of lunges, squats, crunches, and pullups.**
- **Take several 30-minute brisk walks with a backpack every week to build strength and get your body familiar with walking while shouldering a load. Pack light at first, then build up to the load you'll carry on your trip. Wear the boots you plan to take.**
- **Go on at least one warmup hike, ideally 6 weeks before your long trek. Carry the full weight, but cut the distance and elevation gain in half. For more training tips and hiking information, go to www.backpacker.com.**

FITNESS

Size Yourself Up

If you've spent too many years frustrated by your inability to dunk, consider buying a new hoop—one made by Nerf. Or, even better, consult this chart we've compiled with the help of Lincoln E. Ford, M.D., of the Indiana University school of medicine. He actually studied what sports best match different heights.

YOUR HEIGHT	YOUR IDEAL SPORTS	WHY
6' 1"	Basketball, tennis, boxing	You're tall enough to have a long, lethal reach, but not so tall that you can't speed around the court or ring.
5' 11"	Football, softball (preferably center field)	NFL running backs are usually smaller than other players. You can pack powerful muscles onto shorter, speedier legs, so you can explode quickly past tacklers or sprint to snag a line drive.
5' 8"	Distance running, cycling, swimming	Your body mass is naturally lighter because of your height, which is ideal for covering long distances.
5' 6"	Middle-distance running, or, uh, pushup contests	Quick, sudden movements are ideal because your limbs rotate quicker than those of bigger guys.

ADVANTAGE: YOU

Q: I've always been one of the strongest guys in my gym. Now that I've turned 40, the manager of the gym is trying to talk me into competing in Masters powerlifting competitions. Is this a smart thing to do at my age? How do I get ready for this?

P. M., FT. LAUDERDALE

A: Besides being a great way to stay in shape, actively competing in powerlifting will keep you motivated and focused on your training. But because powerlifting centers on lifts like squats and deadlifts, many people erroneously think it's dangerous, especially if you take it up at age 40. Truth is, as long as you always emphasize proper technique over how much weight you lift, you should be fine.

To prepare for this kind of competition you need to focus your efforts on the big core lifts like squats, deadlifts, and bench presses. In addition, you should include what are known as "assistance lifts," which strengthen the surrounding muscles. This means exercises like close-grip bench presses and overhead presses for shoulder and triceps strength, along with good mornings and reverse hyperextensions for lower-back strength.

HARD TRUTH

It's time to walk the walk

Which of these abilities would you most like to have?

Run a 4-minute mile
25%

Bench-press 300 pounds
24%

Dunk a basketball
21%

Throw a 90-mph fastball
14%

Hit a 300-yard drive
12.5%

Kick a 50-yard field goal
3.5%

SOURCE: a poll of 2,293 visitors to www.menshealth.com

STAY IN THE GAME

PART SIX

When you were a kid, your most serious "sports injury" was getting beaned in the head during a wicked game of dodgeball. Now that you're adult, you're bigger and stronger . . . and slower . . . and less resilient.

So in this section, we'll tell you how to dodge the most common injuries that can send you to the bench—or even to the emergency room. Then we'll show you how to baby the achy muscles that are a natural result of a game well-played, so you can come back faster, stronger, and better than before.

MH•QUIZ

Test Your Emergency IQ

Along with the benefits you get from exercise, you also run the risk of some pretty nasty injuries. Weight training alone causes nearly 50,000 visits to the emergency room each year. And weekend-warrior mishaps cause many more.

Every one of the scenarios below is serious enough to make calling 911 your first priority. Would you know what to do in the precious minutes before the paramedics arrive? Take this quiz to find out.

1 While out for your morning run, you see another runner sprawled in the grass, moaning and clutching his chest, so you . . .

- **a. Check for a pulse**
- **b. Start CPR**
- **c. Tell him to do his thing in private**

2 You're slicing through fresh powder until you come across another skier, who's exhausted, wheezing, and fighting for breath, so you . . .

- **a. Assume he's just out of shape**
- **b. Give him mouth-to-mouth**
- **c. Get help from a resort staffer**

3 After two players bonk heads during a pickup hoops game, one of them starts raving about his failing marriage, so you . . .

- **a. Tell him to walk it off**
- **b. Ask if he blacked out, even for a moment**
- **c. Recommend a good attorney**

4 It's third and long. The quarterback takes a blow to the neck, so you . . .

- **a. Volunteer to take his place**
- **b. Escort him to the sidelines**
- **c. Don't let him move a muscle**

5 In the gym, the schlub next to you loses his grip on the bench press and drops 200 pounds on his chest, so you . . .

- **a. Tell him to go back to circuit training**
- **b. Offer to give him a spot next time**
- **c. See if he's short of breath**

6 Your rock-climbing buddy takes a nasty spill and starts bleeding profusely, so you . . .

- **a. Apply pressure to the wound**
- **b. Hand him a Band-Aid**
- **c. Reassure him that it's only a flesh wound**

7 One of your front teeth gets knocked out while you're playing a "friendly" game of wiffle ball. You . . .

- **a. Suck it up and act like a man**
- **b. Pick a fight with an opposing team member**
- **c. Consider how different life would be if Kirsten Dunst were the tooth fairy**

ANSWERS

1. **a. Assess the situation.** Does he have a pulse? Is he breathing? If so, keep your hands and your mouth off him; chest compressions or CPR could cause more damage. Is he exposed to the sun? Carefully move him to a shaded area. "Exposure to high temperatures causes your heart to beat more quickly and your blood pressure to drop,

both of which can worsen a heart attack," says David Meyerson, M.D., a cardiologist at Johns Hopkins and a spokesman for the American Heart Association.

2. c. Call the ski patrol. Exercise-induced asthma is a common medical emergency, especially in cold weather. People with asthma usually carry a short-acting rescue inhaler in case of an emergency. But if the skier has forgotten his rescue inhaler or is so incapacitated that he can't get to it, immediately tell a resort staff member. If the resort doesn't have a rescue inhaler, bottled oxygen can help stabilize the person until paramedics arrive with medication.

3. b. Find out whether he passed out. Even a momentary loss of consciousness is a sign of concussion. So are confusion, nausea, dizziness, unsteadiness, and embarrassing emotional outbursts. "If you hit your head hard enough to knock yourself out, there may be underlying bruising or bleeding," says Thomas Waters, M.D., a Cleveland Clinic emergency-room physician. Even if the player didn't knock himself out, he should stay out of the game until his head clears.

4. c. Keep him as still as possible. Never try to move someone with a neck injury. Permanent paralysis can result if an injured person even tries to lift his head. Make the QB lie still and, if necessary, restrain him until paramedics arrive with a cervical collar. *Emergency tip:* Although severe neck pain is a sign of spinal-cord injury, it's especially worrisome when accompanied by any numbness or tingling elsewhere in the body. Sometimes these symptoms take 24 hours to develop.

5. c. Check his respiration. Shortness of breath and/or extreme chest pain is a sign of a punctured lung. Get your workout pal to rest and calm down. If there's oxygen available, use it. *Emergency tip:* Such injuries often result in an open chest wound. "If you can hear breathing going through the hole, cover it with a clean dressing taped down on three sides so some air can escape through the fourth side," Dr. Waters says.

6. a. Put pressure on him. Uncontrolled bleeding from a severed vein or artery can quickly result in shock and death. If there are no broken bones, elevate the injured area to help slow the bleeding. Then place a sterile dressing or clean cloth on the wound, and apply direct pressure for at least 10 minutes. If the dressing becomes soaked with blood, don't remove it. Instead, place another bandage on top. "Tourniquets should only be applied as a last resort," Dr. Waters says.

7. a. Finish the play, then drop to the ground and try to locate your recently departed incisor. Once you find the thing, douse it with cool water (too hot or too cold and you'll damage the exposed tissue) and put it back in the socket. "This will help provide initial stabilization that will greatly enhance the success of reimplantation," says Keith Kirkwood, D.D.S., Ph.D., of the SUNY Buffalo school of dental medicine. Now go get reimplanted. And next time, slide home feet first.

—RICK ANSORGE

BY SKYLER KENSHO

More Strength, Less Suffering

Don't let injuries sideline you in the weight room. Try these simple solutions for trouble-triggering lifts

When the weight plate landed on your big toe, you knew exactly what the problem was—you were paying attention to her hams instead of your hands. The most common weight-lifting injuries, however, are much more difficult to diagnose. They result from doing exercises that aren't quite right for your unique musculature, or from aggravating a preexisting injury, says Ken Kinakin, a sports chiropractor in Toronto and founder of the Society of Weight-Training Injury Specialists. A lift that may build fast muscle for your friend or

Build muscles like his with these alternative lifts—but please, spare us the pose.

trainer, for example, could bring nothing but pain to your shoulder, back, or knees simply because you're built a certain way.

The worst thing you can do is to keep lifting through the pain. The second-worst thing is to avoid exercising the painful parts altogether. "That's like putting your car in the garage if your tires are out of alignment. A month later, they'll still be out of alignment," says Kinakin.

A better strategy: If a certain lift hurts, treat any injuries, and try substituting another movement that works the same body part from a different angle. Need some suggestions? Following are alternative exercises for a lifter's most annoying pain zones.

Shoulder Pain

Key culprit: the shoulder press. The shoulder-press machine found in most gyms is not built for everybody. Heck, it's not built for most people. It forces lifters' arms into an unnatural motion that causes "the small, vulnerable muscles of the rotator cuff to get pinched between the bones of the shoulder joint," says Nicholas DiNubile, M.D., an orthopedic surgeon and a consultant to the Philadelphia 76ers. The traditional barbell shoulder press can cause the same problem. Over time, these lifts can trigger rotator-cuff tendinitis.

To get the benefits without the pain, try the touchdown shoulder press instead. Grasp two dumbbells, palms facing each other. Now, press them straight overhead as if you were signaling a touchdown. Keeping your palms facing in and arms directly above your shoulders eliminates the pinch. If this still bothers you, try raising one arm at a time, alternating arms.

IF THIS HURTS . . .

TRY THIS . . .

IF THIS BOTHERS YOU . . .	IT'S PROBABLY BECAUSE . . .	SO TRY THIS INSTEAD . . .
Lateral raise	Your upper-arm bone is pinching the connective tissues inside your shoulder joint.	Bent lateral raise: Lie chest-down on an incline bench set between 45 and 60 degrees. Raise dumbbells out to your sides.
Barbell upright row with a narrow grip	See above.	Wide-grip upright row; or use dumbbells and alternate arms on each repetition.
Smith-machine bench press	A normal barbell bench press uses an arcing motion—you lift the bar back and up. With a Smith machine, you can only lift it up, pinching your shoulders as described above.	Barbell bench press.
Barbell bench press	The motion is aggravating a preexisting injury, usually on your dominant side (i.e., your right shoulder if you're right handed).	Dumbbell bench press: Dumbbells allow a more natural motion. Keeping your elbows in close to your torso will leave the joint less vulnerable to strain.

Lower-Back Pain

Key culprit: the squat. The squat is always implicated—unfairly—in lower-back injuries. It's actually a very safe and extremely effective exercise if it's done properly. But a lot of men lean forward too far, which puts strain on the lumbar region. The simple fix: Try the Zercher squat. Hold a barbell in the crook of your elbows or a dumbbell in front of your chest. Your torso will stay more upright. Now squat until your thighs are parallel to the floor.

IF THIS HURTS . . .

TRY THIS . . .

IF THIS BOTHERS YOU . . .	IT'S PROBABLY BECAUSE . . .	SO TRY THIS INSTEAD . . .
Smith-machine squat	The machine is forcing your lower back out of its naturally arched alignment, weakening its stability.	Barbell squat.
Stiff-legged deadlift	You're leaning forward too far and taking your lower back out of its natural alignment.	Romanian deadlift: It's almost the same thing, except you stop lowering the weight when your back starts to round unnaturally.
Bent-over barbell row	You could have a joint problem, or the muscles in your lower back are fatiguing too quickly because they're weak.	Seated cable row with a variety of grips—wide, narrow, medium, overhand, and underhand—or the one-arm dumbbell row.

Dumbbell Injuries

Learn from these boneheaded mistakes collected during an informal poll of exercisers at Powerhouse Gym in Chatsworth, California.

Anthony: "This guy was trying to determine his one-rep max on the bench—by himself. He tore his pec right off his shoulder, and it balled up like a melon in the middle of his chest."

Aida: "Once I was running on the treadmill and turned to say hi to a friend of mine, but tripped and shot off the back of the machine. I got a bloody nose and broke my thumb."

Marcus: "Some guy caught his gym-bag strap on a weight tree, fell, and knocked himself out on a plate."

Charlotte: "I had a boyfriend who had a bench in his basement. He broke his nose by dropping the bar on his face. After it healed, he did the same thing again! Boys."

Chris: "I was having a smoothie after my workout and was looking at this chick while I was leaning over to take a sip—and jammed the straw right in my eye. I had to go to the emergency room with a corneal abrasion and a partially detached retina."

Knee Pain

Key culprit: the leg extension. Leg-extension machines are sneaky saboteurs. Your knees aren't designed to support heavy weights at the odd angle this machine forces on them. The leg extension is, however, a great exercise for rehabilitation if you use very light weights. But if you're trying to build muscle, skip it and use the leg-press machine, which works your quadriceps and the knee-supporting tendons even better.

TOUGH TALK

"Overtraining can hinder any gains, cause injury, and discourage you from your goals. Since you actually build size while you're resting, I also try to get 8 hours of sleep a night."

MIKE BROWN, *MEN'S HEALTH* BELLY-OFF CLUB MEMBER, ON LOSING 35 POUNDS

IF THIS BOTHERS YOU . . .	IT'S PROBABLY BECAUSE . . .	SO TRY THIS INSTEAD . . .
Lunge	The forward momentum is putting more pressure on your kneecap than it can handle.	Step-back lunge: Step backward as you lower your body, allowing your front knee to bend without as much stress on the kneecap. This shifts some emphasis from your quadriceps to your gluteals and hamstrings, however.
Squat	Your knees drift forward as your weight shifts from your heels to your toes.	Lateral lunge: Lunge to the side, or at a 45-degree angle—whichever you can do without pain—suggests Neil Chasan, a physical therapist in Seattle.

IF THIS HURTS . . .

TRY THIS . . .

BY MYATT MURPHY

Rub Out Muscle Pain

To beat aches and stiffness—and even inspire your muscles to grow—learn the simple science of sports self-massage

Whether you spend your Saturdays dunking, throwing, biking, or just mowing, chances are you and every other active guy on the planet have one thing in common: muscle pain, and plenty of it.

A professional athlete would spend an hour packed in ice, take a spin in the whirlpool, work through a series of stretching exercises with the trainer and maybe pick up a prescription for one of the team doctor's "feel-good specials." For a regular guy, muscle pain is more likely to mean a crazed medicine-cabinet excavation in search of that near-empty tube of BenGay you remember from last spring.

You may not have access to all those professionals and their pharmaceuticals, but you can fight muscle soreness with one of their most potent weapons: sports massage. The pros know there's more to massage than just muscle relaxation. It draws out the lactic acid that causes muscle soreness and can improve range of motion, speed muscle recovery, prevent overuse injuries, even soften scar tissue from past injuries.

Don't have the time—or the dough—for this indulgence? No problem, says Joan Johnson, author of *The Healing Art of Sports Massage*. "There's no reason you can't treat yourself to a full-body sports massage anytime you want," she says. "All you need are your own two hands." It may not be as relaxing as the real thing, but then again, nobody else need see you buck naked, either.

This program works through every muscle group, identifying common trouble spots for active men. To keep your hands from tiring, Johnson recommends working on your finger endurance twice a day by squeezing a foam ball, a lump of clay, a tennis ball—anything that won't get you arrested if you squeeze it in public. Start by using your entire hand to squeeze, then work each finger and your thumb individually, until your hands give out.

Do all of the following techniques seated on a mat on the floor. This position will help you relax and let you reach certain parts of your body without straining your back. Also, keep a moist, hot towel nearby to warm your hands. The heat helps loosen the muscles more easily. Keep every stroke smooth, and spend a little extra time on tight or tender areas. And, of course, give equal time to both sides of your body.

Feet

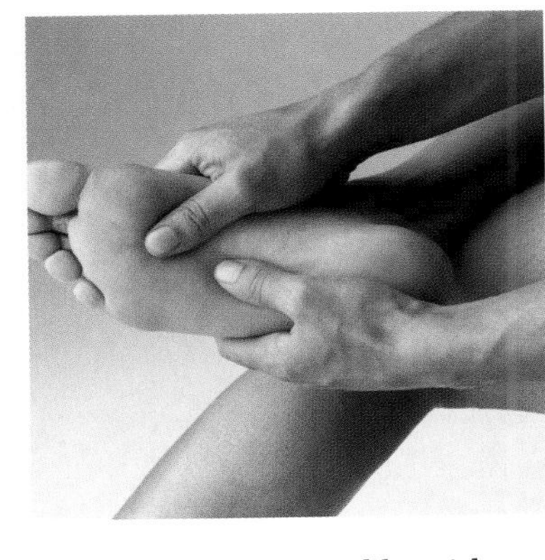

Sit on the floor, legs straight in front of you, and rest one foot over the thigh of the opposite leg, so your legs form a figure 4. Hold your ankle with one hand and slowly rotate the foot clockwise with the other hand in small to large circles. Reverse the motion counterclockwise. Repeat three times in each direction. Next, grab your foot from the sides with both hands (as shown). Begin to stroke lengthwise up and down your sole, pressing your thumbs deep into it. After you've finished with the long strokes, use your thumbs to make a series of small circles up and down the sole. Don't forget to keep your fingers working along the arch. Finish by gently separating and pulling each toe sideways, then back and forth.

Lower Leg

Sports that require you to push off vertically (basketball), horizontally (sprinting), or laterally (hockey) stress the lower legs. Start with the calves. Bend your right leg and grab the bottom of your calf muscle with both hands. Apply pressure with your thumbs and slide your hands up the leg to the back of the knee. Repeat three times. Next, place your thumbs together at the top of your calf. Apply pressure and slowly pull your thumbs away from each other. Lower your hands about a half-inch and repeat, working down your calf until you reach your ankle. Repeat three times. For the shins, grip your ankle with fingers behind your calf and thumbs together in the front. Stroke up the shin, then work back down in a series of small circles.

Quadriceps

This massage will be especially therapeutic after your first day on the slopes. To limber up the big muscles in the front of the thigh, squeeze the three middle fingers of your

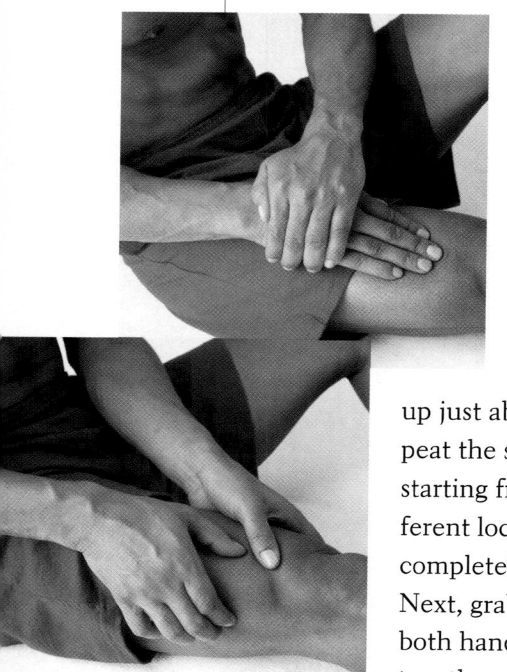

right hand together and press them into the top of your right thigh. Place your left hand over your right hand to help you apply more pressure. Slide your hands down your thigh until they end up just above the kneecap. Repeat the stroke, each time starting from a slightly different location on the thigh to completely loosen the muscle. Next, grab your thigh between both hands with your thumbs together and fingers wrapped around your leg. Begin moving your thumbs in a circular motion as you slide your hands toward your knee. Repeat several times.

Hamstrings

Any athlete whose sport involves running, even just to fetch an errant lawn dart, is subject to tight hamstrings. To work them out, lie flat on your back with your right foot over your left knee. Grab your right leg just above the knee with both hands, with your fingers pressing into the back of your leg

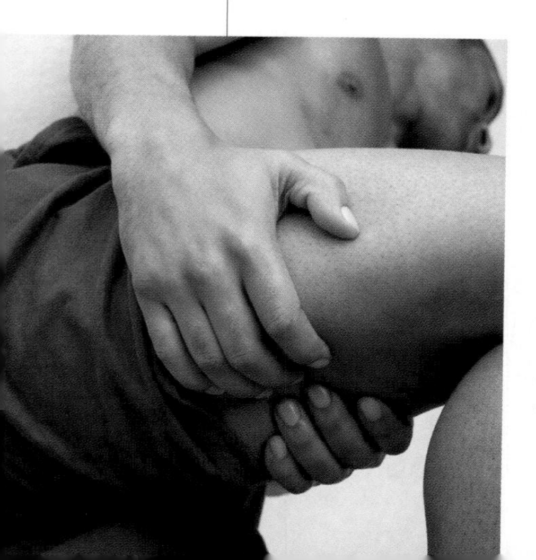

and your thumbs on top by your kneecap. Run your hands up your thigh, using your fingers to apply pressure as you go. Repeat several times. Finally, press the fingers of either hand into the middle of your hamstrings and slowly rub across the leg from side to side. (Apply enough pressure that your fingers don't slide across your skin.) Move your fingers every few seconds to work the entire muscle. For all of these motions, avoid putting direct pressure on the very back of the knee, where fragile tendons and ligaments lurk.

Lower Back

Sports that twist the body at the waist (golf, racquetball, girl watching) can really wring out the lower back, but let's face it: Once you're north of 30, your lower back always benefits from a little loosening. Start by lying on your back with your knees bent, feet flat on the floor. Stick a tennis ball directly under your lower back and place as much of your body weight as you can on the ball. Hold for a few seconds, then lift yourself and readjust the position of the ball. Continue to lower yourself onto the ball to apply pressure to all areas of the lower back.

Upper Back

Sports that require you to push off with the arms, like cross-country skiing, can make your upper back so stiff, a straitjacket would feel more comfortable. This also applies to any throwing sports like baseball or football. To loosen up, place your left hand behind your head so that your left elbow points upward. This will keep your arm out of the way while you work the left side of your body. Your fingertips should be pressed together to help you apply deeper pressure into the muscles. Press your right hand against the left side of your back, directly below your left armpit, and stroke downward toward your waist. Once you reach the bottom, lift your hand and place it at a different location below your left armpit. You can also go across the back muscles, starting from the side and moving toward the center of the back, using short strokes as you go.

Neck

The neck is a spot where tension always seems to build up, even if your day consists of doing nothing but sitting at your desk and listening to your boss scream. To massage the right side of your neck, place the fingers of your right hand into the trapezius muscle, just below the base of your skull. Press into the muscle and slowly drag your fingers down and over toward your right shoulder while simultaneously tilting your head to the left. Your left ear should approach your left shoulder. Repeat this motion several times.

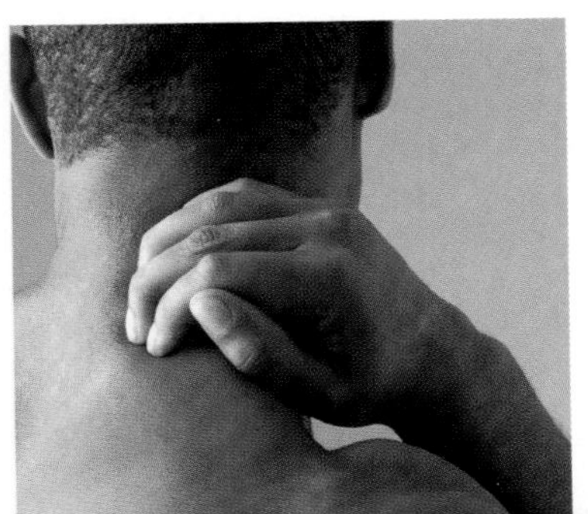

Shoulders

Okay, Atlas, time to shrug off that burden. Start by bringing your left hand across your body and placing it on your right shoulder. Take your right hand and cup the bottom of your left elbow. This will keep your left hand stable when you start to massage. Bring the fingers of your left hand together and press them deep into your shoulder muscle. Slowly rock your fingers back and forth into the muscle for a few seconds, then place your fingertips a half-inch away and repeat. Continue this press-and-rock motion until you've thoroughly worked the entire shoulder muscle.

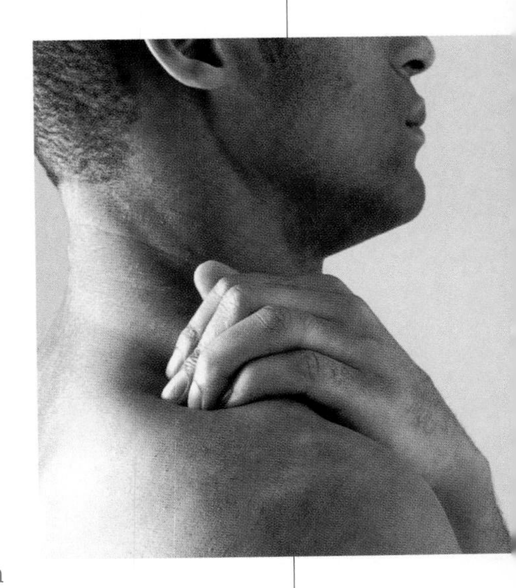

Chest

Trying to impress that cute aerobics instructor with how much you can bench can make waking up the next morning a painful

experience. To begin this massage, assume the same starting position you used to work your upper back—right hand behind your head, elbow pointing upward. Next, press the middle three fingers of your left hand together. Now you're ready to start. Begin by pressing the fingertips of your left hand into the area directly below your right nipple. Now gently move your hand upward toward your right shoulder, maintaining a light pressure. Once you reach your shoulder, lift your hand and place it below the nipple again, this time a half-inch away in either direction from where you originally started. Repeat the process, making sure to work through the entire area of the muscle.

Triceps

This massage will help you recover after any activity where you throw, hit, serve, or pass (such as, say, working as a bouncer in a sports bar). Bend your left arm at a 90-degree angle and rest your left hand on your stomach. Wrap your right arm around yourself and cup your right hand over the back of your left arm, just below the shoulder. Press your right hand into the triceps muscle and slowly move it down your arm toward the left elbow. Straighten your left arm as you go. (The area just above the elbow can be tender, so take it slow.) Your right hand should end up cupping your left elbow, with your left arm straight down at your side. Bend your left arm back into a 90-degree position and repeat three times.

Biceps

Pushed yourself a little too hard in the gym? To give yourself a shot in the arm, start by using your left hand to grab your right arm just above the elbow, so that your thumb points up toward your right shoulder. Your fingers should wrap around the outside of your arm and rest on the outside of your triceps. With your right arm down at your side, gently press your thumb into the biceps muscle and stroke upward toward your shoulder. Repeat several times. Next, reach your hand under your arm and place your thumb at the top of the bi-

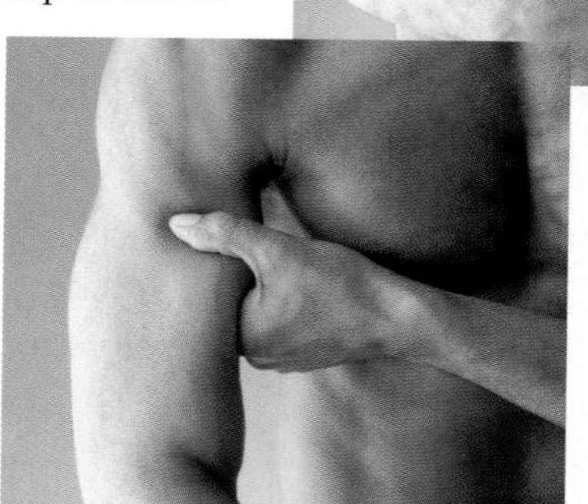

ceps muscle below the shoulder. Your fingers should rest lightly underneath your arm. Press down gently with your thumb and push it from side to side across the tendon. Repeat several times. Pay extra attention to your dominant arm (the one you throw or hit with).

TOUGH TALK

"Sometimes you have to step away today to make sure you can play tomorrow."

SHAWON DUNSTON, ST. LOUIS CARDINALS SHORTSTOP

Forearms

Maybe you don't spend your Saturdays hanging from a sheer cliff face (or maybe you do), but no matter what your sport, your forearms can take a beating. Swinging a tennis racket, lugging a dumbbell, even riding a bike for a long stretch of time will build tension. Work it out by pressing your right thumb into the inside of your left forearm just above the wrist. Push it up along the forearm until it rests just below the bend in your elbow, then pull it back down, keeping tension on the forearm all the way. To work the other side (the hairy side), press your thumb into your forearm and begin opening and closing your fist. You'll feel the muscles writhe under your thumb.

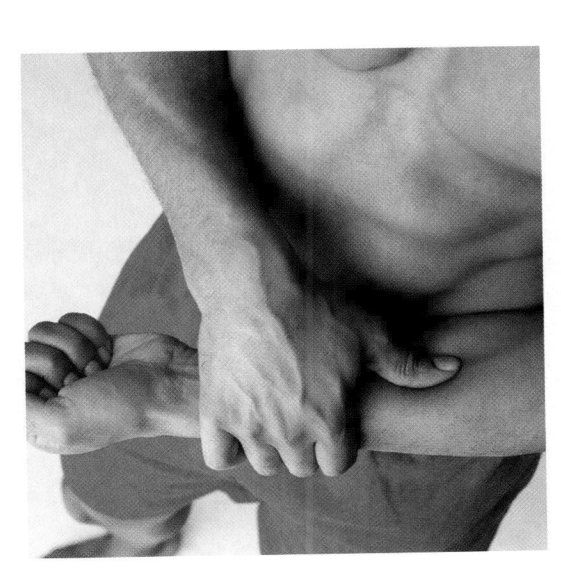

Hands

All this massage may stiffen your hands, so give them a rub, too. Begin by gently pulling each of your fingers with the thumb and fingers of your opposite hand. Gently stroke each finger as you go, applying firm but gentle pressure to any sore or tender areas. To work out the palm, loosely clasp your hands together by intertwining your fingers. Touch the thumb of your massaging hand to the area just below your opposite thumb and apply direct pressure for several seconds. Keep moving your massaging thumb around in a spiral, applying short bursts of pressure each time, until your thumb ends up in the center of your palm. Finish by stroking your thumb up and down into your palm.

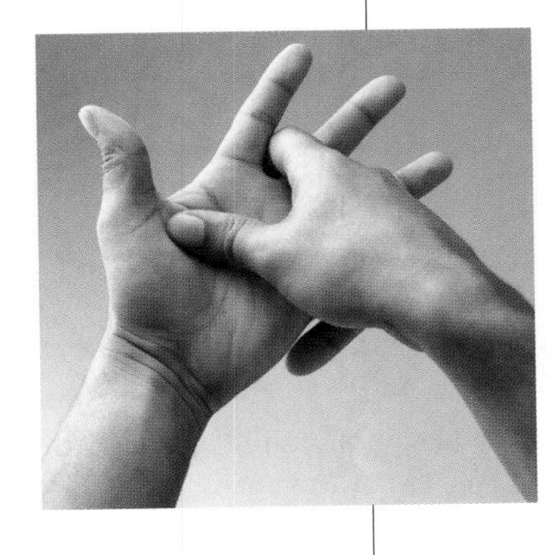

Trainer's Forum

with MICHAEL MEJIA

SLOW GO

Q: I was in pretty good shape for a few years but haven't exercised at all for about 3 months. How do I get back into my regular routine? And how quickly?

W. F., ELIZABETH, NEW JERSEY

A: Suck it up and start slow. I know that sounds like a cliché, but no way will you be able to pick up where you left off—so don't bother trying. At best you'll end up incredibly sore, and at worst seriously injured.

The fact that you were previously in good shape makes you one step ahead of the guy who's just starting out. So my guess is that after 6 to 8 weeks of the right type of training, you'll be back up to speed. Follow these simple rules:

For the first 3 to 4 weeks, keep your weights relatively light (40 to 60 percent of your one-rep max), and your reps high (12 to 20). This will help strengthen your connective tissue so you can progress to heavier weights later on.

Avoid training to the point of failure. End your sets knowing you still have another rep or two in the tank.

It's worth repeating: Progress slowly.

Make small increases to the intensity or duration of your workout—but never both at once.

HARD TRUTH

A Canadian study found that golfers who tightened their abdominal muscles at the start of their swing had less back pain than those who didn't.

GUY WISDOM

Heating Elements

Nothing like getting a winter jump on golf, tennis, or baseball. But a vigorous warmup that raises the body's core temperature is crucial to avoiding muscle pulls and back spasms. Whether it takes 5 minutes or 15, wait for your ready signal: a mild sweat. Here's how to hurry that along.

▶Stay indoors for your warmup and put that warm air to use. Find a corner of the clubhouse for aerobic exercises and dynamic stretches, like windmills and empty-handed swings. Apologize for inadvertent fat lips.

▶Leave your sweatshirt, sweater, or coat on—or all three—during your warmup. Forget style—you just need to raise your temp. Despite what Mom told you, going outside while sweating won't make you ill.

REMEDIES

Rest for Tennis Elbow

A yearlong Dutch study of 185 men and women with tennis elbow found that traditional "wait and see" treatment—rest plus anti-inflammatories—is just as effective as physical therapy and better than newer options like steroid injections.

SORE SIGN

Q: My muscles are hardly ever sore after a workout. Does that mean I'm not getting the results I should? Is soreness necessary for increases in muscle strength and size?

M. J., SURREY, BRITISH COLUMBIA

A: Soreness is overrated. I say this because soreness is the result of unfamiliar, intense exercise. Your muscles could hurt as much after the annual company softball game as after a tough workout. And we all know a couple hours of "beer ball" isn't going to pack on the muscle.

Now, while soreness definitely isn't necessary, a little is usually a good indication that you're on the right track. Never being sore can be an indication that your body has become completely accustomed to the training stimulus. Once this happens, you can forget about making any new gains in size or strength. Change your program every 4 to 6 weeks and constantly push yourself to do a little bit more each time you're in the gym. This way you'll be just sore enough to know you're still making progress.

MIND/BODY

It's a Guy Thing

Ever notice that when you and a buddy are zoned out playing Madden 2001 and your wife reminds you it's her birthday by whapping you upside the head . . . it doesn't hurt? Here's why. Athletic competition dulls us to pain—it's called stress-induced analgesia. A study at Haverford College in Pennsylvania found that this effect extends to the cyber realm. Researchers tested pain tolerance of men and women after they participated in a track meet and after they played video games. Both sexes had decreased pain sensitivity after the track meet, but only the men got a pain-killing buzz from video games.

ANKLE WAITS

Q: I sprained my ankle sliding into second base. I know I can't play ball for a while, but what *can* I do to stay in shape?

B. R., HUTCHINSON, KANSAS

A: I'm sure I don't need to tell you this, but make sure to get your doc's okay before you start any exercise program after an injury. Once you've got the green light, your biggest challenges will be lower-body training and cardiovascular conditioning. Obviously, upper-body work won't pose much of a problem.

In terms of strength training, stay away from exercises that load the ankle and are weight bearing in nature. This means you'll have to replace lifts like squats, deadlifts, and lunges with leg extensions and leg curls. They're not the most powerful lower-body exercises you can do, but they'll work until your ankle heals.

Cardio can be a little trickier. Once again, avoid putting pressure on your ankle. That means running and stairclimbing are out. Swimming, riding a stationary bike, or using an upper-body ergometer are probably your best bets for getting your heart rate going.

Credits

Cover Photograph

Alan Donatone, photographed by **Mitch Mandel/Rodale Images**

Interior Photographs

Pages v, 45, 47, 48, 86, 88, and 89: **Mitch Mandel/Rodale Images**
Page vi (top left), 93, 102, 103, 110, 118, 119, 134, 135, 142, and 143: **Richard Corman**
Pages vi (top right) and 165: **David E. Klutho/Sports Illustrated**
Pages vi (bottom right), 208–9, 210, 211, 212, 213, and 215: **Danny Rothenberg**
Pages 1 and 32: **Dorit Thies**
Pages 4, 5, 6, 9, and 11: **Carlos Serrao**
Pages 14–15: **Steven Lippman**
Page 24: **Getty Images**
Page 35: **Frank Trapper/Corbis Sygma**
Page 36 (left): **Otto Greule/Allsport**
Page 36 (right): **Walter McBride/Retna**
Page 37: **Lorenzo Cinglio/Corbis Sygma**
Pages 41, 42, and 44: **Laura Johansen**
Pages 52, 53 (left column), and 172: **Coolife**
Page 53 (right column): **Mark Platt**
Page 54: **Andrew Southam**
Pages 57, 58, and 59: **Jessica Wecker**
Pages 60, 61, and 62: **Joseph Rodriguez**
Page 64: **AP World Wide Photos**
Pages 68–69, 70 (bottom), 71, 74, and 77: **Joseph Oppedissano**
Page 70 (top): **Steven A. Downs/Archive Photos**
Pages 72, 80, 91, 96, 97, 98, 99, 100, 101, 104, 105, 106, 107, 108, 109, 112, 113, 114, 115, 116, 117, 120, 121, 122, 123, 124, 125, 128, 129, 130, 131, 132, 133, 136, 137, 138, 139, 140, 141, 144, 145, 146, 147, 150, 151, 152, 153, 154, 155, 223, 224, and 225: **Beth Bischoff**
Page 73: **George Rose/Gamma Liaison**
Pages 79, 81, 126, 127, 148, and 149: **Mark Havriliak**
Page 90: **Eric Kamp**
Pages 94 and 95: **Darryl Estrine**
Pages 156 and 218: **Linda Churilla**
Page 161: **Tom Ratalovich**
Page 162: **Davis Factor/Corbis Outline**
Page 163: **Ron Turenne-NBAE/Getty Images**
Page 166: **Michael Grecco/Icon**
Pages 169 and 170: **Mark Seelen**
Pages 174, 176, and 178: **Sue Williams**
Page 180: **Mark Hanauer**
Page 182: **Jeff Carlick**
Page 183: **Sean Murphy**
Page 184: **Visko Hatfield**
Page 189: **Girl Ray**
Pages 191 and 194: **Image Bank**
Pages 196 and 197 (top; bottom middle and right): **Mitchel Gray**
Page 197 (bottom left): **Tony Stone**
Page 216: **Joaquin Palting/Corbis**
Page 222: **Robert Trachtenberg**
Page 227, 228, 229, 230, and 231: **Francisco Mosto**
Page 232 (left): **Paul Viant-VCL/FPG**
Page 232 (right): **John Hamel/Rodale Images**

Illustrations

Pages vi, 90, and 233: **Kelly Alder**
Pages 16, 17, 18, 19, 20, 22, 50, 51, 171, 173, 175, 176, 178, and 181: **John Hull**
Pages 23, 27, and 168: **Getty Images**
Page 30: **Mark Matcho**
Pages 38 and 40: **Hanoch Piven**
Pages 82, 83, and 84: **Robin Kachantones**

Index

<u>Underscored</u> page references indicate boxed text. **Boldface** references indicate photographs or illustrations.

C

D

E

F

G

P

Q

R

S

T

X

Y

Z